Savoring San Francisco

Savoring San Francisco

recipes FROM THE CITY'S *neighborhood* RESTAURANTS

second edition

CAROLYN MILLER & SHARON SMITH

PHOTOGRAPHS BY DAVID WAKELY

Published by Silverback Books, Inc.,
55 New Montgomery, Suite 503,
San Francisco, California 94105

First edition 2000
Second edition 2005

Recipe for Apricot-Cherry Crisp reprinted from *Field of Greens,* by Annie Somerville,
with permission from Bantam Books.

Project editor: Sharon Smith
Cover design: Sharon Smith and Kate Basart
Interior design: Kate Basart
Proofreaders: Carol Lastrucci, Elaine Merrill
Indexer: Sylvia Coates
Page layouts: Joan Olson
Neighborhood map: Joan Olson
Cover photographs, David Wakely: front: Slanted Door *(top),* Plouf *(bottom left),*
Moose's *(bottom right);* back: Castro neighborhood

Library of Congress Cataloging in Publication Data is available upon request.

ISBN: 1–59637–042–4

Printed and bound in China

Contents

Map of San Francisco Neighborhoods   vi

Restaurants by Neighborhood   vii

List of Recipes   viii

Preface   xi

Introduction   xii

Union Square/Downtown   1

Jackson Square/Financial District   21

North Beach/Chinatown   47

Fisherman's Wharf/The Embarcadero/South Beach   77

Russian Hill/Nob Hill/Polk Street   101

The Marina/Cow Hollow/Pacific Heights   121

Civic Center/Hayes Valley   149

South of Market/Potrero Hill   163

The Mission/Bernal Heights   199

Upper Market/The Castro/Noe Valley   231

The Haight/Cole Valley   249

Presidio Heights/The Richmond/The Sunset/Forest Hills/West Portal   265

List of Contributors   285

Ethnic Index   289

General Index   291

Acknowledgments   302

San Francisco Neighborhoods

Restaurants by Neighborhood

UNION SQUARE/ DOWNTOWN
Colibrí Mexican Bistro
Farallon
Grand Cafe
Kuleto's Italian Restaurant
Le Colonial
Postrio
Scala's Bistro

JACKSON SQUARE/ FINANCIAL DISTRICT
Aqua
Bix Restaurant
Bocadillos
Globe
Kokkari Estiatorio
Palio D'Asti
Plouf
Rubicon
Tadich Grill

NORTH BEACH/CHINATOWN
Albona Ristorante Istriano
Café Jacqueline
Da Flora
Enrico's Sidewalk Cafe
Great Eastern
Helmand
L'Osteria del Forno
Moose's
Rose Pistola

FISHERMAN'S WHARF/ THE EMBARCADERO/ SOUTH BEACH
Hog Island Oyster Company
Jack Falstaff
La Suite
Pipérade
Shanghai 1930
Slanted Door
Taylor's Automatic Refresher
Town's End Bakery and
    Restaurant

RUSSIAN HILL/NOB HILL/ POLK STREET
Antica Trattoria
1550 Hyde Café and Wine Bar
La Folie
Le Petit Robert
Pesce Seafood Bar
Ristorante Milano
Tablespoon
Zarzuela

THE MARINA/COW HOLLOW/ PACIFIC HEIGHTS
A 16 Restaurant and Wine Bar
Betelnut Peju Wu
Cafe Kati
Chez Nous
Greens Restaurant
Isa
Plumpjack Café
Quince
Rose's Cafe
Sociale Caffè and Wine Bar
Vivande Porta Via

CIVIC CENTER/ HAYES VALLEY
Absinthe
Bistro Clovis
Citizen Cake
Suppenküche

SOUTH OF MARKET/ POTRERO HILL
Aperto
bacar restaurant
Baraka
Chez Papa Bistrot
Fringale
Koh Samui and the Monkey
Le Charm French Bistro
Maya
Oola Restaurant and Bar
Pazzia Caffè Pizzeria
    Rosticceria
Restaurant LuLu

South Park Café
Town Hall
Yank Sing

THE MISSION/ BERNAL HEIGHTS
Alma
Charanga
Delfina
Foreign Cinema
The Liberty Cafe and Bakery
Limón
Luna Park
Slow Club
Ti Couz
Universal Cafe

UPPER MARKET/ THE CASTRO/NOE VALLEY
Chow
Firefly
Incanto
Ristorante Bacco
Tallula
2223 Market Street

THE HAIGHT/COLE VALLEY
Cha Cha Cha
Eos Restaurant and Wine Bar
Indian Oven
Rnm
Thep Phanom Thai Cuisine
Zazie

PRESIDIO HEIGHTS/ THE RICHMOND/ THE SUNSET/FOREST HILLS/ WEST PORTAL
Bella Trattoria
Cafe for All Seasons
Chapeau!
Chou Chou Pâtisserie and
    Bistro
Clémentine Cuisine Française
Katia's Russian Restaurant
Mandalay
Park Chalet Garden
    Restaurant

List of Recipes

APPETIZERS/FIRST COURSES

Pissaladière
Oven-Dried-Tomato Tarts with Goat Cheese and Onion Jam
Gnocchi al Tartufo *(Potato Dumplings with Truffle Sauce)*
Warm Piquillo Peppers with Goat Cheese, California Raisins, and Moscatel Vinaigrette
Portobellos Balsamico
Eggplant Caviar
Blood Orange–Glazed Fresh Sardines with Spicy Watercress and Orange Salad
Sicilian Swordfish Rolls
Tuna Tartare with Fried Green Tomatoes and Tabasco
Tuna Confit with Fennel-Rucola Salad and Anchovy Vinaigrette
Seared Day-Boat Scallops with Sunchoke Purée
Crab Cakes
Grilled Fresh Calamari with Warm White Bean Salad
Hog Island Oysters Rockefeller
Shrimp Goldfish
Minced Duck in Lettuce Petals

SOUPS

Asian Pear Ajo Blanco
Spring Asparagus Soup with Mint and Red Radishes
Cranberry Bean and Dandelion Soup
Gazpacho Andaluz
Caramelized Garlic Soup with Dungeness Crab and Upper Market Street Wild Anise
Italian Fish Soup *(Cacciucco)*

SALADS

Grapefruit Salad with Jicama
Grilled Corn Salad
Grilled Fuyu Persimmon and Red Oak Leaf Lettuce Salad with Candied Pecans
Marinated Shrimp with Peach and Cucumber Salad

SIDE DISHES

Spätzle
Gnudi *(Spinach-Ricotta Gnocchi)*
Macaroni Gratin
Melanzane al Forno *(Baked Herbed Eggplant with Capers and Olives)*
Saag Aloo *(Spinach and Potatoes with Onion, Ginger, and Garlic)*

MAIN COURSES

Pasta, Risotto, Polenta, Crepes, and Pancakes

Emerald Fire Noodles
Portobello Mushroom Pasta
Tagliolini Pepati *(Tagliolini with Spicy Roasted-Tomato Sauce)*
Pappardelle di Zafferano con Salsa di Agnello *(Saffron Pappardelle with Lamb Sauce)*
Sausage Ravioli in a Red Bell Pepper Sauce
Crespelle alla Boscaiola *(Crêpes with Porcini, Ham, and Béchamel Sauce)*
Seafood Risotto
Swedish Oatmeal Pancakes with Pears and Almonds

Vegetarian

Pipérade
Pumpkin Curry Tofu
Spring Vegetable Potpies with Parmesan Crust and Creamy Herb Gravy

Fish

Whole Fish with Tomato and Fennel Ragout à la Niçoise
Bronzini à la Provençale
Potato-Wrapped Bluenose Sea Bass
Fennel-Crusted Golden Trout
Huachinango a la Talla *(Red Snapper with Chipotle Rouille and Warm Cabbage Salad)*
Salmon Salad Cozies with Arugula, Tomatoes, and Aioli
King Salmon with Dungeness Crab Fondue
Kale-Wrapped Wild Salmon with Red Bell Pepper, Almond, and Garlic Sauce
Grilled Salmon Paillards on Bucatini with Watercress and Chiles de Árbol Aglio e Olio
Balsamic-Glazed Grilled Salmon with Mashed Potatoes, Corn Salsa, and Oregano Butter
Ahi Tuna au Poivre with Chanterelles, Niçoise Olives, and Artichokes
Ahi Burgers with Ginger-Wasabi Mayo

Shellfish

Hangtown Fry
Cioppino
Crab in Black Bean Sauce
Polenta alla Coda di Rospo *(Stewed Monkfish, Clams, and Mussels over Soft Polenta)*
Wok-Roasted Mussels with Asian Aromatics
Porcini-Crusted Scallops with Mushroom Ragout

Chicken

Herb-Marinated Brick Chicken with Heirloom Tomato Jam and Garlic Mashed Potatoes
Pollo alla Marsala con Spinaci Siciliani *(Chicken Marsala with Sicilian Spinach)*
Chicken Fricassee with Glazed Shallots, Garlic, and Sherry Vinegar Sauce
Mango Chicken

Lemongrass-Marinated Chicken with Wok-Tossed Asian Vegetables
Mexican Chicken Salad
Chicken Potpies
Chicken Hash à la Bix

Duck
Duck à l'Orange Provençale
Duck in Pipian Sauce

Rabbit
Coniglio in Agrodolce *(Braised Rabbit in a Sweet and Sour Glaze)*

Veal
Veal Filet with Blue Cheese–Potato Gratin and Red Wine Sauce

Beef
Braised Short Ribs with Celery and Herb Salad
Lomo Saltado *(Sautéed Beef with Fried Potatoes)*
Thaitanic Beef
Braised Oxtails with Garlic and Feta
Picadillo Cubano with Black Beans *(Cuban-Style Ground Beef with Green Olives and Raisins)*

Pork
Roasted Pork Loin with Figs and Marsala
Three-Mustard-Crusted Pork Tenderloin with Soy-Braised Cabbage
Pork Tenderloin with Mustard Sauce, Sage, Onion Confit, and Grapes
Brined Pork Chops with Red Sauerkraut and Juniper Butter

Lamb
Chowpan *(Grilled Marinated Rack of Lamb with Sautéed Eggplant and Pallow)*
Grilled Herbes de Provence Lamb Chops with Lavender Salt
Grilled Lamb Skewers with Couscous "404" and Spicy Chickpea Stew
Shepherd's Pie

DESSERTS
Coconut Tapioca with Passion Fruit Sorbet, Basil Infusion, and Coconut Tuiles
Chocolate Pots de Crème
Orange Crème Brûlée
Lemon Soufflé
Huckleberry Soufflé
Dessert Crêpes with Caramelized Pears and Crème Fraîche
Far Breton with Dried Plums
S'More Brownies
Pear Tarte Tatin
Coconut Cream Pie
Apricot-Cherry Crisp

Preface

When the first edition of *Savoring San Francisco* was published in 2000, the city was at the height of the dot-com boom. The neighborhoods were full of moving vans unloading furniture for the newest San Franciscans, and high-tech start-ups were buying old buildings and evicting the tenants, leading to the creation of a new verb: to be "dot-commed" meant your business had lost its space. It was our own late-twentieth-century version of the Gold Rush. And though omelettes weren't being sold for a stash of gold nuggets, the restaurant business was booming, too. New eating places opened across the city in areas like the Mission and South Park, near the hot spots of the dot-com phenomenon, and old restaurants were thriving.

Then, without warning, the boom went bust, and the new companies moved out of their office spaces, leaving some of them still vacant today. More moving vans were double-parked in the streets again, but this time people were moving away from the city. And more than the usual number of restaurants, in a notoriously volatile business, closed their doors.

Five years later, San Francisco is achieving some equilibrium. The face of the city has changed, due to construction projects begun after the 1989 earthquake, and the ambitious restoration and building programs of former mayor Willie Brown. A dynamic, hands-on young new mayor is shaking up the status quo, and the restaurant scene is healthy, with new places opening every month.

This second edition of *Savoring San Francisco* reflects those changes, with thirty-three new restaurants, many of them replacing eating establishments that have closed. The majority of the favorite, time-tested restaurants that appeared in our first edition are included again, though often with a new recipe, so that over half of the recipes in this book are new. The revised *Savoring San Francisco* captures the vibrant, fluid, and bustling San Francisco restaurant scene, with its enduring combination of innovation and tradition, and above all, its fascination with and respect for good food.

Introduction

It's late afternoon in San Francisco, and from the Embarcadero to the ocean and the bay to the Outer Mission, the town is like a vast dinner party waiting to begin. In thousands of restaurants of every size and kind, the tables are set, the stocks and sauces have been made, and the vegetables are prepped. The kitchen may be humming, but the dining chairs are empty and the room is quiet and waiting. If it's one of those rare warm nights in spring, summer, or early fall, half of the tables may be out on the sidewalk, and the wait staff and even the line cooks may be there too, catching a breath of air before the customers arrive. If it's foggy, cold, or raining, the lights of the restaurant and the aromas of its food are beckoning to people passing by in the streets of a city where fine restaurants and good food are a cherished way of life.

Right from the start, San Francisco was a restaurant town. Even before it was named San Francisco, when it was still a motley collection of not quite fifty adobes, frame buildings, and shanties called Yerba Buena, John Henry Brown, a former British sailor, opened the town's first hotel and restaurant, near the corner of what is today Kearny and Clay. The year was 1846. The population was around one thousand, the country was at war with Mexico over possession of Texas and California, and Yerba Buena had just been declared part of the United States by a detachment of men from the USS *Portsmouth*. The officers and sailors needed a place to stay when they came ashore, and John Brown figured that the ocean winds and tides would soon bring even more visitors needing food and lodging. Some of the men from the *Portsmouth* offered to make a sign for the new hotel if Brown would name it after their ship, and so the Portsmouth Hotel (and the town's first sign) was born.

Soon, John Brown had more customers than he could handle, but in his wildest dreams he couldn't have foreseen what happened next: Two years later, after Yerba Buena had been renamed after San Francisco Bay, a few flakes of gold were found in the American River, in the foothills of the Sierra mountains. By early 1850, the population of the town was estimated at around thirty thousand, and the housing stock included elegant hotels and a wide variety of restaurants, including some serving the finest Parisian dishes.

The San Francisco restaurant boom hasn't stopped since. In 1875, the city had between two and three hundred eating places, more than any other city in the country, a distinction it still holds today, though the number of restaurants has grown to around thirty-five hundred, or roughly one for every two hundred residents.

Fine food has always been an object of desire in San Francisco. In a setting of great natural abundance, rich with game, fish, and shellfish, the

new town was an El Dorado for fortune hunters, entrepreneurs, and adventurers of every stripe, all of them people who were willing to gamble on the future and who wanted to live large lives in the present. Hedonism was the order of the day, and food and wine were two of the most obvious rewards for a life of risk-taking in an isolated town on the far edge of the continent.

San Franciscans are still obsessed with food. Where citizens of some other cities are consumed with sports, politics, society, show business, or sex, in San Francisco a surprising number of conversations sooner or later turn to the subject of food. It's estimated that people who live in the city go out to dinner an average of three nights a week. Restaurants are part of our entertainment, a kind of theater in which the sets and players and the props are constantly changing. There's an unspoken competition among some people to get to the newest restaurant first. Reviews of the latest places are as eagerly read as the reviews of the latest movies or best-sellers. The San Francisco *Chronicle* has what is arguably the country's best food section, with a column ("The Inside Scoop") by GraceAnn Walden that records the dizzying pace of change among the restaurants: which new ones have opened; which ones have closed; who is changing their decor, menu, chef, focus; which are now the hottest places in town; where the latest hot chefs have gone. San Francisco may even be the origin of the word *foodies*, which describes those people who consider the kind and quality of the food they eat right up there in importance with the air they breathe.

Food is one of San Francisco's major industries. The wealth of good restaurants here are a major draw for tourists, businesspeople, and conventioneers. Chefs are not only celebrities, but major players in the city's charities as well, donating vast amounts of both food and time to events year-round. Food vendors are equally celebrated, with chefs seeking the best, the newest, and the freshest wines, cheeses, and produce. To keep these exquisite foodstuffs from going to waste, an organization called Food Runners collects leftover food from restaurant kitchens every night and delivers it to homeless shelters. And, to complete the cycle, many homes and restaurants recycle their food scraps into green plastic bins provided by Norcal Waste Systems, who retrieve them and convert the contents into Four Course Compost.

California has built its food reputation on local, seasonal foods, and the organic food movement is strong here, with farmers' markets and Community Supported Agriculture farms that bring just-picked foods directly from the farm to the consumer by subscription. Some of the most important trends in American cooking today either originated in the San Francisco Bay Area or were given impetus here: organic vegetables and mixed greens, goat cheese and other farmhouse cheeses, organic wines, artisan breads.

San Francisco is as proud of its diversity as it is of its food, and that diversity has always been reflected in the mixture of cuisines found on its tables. Even before gold was discovered, Yerba Buena hosted a wildly mixed population: Mexicans, Spaniards, English, Dutch, Irish, Scots, Russians, French, Sandwich Islanders, Kanakans, and more. The lure of gold brought people from every direction, by land and by sea: South Americans, Chinese, Malays, Filipinos, Italians, Greeks, Japanese. Many of the forty-niners, of course, were not miners at all, but people who made their money by feeding, clothing, and housing miners, would-be miners, and former miners. Among these were the proprietors and chefs of French, English, German, Chinese, and Italian restaurants.

The epitome of fine dining then was believed to be Parisian, and some of the best-known French restaurants were started by chefs who were brought here in the retinue of rich East Coast investors. French food is still a major force in San Francisco dining, as *Savoring San Francisco* indicates. But today it's not all classic French cuisine; exotic global ingredients are creeping into traditional French dishes, and some of the most interesting places in town call themselves New French or California-French. And then there's "fusion" cuisine, which usually means Asian fusion, a combination of European and Asian cooking techniques and ingredients.

Some of the food in the city is so innovative it's hard to know what to call it, though you can always fall back on that old standby, California cuisine, a name invented to describe cooking that combines seasonal and regional foods with global foods and seasonings in surprising ways. Cal-Med is a newer designation, emphasizing foods that are grown in the Mediterranean climate of California and used in neo-classic Mediterranean dishes.

At the same time, San Francisco is home to traditional ethnic cuisines ranging from Afghan to Vietnamese, and including Bolivian, Peruvian, Cambodian, Egyptian, Turkish, Persian, Senegalese, South African, Eritrean, Nepalese, and Tibetan. You'll also find regional variations of ethnic cuisines, such as Hakka, Shanghainese, and Hunanese Chinese restaurants, and Istrian, Lucchese, Venetian, and Sicilian Italian places. Then there are the hybrids and the unique-niche categories, including the only-in-San-Francisco's: Portuguese-Hawaiian (Tita's), white trash/microwave (Butter), Old San Francisco (the Fly Trap), and organic *raw* vegan food (the Gratitude Cafe, Alive!), among others.

Many of the finest and most expensive restaurants in the city are clustered in the downtown area, close to the big hotels and Moscone Center. But we organized this book by neighborhoods to give readers a flavor of the city as a whole, and to highlight something that every resident of the city knows: You can find amazingly good food no matter where you are in San Francisco. Tourists who venture beyond the city center will find a wealth of distinct neighborhoods, like villages within the city. We hope that those who really want to know San Francisco will venture beyond the downtown area to explore the streets and restaurants of these other parts of town. For although many of the restaurants in this book are small and chef-owned, and "neighborhood restaurants" in the sense that they are a focus for people living nearby, every restaurant included here is also a destination restaurant, a place that San Franciscans are willing to navigate all the way across the city to visit.

We chose our contributors based on the San Francisco *Chronicle*'s annual listing of the best restaurants in the Bay Area, and filled in the blanks based on the latest city and restaurant guides, including the *ZAGAT Survey,* leaning, when necessary, toward our own personal favorites. A few restaurants declined to give us recipes, but most chefs were delighted to contribute, despite the time and effort it took from their demanding profession.

Our aim in choosing contributors was to show the wide range of good restaurants found all over San Francisco, from chic boutique-hotel restaurants to tiny storefronts that have been around for years. We included a range of cuisines as well, picking what we thought were among the best of the city's many ethnic places. For reasons of length and organization, we chose the arbitrary number of one hundred restaurants and twelve neighborhoods. This means that many, many good restaurants in the city are not represented by recipes, and that our twelve neighborhoods are all really clusters of smaller neighborhoods that fit together geographically. We tried to make up for omissions by adding a list of "Other Neighborhood Stars" to each neighborhood introduction, but we inevitably left out many restaurants that both visitors and locals love. We did not include places that are known mainly for their location, history, or visibility; tourists will find these restaurants listed in every city guide. Our first and most important criteria was simply that every restaurant included in this book serve consistently fine food.

As for the recipes themselves, we tried to present a balanced range, from appetizers to desserts, from traditional favorites to surprising and innovative dishes, and from simple, easy-to-make recipes to those that will provide some challenge for the home cook. A list of recipes (page

viii) and a general index (page 291) will help you find the dishes you want to prepare, while a list of contributors (page 285), a list of restaurants by neighborhood (page vii), and an ethnic index (page 289) will help you find the restaurants you want to visit.

Due to the volatility of the San Francisco restaurant scene, by the time this book reaches print, a few of the restaurants included may have closed, or have changed hands, name, decor, and/or chef. Because so many chefs change their offerings with the seasons and the years, the recipe you find here may not appear on a restaurant menu when you visit. But this cook-book will give you an idea of the kind of food each eating place serves, and a taste of San Francisco as it is now, in some of its oldest and newest restaurants, in the early years of a new century. If you can, make your way into one of the city's unique neighborhoods and join the party. If you're having your own private feast at home instead, wherever you may be, follow one of the recipes in these pages. In either case, we hope you will enjoy savoring San Francisco.

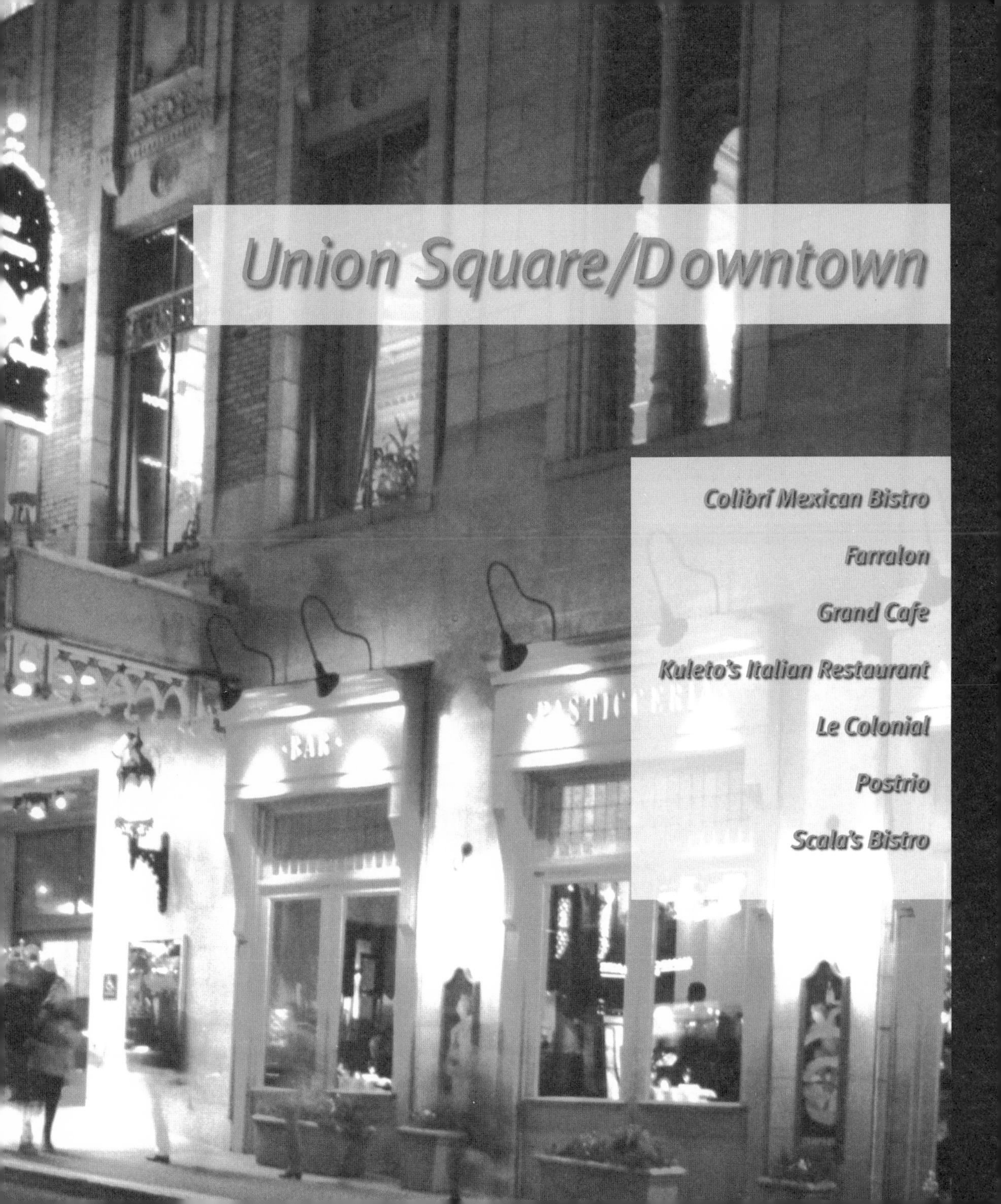

Union Square/Downtown

Colibri Mexican Bistro

Farralon

Grand Cafe

Kuleto's Italian Restaurant

Le Colonial

Postrio

Scala's Bistro

THE CENTER OF DOWNTOWN SAN FRANCISCO is a small public space where meetings were held during the Civil War in support of the Union Army, giving the square its name. In 2002, after much public discussion and a closure of two years, Union Square was finally redesigned  and refurbished, and today only the Dewey Monument and, unfortunately, the underground garage remain. In place of the somewhat shabby, bleak former space, largely blocked off by dark hedges, the square is now an expanse of granite, flowers, and palm trees, where a mix of tourists and downtown workers can enjoy the sunshine on the park benches or relax at Emporio Rulli, an Italian cafe with outdoor seating. ⟶ MANY OF THE CITY'S MOST ELEGANT DINING PLACES are in buildings near the square. These are the restaurants well-heeled tourists and businesspeople frequent, and where San Franciscans go for special occasions. A large number of them, such as the Dining Room at the Ritz-Carlton, Campton Place, Masa's, Postrio, Scala's Bistro, Michael Mina, and Grand Cafe, are in hotels, but they are so well known for their food, setting, and service that they are thought of as restaurants on their own, not hotel restaurants. Mixed in among these world-class eateries, and in the alleys and side streets, are smaller, less-well-known spots where San Franciscans flock for breakfast, lunch, and dinner. As in the city's other neighborhoods, restaurants here offer a wide range of cuisines, from down-home American food (Dottie's); to casual French food in a fifties cafe brought straight from Paris, authentic down to its salt shakers (Café Claude); to classic Italian cuisine (Kuleto's). ⟶ AT LUNCHTIME, BOUTIQUE-LINED MAIDEN LANE, once a notorious alley of brothels named Morton Street, gives itself over to other pleasures and fills up with bright tables, chairs, and umbrellas set right on the pavement. You can find similar clusters hidden away in Claude Lane, and in Leidesdorff and Belden Streets in the adjacent Financial District. Once shadowy settings for detective dramas by Dashiell Hammett, today these urban alleys are no more dangerous than an order of *pommes frites.* FUELED BY COMMERCE AND THE VAGARIES OF FASHION, the shops and businesses of Union Square and the downtown area are constantly changing. Many of the old family-run businesses, like the White House, I. Magnin, Joseph Magnin, and City of Paris department stores are gone, replaced by national and international chains like Macy's and Nike. But the lure of San Francisco's downtown continues. TO THE EAST OF THE SQUARE, the downtown blocks gradually merge into the Financial District; to the north, the streets, lined with small apartment houses, begin their abrupt rise to Nob Hill, while to the west the blocks blend into the Tenderloin, a dicey area that is being changed by an infusion of Vietnamese families, boutique hotels, and clubs. So many Vietnamese restaurants are here that part of the area is called Little Saigon. Because the American Conservatory Theater and several smaller theatrical houses dot the blocks closer to Union Square, this area is known as the Theater District. And a recent influx of Indian and Pakistani restaurants is adding new flavors to the neighborhood table. TO THE SOUTH, the shops, hotels, and restaurants of downtown spill over to Market Street, which runs at an angle to the northern blocks. Here, on the south side of the thoroughfare, though technically part of SoMa (South of Market), the city continues to reinvent itself, and new hotels, restaurants, and shops are adding to the excitement of downtown San Francisco.

OTHER NEIGHBORHOOD STARS

Anjou

Cafe Claude

Campton Place

Canteen

Cortez

The Dining Room at the Ritz-Carlton

Dottie's True Blue Cafe

Fleur de Lys

Masa's

Michael Mina

Shalimar Gardens

Duck in Pipian Sauce

SERVES 4 AS A MAIN COURSE

Colibrí
Mexican Bistro
438 Geary Street (at Mason)

One of the most recent entries in the very short list of upscale Mexican restaurants in San Francisco, Colibrí is as bright and lively as its namesake, the hummingbird. In this twenty-first-century version of a nineteenth-century cantina, you can dine on authentic family recipes from central Mexico, served small-plates style. Executive chef Alex Padilla and chef de cuisine Alex Placencia use only high-quality fresh ingredients in bringing this regional cuisine to downtown San Francisco. Guacamole prepared at your tableside, fresh tortillas made by hand in-house, and intensely flavored dishes like this duck in a green sauce with its roots in Aztec and Mayan cooking are only some of the delights offered up in this colorful space.

Note: For a milder sauce, seed the chilies. Serve this dish with rice seasoned with garlic.

PIPIAN SAUCE

$\frac{1}{2}$ tablespoon raw peanuts

$\frac{1}{2}$ tablespoon raw almonds

$\frac{1}{4}$ cup raw pumpkin seeds

1 tablespoon canola oil

2 small tomatillos, husked, rinsed, and coarsely chopped

1 green serrano chili

$\frac{1}{2}$ green jalapeño chili

$\frac{1}{4}$ small white onion, coarsely chopped

1 small garlic clove

$\frac{1}{2}$ tablespoon raw sesame seeds

$\frac{1}{4}$ cup packed spinach leaves

1 corn tortilla, torn into pieces

4 cups chicken broth

1 bunch fresh epazote, stemmed (available in Latino markets)

$\frac{1}{4}$ bunch cilantro, stemmed

Salt to taste

1 whole duck breast
Salt and freshly ground pepper to taste
Cilantro sprigs and raw sesame seeds for garnish

- To make the sauce: In a dry skillet over medium-low heat, separately toast the peanuts, almonds, and pumpkin seeds, stirring constantly, until fragrant and lightly browned, about 3 minutes. Pour them into a bowl to cool.

- In a large skillet or sauté pan, heat the oil over low heat. Add the tomatillos, chilies, onion, garlic, sesame seeds, and the toasted nuts and sauté until the vegetables are heated through and the onion is translucent, about 5 minutes.

- Transfer the mixture to a blender and purée until smooth. Strain through a coarse-meshed sieve and transfer to a saucepan.

- In the blender, combine the spinach, tortilla, and chicken broth and purée until smooth. Add the epazote and cilantro and purée again until smooth. Strain through a coarse-meshed sieve and add to the mixture in the pan. Simmer over medium-low heat for 30 minutes, or until the flavors blend. Season with salt. Remove from heat and let stand while preparing the duck.

- Season the duck breast with salt and pepper. In a large skillet or sauté pan over low heat, cook the duck, skin side down, for about 20 minutes, or until the skin is crisp. Turn and cook for 3 minutes on the other side. Remove from heat and let rest for 2 minutes.

- Cut into ¼-inch-thick slices. Divide the slices among 4 warmed plates and pour some sauce over each serving. Garnish with cilantro sprigs and a few sesame seeds and serve.

Blood Orange–Glazed Fresh Sardines

with Spicy Watercress and Orange Salad

SERVES 4 AS A FIRST COURSE

Farallon

450 Post Street (between Mason and Powell)

A meal at Farallon, named for the islands just beyond the Golden Gate, is a bit like dining in an underwater dream world, complete with sea urchins floating overhead and kelp streamers twisting up from the ocean floor. Nationally known restaurant designer Pat Kuleto outdid himself in fashioning this one, and Mark Franz's cuisine more than lives up to its surroundings, as this salad blending the bite of watercress and the raspberry sweetness of blood oranges with fresh sardines illustrates. A true bonus here is the wonderful dessert list from acclaimed pastry chef Emily Luchetti, who came, like Franz, from the old Stars.

2¹/₂ cups fresh blood-orange juice (about 8 oranges)
1 red bell pepper, seeded, deribbed, and finely diced
1 red Fresno or Anaheim chili, seeded, deribbed, and finely diced
2 tablespoons green peppercorns, drained and chopped
¹/₄ cup fresh lemon juice
1 bunch chives, minced
¹/₂ cup grapeseed oil
Salt and freshly ground pepper to taste
12 fresh Monterey sardines, boned
2 bunches spicy watercress, pepper cress, or watercress, stemmed
4 blood oranges, peeled and segmented (see note)

In a small, heavy nonreactive saucepan, bring the orange juice to a slow boil over medium heat and cook until reduced to about 1¹/₂ cups. Set aside to cool.

In a small bowl, combine ¹/₄ cup of the reduced orange juice, the bell pepper, chili, green peppercorns, lemon juice, chives, and grapeseed oil. Whisk to blend. Season with salt and pepper. Set aside.

- Just before serving, preheat the broiler. Line a broiler pan with aluminum foil and oil the foil. Open the sardines flat and place them, skin-side up, on the prepared pan. Reserve ⅓ cup of the remaining reduced orange juice for garnish. Brush the sardines with the remaining reduced orange juice and sprinkle with salt and pepper. Broil the sardines 6 inches from the heat source for 1 minute, or until browned on top and opaque throughout.

- To serve, in a large bowl, combine the watercress and blood orange segments. Toss with just enough vinaigrette to lightly coat the watercress. Place 3 sardines on each serving plate. Spoon some of the vegetables from the vinaigrette onto each of the sardines. Place a mound of salad on top of the sardines. Drizzle some of the reserved reduced orange juice on the plate around each serving and serve at once.

Peeling and Segmenting Citrus Fruit: To peel, use a large knife to cut off the top and bottom of each fruit down to the flesh. One at a time, set a fruit on end on a cutting board and use the knife to cut off the peel downward, revealing the flesh and following the curve of the orange. To segment, holding the fruit over a bowl, use a large knife to cut between the membranes of each segment to release the segments into the bowl. If the juice is needed as well, squeeze the membranes over the bowl.

Bronzini à la Provençale

SERVES 6 AS A MAIN COURSE

Grand Cafe
Hotel Monaco, 501 Geary Street
(at Taylor)

It's not just grand, it's enormous, in the old tradition of great hotel dining rooms, although it's attached to one of the city's newer boutique hotels. There are palm trees, huge Art Deco–style light fixtures, and an open kitchen in this former ballroom space, but somehow the seating is intimate, especially if you choose one of the booths. The food here lives up to its expansive setting, as in this celebration of the best of Provençal cuisine: French sea bass served atop basil-scented couscous, with a confit of bell peppers.

BASIL OIL

Leaves from 1 bunch basil
¹/₂ cup extra-virgin olive oil
Salt and freshly ground pepper to taste

PEPPER CONFIT

2 red bell peppers
1 yellow bell pepper
1 large sweet white onion, such as Maui, halved
¹/₂ cup extra-virgin olive oil
Pinch of ground coriander
Pinch of ground cumin
Salt and freshly ground pepper to taste

COUSCOUS

2 cups couscous
2¹/₄ cups low-salt chicken broth
Salt and freshly ground pepper to taste

FISH

1 tablespoon extra-virgin olive oil
Six 5- or 6-ounce bronzini (French sea bass, or loup de mer),
striped bass, or black bass fillets
Salt and freshly ground pepper to taste

2 tomatoes, peeled, seeded, and finely diced (see page 12)
6 oil-cured black olives, pitted and sliced
6 tablespoons extra-virgin olive oil
Salt and freshly ground pepper to taste
6 fresh basil leaves

- To make the basil oil: In a medium saucepan of boiling water, blanch the basil leaves for exactly 1 minute. Using a wire skimmer, transfer them to a bowl of ice water. Drain and dry the leaves on paper towels. In a blender, combine the basil and olive oil. Blend on high speed until smooth. Season with salt and pepper.

- To make the pepper confit: With a vegetable peeler, peel the red and yellow pepper. Seed the peppers and cut into julienne (2 inches long and ⅛ inch thick). Place the onion cut side down and cut it into vertical slices. In a small saucepan, heat the olive oil over low heat until fragrant. Add the peppers, onion, coriander, cumin, salt, and pepper. Cook, stirring occasionally, until the mixture has the consistency of marmalade, 20 to 25 minutes. Set aside and keep warm.

- To make the couscous: Put the couscous in a large bowl. In a small saucepan, bring the chicken broth to a boil. Pour the broth over the couscous, stir in the salt and pepper, and cover with plastic wrap. Let stand for 10 minutes.

- Meanwhile, in a large sauté pan or skillet, heat the olive oil over medium-high heat. Season the fillets on both sides with salt and pepper. Add to the pan, skin side down, and reduce heat slightly. Cook for 3 to 4 minutes on the skin side only.

- To make the garnish: In a small bowl, combine the tomatoes, olives, olive oil, salt, and pepper. Stir well.

- To serve, stir the basil oil into the couscous. Mound in the center of 6 warmed plates. Place the fish on top of the couscous. On the side of the couscous, place a quenelle of the pepper confit. Sprinkle the garnish around the plate and place a basil leaf on top of each fillet.

Herb-Marinated Brick Chicken
with Heirloom Tomato Jam
and Garlic Mashed Potatoes

SERVES 4 AS A MAIN COURSE

Kuleto's Italian Restaurant
Villa Florence Hotel,
211 Powell Street
(between Geary and O'Farrell)

Named after the former owner, restaurant designer Pat Kuleto, this bustling Italian restaurant is right in the center of the downtown action, next to the cable car line and close to Market Street, meaning it's always full of people and energy. Open all day long, it's a great place to grab a cappuccino and pastry in the morning, have lunch while shopping, or dine before a show on lusty dishes like this brick chicken.

HEIRLOOM TOMATO JAM

1 pound Brandywine or other dark red heirloom tomatoes,
peeled and seeded, juice reserved (see note)
Grated zest and juice of $^1/_2$ lemon
$^1/_4$ tablespoon grated fresh ginger
$^1/_4$ teaspoon salt
1 cup sugar
$^3/_4$ teaspoon freshly ground coriander

$^1/_2$ tablespoon minced fresh thyme
$^1/_2$ tablespoon minced fresh oregano
$^1/_2$ tablespoon minced fresh sage
$1^1/_2$ tablespoons minced fresh flat-leaf parsley
$1^1/_2$ tablespoons kosher salt
1 teaspoon freshly ground pepper
$^1/_2$ tablespoon minced garlic
1 teaspoon minced shallot
Four 8-ounce boneless chicken breast halves, skin on
1 tablespoon olive oil
Minced fresh chives for garnish
Garlic Mashed Potatoes for serving (page 12)

- To make the tomato jam: Chop the tomatoes coarsely. Put them and their reserved juice in a large, heavy saucepan. Add the zest and juice of the lemon. Stir in the ginger and salt. Bring to a boil over medium-high heat, stirring occasionally. Reduce heat to low and simmer uncovered, stirring occasionally, until the tomato pieces are soft, about 15 minutes. Stir in the sugar. Increase the heat to medium-high and cook, stirring almost constantly, until thickened to jam consistency, about 10 minutes. The jam is done when a spoonful placed on a plate and set in the freezer congeals in about 30 seconds. Stir in the coriander. Remove from the heat and let cool.

- In a small bowl, combine the herbs, salt, pepper, garlic, and shallot. Rub the mixture onto both sides of the chicken breasts. Place in a baking dish, cover with plastic wrap, and refrigerate for 24 hours. Remove from the refrigerator 30 minutes before cooking.

- Preheat the oven to 500°F. In a large ovenproof sauté pan or skillet, heat the olive oil over medium-high heat. Add the chicken and sauté until golden brown, about 2 minutes on each side. Turn off the heat. Weight the chicken down with another heavy ovenproof pan and put the two pans in the oven. Roast for 10 minutes, or until the juices run clear.

- Transfer the chicken to warmed plates and top each with a spoonful of tomato jam. Garnish with chives and serve at once, with the garlic mashed potatoes.

Garlic Mashed Potatoes

SERVES 4 AS A SIDE DISH

2 pounds russet potatoes, peeled and cut into 2-inch chunks
2 teaspoons salt
3 garlic cloves
¼ cup heavy cream
2 tablespoons milk
4 tablespoons unsalted butter
¼ teaspoon freshly ground pepper

- In a large saucepan, combine the potatoes, garlic, and 1 teaspoon of the salt. Add water to cover. Bring to a boil, then reduce heat to a simmer and cook until the potatoes are fork-tender, about 15 minutes. Meanwhile, in a small saucepan, combine the cream, milk, and butter and heat over low heat.

- Drain the potatoes and garlic and return them to the pan. Heat over low heat for a few seconds to cook off excess water. Push the potatoes through a ricer into another saucepan, or mash in the same pan with a potato masher. Add the cream mixture and stir until smooth. Stir in the remaining 1 teaspoon salt and the pepper. Taste and adjust the seasoning. Cover and keep warm in a low oven or over hot water for up to 30 minutes, if necessary. Serve warm.

Peeling and Seeding Tomatoes: Drop the tomatoes into a pot of boiling water for 5 to 10 seconds. Using a wire skimmer, transfer immediately to a bowl of ice water. Peel off the skins and remove the stems. Halve the tomatoes and squeeze the seeds into a sieve set over a bowl. Discard the seeds and reserve the juice.

Heirloom Vegetables and Fruits

They may be lumpy or lopsided; they may be small and knobby; they may be bizarre colors you're not used to, but they will almost always have more flavor and aroma than the perfect, tasteless vegetables packaged in plastic in the supermarket. Wherever you find them, they won't be far from the ground where they were grown; heirloom vegetables and fruits have not been bred to withstand a long time on the shelf or in storage, or a long trip from the farm. This is the quirky produce that got left behind when fruits and vegetables were hybridized to look uniform and to withstand time and travel. Unfortunately, nuance and intensity and variety were left behind at the same time.

Heirloom fruits and vegetables have been brought back by dedicated and stubborn growers. Look for this idiosyncratic produce at farmers' markets and farmstands, and in organic markets like Real Food and Whole Foods. The tomatoes will range from purple/black (Brandywine) to fully ripe green with stripes (Green Zebra); the potatoes may be blue or shaped like fingers; and one variety of apples may be small and available for only a few weeks in the fall (Gravenstein), but you can bet that they will be organically grown and pesticide free, and that they will add unique flavor and color to your kitchen and your table.

Lemongrass-Marinated Chicken
with Wok-Tossed Asian Vegetables

Le Colonial

20 Cosmo Place (between Post and Taylor)

Even though it's hidden away on little Cosmo Place, this elegant colonial-style restaurant and its beautiful upstairs bar are always full, especially now that chef Mike Yakura has taken over the kitchen. The atmosphere is tropical and romantic, and the excellent French-Vietnamese food is seductive and exotic, like this stir-fry of chicken scented with lemongrass and vegetables spiced with black bean sauce. Serve it with steamed jasmine rice and cold Asian beer.

Notes: Fresh lemongrass is sold at most Asian produce stores and at many large chains. Look for stalks that are firm and pale yellow. Black bean sauce is sold in jars in Asian markets and many supermarkets.

MARINADE

5 stalks lemongrass (white part only), peeled and crushed

4 garlic cloves

3 shallots

1/2 cup fish sauce

1 tablespoon soy sauce

1 tablespoon ground pepper

2 tablespoons sugar

2 skinless, boneless chicken breast halves, cut into bite-sized pieces

3 skinless, boneless chicken thighs, cut into bite-sized pieces

ASIAN VEGETABLES

2 tablespoons unsalted butter or canola oil

4 baby bok choys, julienned

1 carrot, peeled and julienned

1 small white onion, sliced

10 ounces shiitake mushrooms, stemmed and sliced
1 cup Chinese long beans, cut into 1-inch pieces
2 tablespoons black bean sauce

3 tablespoons canola oil
Cilantro sprigs for garnish
Steamed jasmine rice for serving

- To make the marinade: Coarsely chop the lemongrass, then transfer to a food processor and chop until fine. Add the garlic and the shallots to the food processor and continue chopping until the pieces are small. Put the mixture in a large bowl and whisk in the fish sauce, soy sauce, pepper, and sugar. Add the chicken to the bowl, mix well, cover with plastic wrap, and let stand at room temperature for 1 hour.

- To prepare the vegetables: In a small wok or a large sauté pan or skillet, melt the butter or heat the oil over high heat. Add the vegetables and stir-fry until crisp-tender, about 30 seconds. Add the black bean sauce and continue to stir-fry until all the vegetables are coated, about 15 seconds. Remove from heat and transfer the vegetables to a platter. Keep warm in a low oven.

- Wipe out the wok with paper towels. Return it to the stove and heat the canola oil over high heat. Add the marinated chicken and stir-fry until lightly browned, 2 to 3 minutes. Add the chicken to the plate with the vegetables, garnish with cilantro, and serve at once, with steamed jasmine rice.

Italian Fish Soup

(Cacciucco)

Postrio

Prescott Hotel, 545 Post Street
(between Mason and Taylor)

Postrio has lost none of its excitement over the years; the stairway down into the restaurant is as dramatic, the decor (by Pat Kuleto) is as stunning, and the food is as sensational as the day the place opened. For several years, Postrio was a spawning ground for chefs who went on to open their own excellent restaurants in San Francisco. The current chefs, brothers Mitchell and Steven Rosenthal, however, take turns continuing Postrio's tradition of contemporary American cuisine while also helming Town Hall (page 192) on the other side of Market Street. Here is their version of *cacciucco*, the Italian fisherman's soup that evolved into cioppino when it came to San Francisco.

$^1/_2$ cup extra-virgin olive oil

3 garlic cloves, thinly sliced

1 teaspoon red pepper flakes

1 tablespoon tomato paste

16 mussels, scrubbed and debearded

8 ounces large rock shrimp in the shell

6 ounces bay scallops or halved sea scallops

$^1/_2$ cup dry white wine

6 cups Lobster Stock (recipe follows)

1 tablespoon chopped fresh oregano

GARNISH

Chopped fresh flat-leaf parsley

Extra-virgin olive oil for drizzling

In a stockpot, heat the oil over medium heat and sauté the garlic until lightly browned. Add the pepper flakes, tomato paste, seafood, and white wine and cover immediately. Cook for 2 minutes. Remove the lid, add the stock, and cook, uncovered, for about 5 minutes, or until the shrimp are pink, the scallops are opaque, and the mussels have opened (discard any that do not open). Stir in the oregano. Ladle the soup into warmed shallow soup bowls. Garnish with parsley, drizzle with olive oil, and serve hot.

Lobster Stock

MAKES 6 CUPS

8 cups water
1¹/₂ pounds lobster shells, rinsed
¹/₂ cup dry white wine
¹/₂ carrot, peeled and chopped
1 celery stalk, chopped
1 leek (white part only), chopped
2 parsley sprigs
2 thyme sprigs
4 peppercorns
1 tablespoon tomato paste

In a small stockpot, combine all the ingredients and bring to a boil over high heat. Reduce heat to a simmer and cook for about 45 minutes, or until the stock is well flavored. Strain through a fine-meshed sieve, pressing on the solids with the back of a large spoon. Let cool, then cover and refrigerate for up to 2 days. To keep longer, bring to a boil every 2 days, or freeze for up to 2 months.

Fish Stock or Shrimp Stock: Substitute fish bones and parts or shrimp shells for the lobster shells in the above recipe. If making fish stock, delete the tomato paste.

Gnudi

(Spinach-Ricotta Gnocchi)

SERVES 8 AS A FIRST COURSE, 4 AS A MAIN COURSE

Scala's Bistro

Sir Francis Drake Hotel,
432 Powell Street
(between Post and Sutter)

Outside, tourists, locals, and the Sir Francis Drake doorman, clad in his brilliant red Beefeater costume, are doing a kind of line dance on the sidewalk, and the cable cars are clanging by on their way to Market Street and Aquatic Park. Inside this elegant, high-ceilinged trattoria, people are indulging in chef Staffan Terje's robust Italian and French Provençal cuisine, like these satisfying gnocchi. Come here for lunch, or for dinner before or after the theater, and enjoy being one remove from the heart of the downtown / Union Square bustle.

Note: If you are unable to find Bellwether Farms ricotta cheese or other dense Italian-style ricotta, you will need to empty the ricotta into a colander lined with cheesecloth and placed over a bowl to let the cheese drain for 4 hours. Most American cheese is otherwise too watery for this recipe.

2 bunches spinach, stemmed and well rinsed
1 pound Bellwether Farms whole-milk ricotta cheese
1 cup (4 ounces) grated Parmesan cheese
1 cup pastry or cake flour, sifted
1 large egg, beaten
1 large egg yolk
1 tablespoon kosher salt
1 teaspoon freshly ground pepper
1 teaspoon freshly grated nutmeg
Olive oil for coating
Tomato sauce (page 168) or melted butter and grated Parmesan for serving

- Put the still-wet spinach in a large pot, cover, and cook over medium-low heat until wilted, 2 to 3 minutes. Transfer to a colander and let drain until cool to the touch. Squeeze dry, one small handful at a time. Transfer to a cutting board and use a chef's knife to cut the spinach very finely.

- In a large bowl, combine the spinach and all the remaining ingredients except the olive oil and tomato sauce (or butter and Parmesan). Gently mix with your hands until a soft dough has formed. Do not knead the mixture. Divide into 4 pieces. On a lightly floured work surface, roll each piece into a rope about ½ inch thick. Cut each rope into 1-inch pieces and dust lightly with flour.

- In a large pot of salted, slowly boiling water, cook the gnocchi in batches until they rise to the surface. Using a wire skimmer, transfer to ice water to cool. Drain and toss with olive oil to prevent sticking. Heat gently in the sauce and serve in warmed bowls, or serve in the bowls, topped with the melted butter and Parmesan.

Jackson Square /
Financial District

Aqua

Bix Restaurant

Bocadillos

Globe

Kokkari Estiatorio

Palio D'Asti

Plouf

Rubicon

Tadich Grill

THE OLD BRICK BUILDINGS ARE CHARMING, the streets are clean, the windows are filled with pricey antiques, but beneath the pavement of the Jackson Square district—and the adjacent Financial District—beats the old, wild heart

of the city. When you walk through these streets, you're walking over buried ships, a lost lagoon, the foundations of the first buildings constructed in San Francisco, and the remains of one of the most frenzied get-rich-quick meccas in human history. If you stroll down Montgomery Street, you're walking over the shoreline of the little cove that stretched from Alta Loma (now called Telegraph Hill) to Rincon Hill (later cut down to form a base for the southern end of the Bay Bridge). ⟶ BELOW MONTGOMERY STREET stretched mudflats that were covered with water at high tide; soon they were filled in with wharves that extended the streets out to the ships rocking in the harbor. When the ships were abandoned during the Gold Rush, their crews gone off to seek their fortunes in the mountains, they were turned into shops and restaurants, or sunk for fill. ⟶ ALMOST ALL THE BUILDINGS FROM THAT TIME ARE GONE NOW; most of those remaining are in the Jackson Square district. One or two stories high, they are made of unreinforced brick and have managed to ride out every earthquake since they were constructed, including the Big One in 1906. Many of the other buildings in this area were put up just after the Great Quake; in some of them, you can see exposed walls of broken bricks, for they were built of earthquake rubble. ⟶ THIS IS A NEIGHBORHOOD FOR STROLLING and imagining the past. Brass plaques on the sides of buildings throughout the area mark significant sites, from the first literary weekly in the city (with Mark Twain and Bret Harte on staff) to the Old Ghirardelli Building, the original location of the company before it moved to Ghirardelli Square. Pacific Street was the center of the infamous Barbary Coast, named after the pirate-ridden coast of North Africa and one of the most degenerate places on earth for a period of more than fifty years following the Gold Rush. Both visitors and residents alike should make it a point to follow the 3.8-mile-long Barbary Coast Trail established in 1997. Far more than just a tour of the Coast, it runs from the Old Mint south of Market to Maritime Park and is marked by brass plaques in the sidewalks. A Barbary Coast Trail walking map and/or guidebook will lead you from site to site and make the past spring to life in the midst of the present. ⟶ UNLIKE THE RECLAIMED AREAS OF SOME CITIES, Jackson Square has never been turned into an Old Town, for despite all its

charm and quietude it is still very much a part of the current city of San Francisco. Law offices, design firms, antiques shops, and restaurants fill the high-ceilinged rooms. From the start, these two neighborhoods were the commercial part of San Francisco, and today the Financial District sprouts on the eastern and southern edges of Jackson Square, where the buildings change

from small and ornate to huge, sleek highrises housing banks and other financial institutions. ⟶ SPRINKLED IN BETWEEN ARE RESTAURANTS. In a little alley that runs between Bush and Pine, facing the enormous, dark Bank of America building, is a cluster of eating places that include French bistros (Plouf and Café Bastille), two Italian trattorias (Cafe Tiramisù and Brindisi), a Catalonian restaurant (B44), and Sam's, a classic San Francisco seafood spot

OTHER NEIGHBORHOOD STARS

B44 Catalan Bistro

Brindisi Cucina di Mare

Cafe Tiramisù

Myth

Sam's Grill

Silks

dating from 1867, with old-fashioned curtained booths. The two French restaurants on this short stretch are an extension of the nearby Gallic enclave of Café Claude, Le Central, and Café de la Presse, which lies across the way from the French Consulate and the Notre Dame de Victoires church on Bush Street. On Bastille Day, these streets are clogged with people and decorated with blue, white, and red banners and balloons. On mild-weather weekdays, Belden and Leidesdorf Streets, which are closed to traffic, are filled with people having lunch at tables and chairs set out on the pavement. ⟶ THE RESTAURANTS IN THIS PART OF TOWN no longer serve bear steak or pigs' feet; red-flocked wallpaper and crystal chandeliers are harder and harder to find; and private upstairs dining rooms are almost nonexistent. But the restaurant scene is still thriving in the many low-key, elegant restaurants of Jackson Square and the Financial District. Leaving the premises late in the evening and walking through the quiet streets toward the lights of North Beach, you may think you can hear the long, rolling rush of waves, or the sound of cards slapping on bare tables, or the strains of fiddle music. You may even think you can smell the smoke from cooking fires, or the faintly bitter smell of baking sourdough bread—but, after all, it's only your imagination.

King Salmon
with Dungeness Crab Fondue

SERVES 4 AS A MAIN COURSE

A stunning restaurant serving food that is equally beautiful. Showered with accolades since it opened in 1991, Aqua is considered the premiere seafood restaurant in a town that prides itself on its preparation of foods from the ocean. Prices are high, but the setting and the sophisticated food from chef Laurent Manrique are worth it. Manrique, formerly of Campton Place, has added a Gallic flavor to the menu since signing on here, as is evidenced by this many-faceted dish of two San Francisco favorites, wild salmon and Dungeness crab.

Aqua
252 California Street
(between Battery and Front)

Note: To simplify this dish, delete the shellfish broth.

SHELLFISH BROTH
8 ounces mixed lobster, shrimp, and crab shells
1 large shallot, coarsely chopped
1/2 head garlic (halved crosswise), outer skin removed
2 thyme sprigs
1/2 bay leaf
1 1/2 tablespoons tomato paste
About 8 cups water or chicken stock
2 tablespoons Cognac or brandy to taste

4 whole pea pods for garnish
1 1/2 pounds green peas, shelled (1 1/2 cups), blanched for 1 minute
1 1/2 pounds fava beans, shelled (1 1/2 cups), blanched for 2 minutes and peeled
1 cup chicken stock, heated
1 tablespoon unsalted butter

SHERRY VINAIGRETTE
1 teaspoon sherry vinegar
2 teaspoons olive oil
Kosher salt and freshly ground pepper to taste

Four 5-ounce wild king salmon fillets, pinbones removed
Olive oil for coating
Salt and freshly ground pepper to taste
6 ounces fresh lump Dungeness crabmeat, picked over for shell
Beurre Blanc (recipe follows)
4 ounces pea shoots

- To make the shellfish broth: In a large pot, combine the lobster, shrimp, and crab shells. Stir well over high heat until all the shells have some color. Add the shallot, garlic, thyme, and bay leaf. Add the tomato paste and stir well until the paste is a shade darker. Add water or chicken stock to cover. Reduce heat to medium and simmer for 20 minutes. Remove from heat and push through a medium-meshed sieve with the back of a large spoon. Stir in the Cognac or brandy. Set aside.

- To make the garnish: Split the pea pods carefully to keep the peas inside the pod intact and the two halves of the pod together at the stem end. Put them in a small skillet of barely simmering water and cook for 2 to 3 minutes. Drain, cool in ice water, drain again, and set aside on paper towels.

- In a blender, combine half of the peas, half of the fava beans, and the hot chicken stock. Purée until smooth. Add the butter and purée again. Season with salt and pepper. Set aside and keep warm.

- In a small bowl, whisk all the vinaigrette ingredients together and set aside.

- Coat the salmon fillets with olive oil. Season with salt and pepper. Heat a grill pan over medium heat. Coat with oil, using paper towels. Add the salmon and cook, skin side down, for 2 minutes, then turn and cook on the second side for 2 to 3 minutes for medium-rare.

- In a small saucepan, combine the crabmeat, remaining peas, and remaining fava beans. Warm over very low heat for a few seconds. Add just enough beurre blanc to make the mixture creamy. Season with salt and pepper to taste.

Place one fourth of the fondue in the center of each of 4 warmed plates. On each side of the fondue, place a spoonful of the pea and fava bean purée. Set the salmon on top of the fondue. Toss the pea shoots with the sherry vinaigrette and set atop the fish. Garnish each serving with a pea pod half. Serve the shellfish broth on the side, for dipping or pouring over.

Beurre Blanc: In a medium saucepan, combine ¼ cup chopped shallots, ½ bay leaf, ¼ bunch thyme, ½ teaspoon black peppercorns, and 1 cup dry white wine. Cook over medium heat to reduce to about 2 tablespoons. Strain into a clean saucepan. Cut ¾ cup (1½ sticks) unsalted butter into tablespoon-sized pieces. Place the saucepan over very low heat and gradually whisk in the butter one piece at a time until the sauce is creamy and thick. Season with salt and pepper to taste. Cover and keep warm over tepid water. Makes about ¾ cup.

Wine Pairing: "Who says red does not go with fish! Step out of the box and try this dish with a 2002 Keyhole Ranch Pinot Noir from Seghesio Family Vineyards. A great balance of fruit and earth, texture and acidity."

—Sommelier Sean Crowley

Chicken Hash à la Bix

SERVES 4 AS A MAIN COURSE

Bix Restaurant

56 Gold Street (between Jackson and Pacific)

Hidden on a narrow alley where gold was assayed during the Gold Rush, Bix has long been delighting San Franciscans who enjoy stepping into another time: the glamorous thirties. In this Art Deco supper club, where you might expect William Powell to come walking down the stairs at any moment, you can listen to jazz, drink Martinis or a wine from their excellent list, and dine on such regional American cuisine as these hash patties made with chicken, grits, and fresh corn, served with a fresh-tomato sauce. Remember this hash for a brunch or lunch dish, and the sauce for topping other savory pancakes or fritters.

POACHED CHICKEN

One 3-pound chicken
3 carrots, peeled and halved crosswise
3 celery stalks, halved crosswise
1 bay leaf
1 tablespoon black peppercorns
1 teaspoon minced fresh thyme
1 tablespoon minced fresh flat-leaf parsley

GRITS

1 1/2 teaspoons unsalted butter
1 1/2 teaspoons minced garlic
1 tablespoon minced red onion
Kernels cut from 3 ears fresh corn, plus milk from scraping cobs with a knife
1/4 cup hominy grits
1/4 cup heavy cream
1/4 teaspoon salt
Pinch of freshly ground pepper

Kernels cut from 2 ears fresh corn
1/4 cup finely chopped green onions, including green parts

Savoring San Francisco

28

2 tablespoons olive oil
¼ cup diced red onion
¼ cup all-purpose flour
1 egg, lightly beaten
Salt and freshly ground pepper to taste

SAUCE

1 teaspoon unsalted butter, plus 2 tablespoons
1 teaspoon minced shallot
½ teaspoon crushed garlic
1 tablespoon tomato paste
4 tomatoes, peeled, seeded, and diced (see note)
Pinch of sugar
1 tablespoon chopped fresh basil
1 tablespoon minced fresh flat-leaf parsley
Salt and freshly ground pepper to taste
½ cup dry white wine

Flour for dusting
2 tablespoons olive oil
Finely chopped green onions, including green parts, for garnish

● To poach the chicken: Put the chicken in a stockpot and add cold water to cover. Add the carrots, celery, bay leaf, peppercorns, thyme, and parsley. Bring to a boil and then turn off the heat. Leave the chicken submerged for 50 minutes, then remove from the stockpot and let cool to the touch. Remove the skin from the chicken and pull the meat from the bones. Cut the meat into ½-inch pieces.

● To make the grits: In a small saucepan, melt the butter over medium heat and sauté the garlic and red onion until fragrant, about 2 minutes. Add the corn and its milk and simmer for 1 minute. Add the hominy grits and cream. Cook, stirring occasionally, until the grits are cooked and thickened, 5 to 7 minutes. Stir in the salt and pepper. Set aside to cool for about 15 minutes.

In large bowl, combine the grits, corn kernels, green onion, and chicken. In a small saucepan over medium-low heat, heat the olive oil and sauté the red onion for about 3 minutes, or until translucent. Add to the grits mixture. Add the flour, egg, salt, and pepper. Stir until blended.

Preheat the oven to 400°F. To make the sauce: In a small saucepan, melt the 1 teaspoon butter over low heat and sauté the shallot and garlic until golden. Add the tomato paste and cook for about 1 minute. Add the tomatoes, basil, parsley, salt, pepper, and wine. Cover and cook until the tomatoes soften and the mixture thickens, about 10 minutes. Stir in the 2 tablespoons butter. Set the sauce aside and cover to keep warm.

Shape the grits mixture into patties and dust with flour. In a large, ovenproof nonstick skillet, heat the olive oil over medium heat until fragrant. Carefully place the patties in the skillet and brown on one side. Turn the patties and place the pan in the oven to bake for 5 minutes. Serve on warmed plates, with the sauce spooned over and the green onions sprinkled on top.

Warm Piquillo Peppers
with Goat Cheese, California Raisins, and Moscatel Vinaigrette

SERVES 8 AS A FIRST COURSE, 4 AS A MAIN COURSE

This sophisticated urban cafe would not be out of place on a trendy street in Biarritz or Bilbao, but it also fits right in on Montgomery Street, next door to the Bubble Lounge. An outpost of Gerald Hirigoyen's Basque restaurant on Battery Street (Pipérade, page 89), Bocadillos is named for the small sandwiches popular in the Basque region and in Spain. The menu includes several interesting versions of these, along with a variety of small plates that sometimes include these meltingly good stuffed peppers, making this a perfect spot for lunch, an after-work drink, or a late-night snack; Bocadillos is also open for breakfast.

Bocadillos
710 Montgomery Street
(at Washington)

8 roasted piquillo peppers (sold in jars in specialty markets)
or red bell peppers

FILLING
1¹/₂ cups fresh goat cheese
¹/₂ cup pine nuts, toasted (see note)
¹/₂ cup golden California raisins, soaked in water to cover
for 3 to 4 hours and drained
3 tablespoons finely snipped fresh chives
3 tablespoons minced fresh basil
¹/₂ teaspoon piment d'Espelette (Basque chili powder), or ¹/₄ teaspoon cayenne
pepper and ¹/₄ teaspoon sweet Hungarian paprika
¹/₄ cup heavy cream

MOSCATEL VINAIGRETTE
3¹/₂ tablespoons moscatel vinegar (a Spanish vinegar) or balsamic vinegar
¹/₂ teaspoon kosher salt
¹/₄ teaspoon freshly ground black pepper

¹/₃ cup extra-virgin olive oil
3 tablespoons golden California raisins,
soaked in water to cover for 3 to 4 hours and drained

GARNISH

Finely snipped fresh chives
4 small handfuls micro greens or baby salad greens

- If using piquillo peppers, drain them. If using bell peppers, preheat the broiler. Cut off the top of each pepper and remove the seeds and ribs, leaving the pepper whole. Place the peppers on a broiler pan and broil about 2 inches from the heat source until blackened, about 5 minutes on each side. Transfer to a paper bag, close the bag, and let cool to the touch, about 10 minutes. Remove the peel.

- Preheat the oven to 375°F. Lay the peppers out on a small baking sheet and set aside. In a large bowl, combine all of the filling ingredients and stir until well blended.

- Gently stuff each of the peppers with an equal amount of the filling mixture and return them to the pan. Place in the oven and bake just until warmed through, 5 to 6 minutes.

- Meanwhile, make the vinaigrette: In a small bowl, combine the vinegar, salt, pepper, and olive oil and whisk well until blended. Stir in the raisins and set aside.

- To serve, place a stuffed pepper on each plate and prop a second one up against it at an angle. Spoon the vinaigrette liberally over the peppers and garnish with snipped chives. Garnish each plate with a mound of micro greens or salad greens. Serve at once.

Toasting Pine Nuts: In a small, dry skillet, stir the pine nuts over medium heat just until golden; take care not to burn. Immediately empty the nuts into a bowl to cool.

Grilled Salmon Paillards
on Bucatini with Watercress and Chile de Árbol Aglio e Olio

SERVES 4 AS A MAIN COURSE

Launched by two veterans of Postrio (page 16), Globe is a casual, small (forty-four-seat) restaurant in a hip setting on the edge of Jackson Square. Chef/owner Joseph Manzare's food is rustic but innovative (he calls it California cuisine with an Italian spirit), and Globe has been a magnet for food-lovers from the minute it opened to enormous buzz in 1997. Because it is one of the few fine restaurants that stay open late (until 1 A.M.), it's a favorite stop for chefs from other restaurants and anyone else out on the town.

Globe
290 Pacific Avenue
(between Battery and Front)

Four 5-ounce wild salmon fillets, pinbones removed
2 tablespoons olive oil
Kosher salt and freshly ground pepper to taste

SALSA VERDE
Pinch of kosher salt
Freshly ground pepper to taste
Grated zest of ¼ lemon
1 tablespoon capers, drained
1 garlic clove
3 heaping tablespoons chopped fresh flat-leaf parsley
3 tablespoons extra-virgin olive oil
1 tablespoon fresh lemon juice

14 ounces bucatini or dried linguine pasta
5 tablespoons olive oil
2 teaspoons minced garlic
Pinch of crushed chile de árbol or red pepper flakes
Pinch of freshly ground pepper

¾ cup chicken stock or canned low-salt chicken broth
2 bunches watercress, stemmed
¼ cup grated Parmesan cheese

- Coat the salmon fillets with the olive oil and season with salt and pepper. Set aside.

- To make the salsa verde: In a mortar, combine the salt, pepper, lemon zest, capers, and garlic. Grind with a pestle to make a paste. Add the parsley, oil, and lemon juice and work everything together for 2 or 3 minutes to make a smooth sauce. Set aside.

- In a large pot of salted boiling water, cook the pasta until al dente, about 10 minutes; drain. At the same time, preheat the broiler or heat a grill pan over high heat. Broil the salmon, skin-side down, on a broiler pan and broil 6 inches from the heat source or cook in the grill pan for 3 minutes on each side, or until opaque and browned on the outside and still slightly translucent in the center.

- While the pasta and salmon are cooking, heat a large sauté pan or skillet over medium heat, add the olive oil, and sauté the garlic just until it starts to color. Add the crushed chile or pepper flakes and ground pepper.

- Add the pasta to the pan with the chile and pepper and cook over medium heat for 1 minute. Add the stock or broth and cook for about 1 minute. Increase heat to high, add the watercress and Parmesan, and toss to mix.

- Divide the pasta among warmed bowls. Place 1 piece of salmon on each serving and top the salmon with 1 tablespoon of the salsa verde. Serve at once.

Braised Oxtails
with Garlic and Feta

SERVES 6 AS A MAIN COURSE

The corner of Jackson and Front may be the closest some of us will ever come to dining in a lavish Greek country home, with a cadre of chefs in the kitchen turning out stellar food. Kokkari, named for a fishing village on the island of Samos, has a huge open fireplace, big windows with wooden shutters that open onto the street, massive wooden beams, a vast wooden table in one room that seats twenty-two, and generous plates of New Greek cuisine. Start with the assorted Greek appetizers with house-made grilled pita, and move on to one of the rustic main-course dishes from chef Erik Cosselman, typified by these savory braised oxtails.

Kokkari Estiatorio
200 Jackson Street (at Front)

Note: This dish is even better if made one day ahead.

Salt and freshly ground pepper to taste
4 to 5 pounds oxtails, trimmed and cut at the joint
Flour for dredging
¼ cup olive oil
½ cup red wine vinegar
About 6 cups beef broth
Cloves from 3 garlic bulbs, crushed
5 thyme sprigs, tied together with kitchen twine
6 bay leaves
1 pound orzo pasta

GARNISH

1½ cups (8 ounces) crumbled feta cheese
1 cup Greek black olives, pitted
Grated zest of 1 lemon
3 tablespoons minced fresh flat-leaf parsley

Preheat the oven to 325°F. Salt and pepper the oxtails. Dredge in the flour to coat evenly; shake off the excess. In a Dutch oven or heatproof casserole, heat the olive oil over medium heat and brown the oxtails on all sides, about 15 minutes. Using a slotted spoon or a wire-mesh skimmer, transfer the oxtails to a plate.

Add the vinegar to the pan and stir over medium heat to scrape up the browned bits on the bottom of the pan. Add the broth. Taste and adjust the seasoning. Bring to a boil and add the garlic, thyme, and bay leaves. Add the oxtails, cover the pot, and bake until the meat is very tender and the pan juices are rich, 3 to 4 hours. Remove the thyme and bay leaves. Spoon off the fat on the surface. If making ahead, let cool, then cover and refrigerate overnight. Remove and discard the congealed fat on the surface. Reheat the oxtails over medium-low heat until heated through.

Just before the oxtails are done, cook the orzo in a pot of salted boiling water until al dente, about 8 minutes. Drain. Transfer to a medium saucepan, cover, and keep warm. To serve, ladle ¼ cup of the pan juices over the orzo. Heat the orzo over medium-low heat for 1 or 2 minutes to heat through. Mound the orzo on warmed plates and spoon the oxtails and some of the pan juices over. Sprinkle with the feta, olives, lemon zest, and parsley to garnish. Serve hot.

Pollo alla Marsala
con Spinaci Siciliani
(Chicken Marsala with Sicilian Spinach)

SERVES 6 AS A MAIN COURSE

This narrow, somewhat formal space with windows on Sacramento Street is brightened with large wall murals of the famous Palio d'Asti, a bareback horse race in Asti, Italy. Chef Daniel Scherotter prepares Italian food for the Financial District crowd, who fill the tables here at lunch and for early suppers after work. His chicken Marsala is topped with a rich, intensely flavored glaze, and served on spinach quickly sautéed with golden raisins and pine nuts, Sicilian style.

Palio D'Asti
640 Sacramento Street
(between Kearny and Montgomery)

6 small (6- to 8-ounce) skin-on boneless chicken breasts, with wing if possible
16 tablespoons (2 sticks) unsalted butter
³/₄ cup pine nuts
¹/₂ cup golden raisins
2 cups sweet Marsala wine
¹/₄ cup canola or grapeseed oil
Salt to taste
2 tablespoons minced shallots
1 tablespoon tomato paste
2 cups chicken broth, simmered for 20 minutes or so
with leftover Parmesan rinds, if possible
1 tablespoon minced garlic
2 pounds baby spinach

- Preheat the oven to 500°F. Using a flat meat pounder or the bottom of a skillet, pound the chicken breasts so they are of equal thickness.

- In a medium skillet, melt 4 tablespoons of the butter over medium-low heat. Add the pine nuts and stir until toasted, about 3 minutes. Remove from heat and set aside. In a small saucepan, combine the raisins and Marsala. Heat over low heat until the raisins are tender, about 8 minutes. Drain, reserving the Marsala.

In a large, heavy sauté pan or skillet, heat the canola or grapeseed oil over medium heat until shimmering. Salt the skin sides of the chicken breasts and add to the pan, skin side down. Do this in batches if necessary to prevent crowding. Cook until browned, about 5 minutes, shaking the pan to prevent sticking. Transfer the chicken, skin side up, to a rimmed baking sheet (jelly-roll pan). Place the baking sheet on the bottom rack of the oven and roast for about 5 minutes, or until opaque throughout.

Pour off the oil in the skillet. Add 4 tablespoons of the butter and melt over medium heat. Add the shallots and sauté, scraping up the browned bits from the bottom of the pan, until browned, about 4 minutes. Stand back and carefully add the reserved Marsala, which will flame up. Shake the pan to put the flames out and cook the Marsala to reduce to a glaze. Stir in the tomato paste until blended. Stir in the chicken broth and cook until reduced to a glaze. Stir in the remaining 8 tablespoons butter. Add salt to taste.

Meanwhile, in a large pot over medium heat, combine the pine nuts, their butter, and the garlic. Sauté for 1 to 2 minutes. Add the spinach, raisins, and salt to taste. Stir frequently until spinach is just wilted. Using a wire skimmer, transfer to a warmed platter. Using tongs, transfer the chicken to the bed of spinach. Add the juices from the baking sheet to the glaze. Pour the glaze over the chicken and serve at once.

Note: The chef says this dish is perfect with a jammy California Zinfandel.

Crab Cakes

SERVES 4 AS AN APPETIZER, 2 AS A MAIN COURSE

Plouf, the sound water makes when it splashes in France, is the perfect name for this Gallic-flavored seafood restaurant, one of a handful of European bistros in this lively one-block-long alley. The charming wait staff wear striped Breton fisherman shirts, and the specialty here is various preparations of mussels, but the crab cakes are also some of the best in the city.

Plouf
40 Belden Street
(between Bush and Pine)

SAUCE
1 cup crème fraîche
2 tablespoons minced fresh chives
1 teaspoon minced lemon zest
1 tablespoon fresh lemon juice

CRAB CAKES
8 ounces fresh lump crabmeat, picked over for shell
1 tablespoon finely diced red onion
1 tablespoon finely diced roasted bell pepper (see page 40)
1 tablespoon finely chopped green onion
1 teaspoon minced fresh cilantro
1 teaspoon minced fresh chives
1 teaspoon minced fresh ginger
¼ teaspoon salt
1 tablespoon fresh lemon juice

Panko (Japanese bread crumbs) for breading
Grapeseed oil or canola oil for frying
4 large handfuls mâche or mixed baby salad greens
Vinaigrette (recipe follows)

- To make the sauce: In a small bowl, combine all the ingredients and stir to blend. Set aside.

- To make the crab cakes: Drain the crabmeat in a fine-meshed sieve to eliminate excess water. In a blender, purée one fourth of the crab. Add this purée to a medium bowl with the remaining crab and all the remaining crab cake ingredients. Portion the crab mixture with an ice cream scoop, flatten the balls into cakes, and dredge them in the panko to coat evenly.

- In a large skillet over medium heat, heat ½ inch oil until the surface shimmers. Add the cakes and fry until golden brown, 2 to 3 minutes on each side.

- To serve, toss the greens with enough vinaigrette to coat them well. Divide among 4 serving plates and place the crab cakes on top. Serve at once.

Vinaigrette

MAKES ½ CUP

½ tablespoon Dijon mustard
2 tablespoons red wine vinegar
6 tablespoons olive oil
½ teaspoon salt
½ teaspoon minced fresh thyme

- In a small bowl, stir mustard and vinegar together. Gradually whisk in the olive oil, then stir in the salt and thyme.

Roasting and Peeling Bell Peppers: Preheat the broiler. Cut the peppers in half and remove the seeds and ribs. Place the peppers on a broiler pan lined with aluminum foil and press them to flatten. Place the pan under the broiler about 2 inches from the heat source and broil until blackened, about 10 minutes. Using tongs, transfer the peppers to a paper bag, close the bag, and let cool for about 15 minutes. Rub off the blackened skin with your fingers.

Dungeness Crab

It's just a coincidence that Dungeness crab and Beaujolais Nouveau come into season at almost the same time, but it's a happy coincidence. The wine—fresh, fruity, and uncomplicated—is a good match for the mild, sweet flesh of crab. Those who scorn Nouveau as little better than grape juice can opt for the classic combination of cracked crab and Chardonnay. Fence-straddlers can choose a dry rosé like Bandol, or a Sauvignon Blanc instead.

Crab season usually opens around November 15, making this shellfish a traditional choice among many San Franciscans for holiday celebrations. For a Christmas-season party, you can't do much better than cold cracked crab, Brie, sourdough bread, and the wine of your choice, with a winter salad like Firefly's Grilled Fuyu Persimmon and Red Oak Leaf Lettuce Salad (page 237). Buy fresh lump Dungeness crabmeat during season (which runs until June) at Swan Oyster Depot, Whole Foods Market, or one of the crab stands at Fisherman's Wharf and make Plouf's crab cakes (page 39) or Rubicon's garlic soup (page 42); it's pricey but worth it not to have to shell your own.

Go out for cioppino on a blustery late fall or early-winter day, or make your own from Rose Pistola's recipe (page 74). Crab in black bean sauce (page 63) and garlic-roasted crab are also San Francisco favorites; either one is a good choice for Christmas Eve or New Year's Eve. Cover the table with newspaper instead of your fine linens, and provide finger bowls and towels at the end of the meal, followed by a knock-out dessert like Fringale's Pear Tarte Tatin (page 177) or Foreign Cinema's Chocolate Pots de Crème (page 210). Pick up your live Dungeness crabs in Chinatown or on the Wharf, keep them in the refrigerator in a paper bag, and cook them the same day you buy them. And remember: Crab season comes but once a year.

Caramelized Garlic Soup
with Dungeness Crab
and Upper Market Street Wild Anise

MAKES 6 FIRST-COURSE SERVINGS

Rubicon

558 Sacramento Street (between Montgomery and Sansome)

Opening with a slate of celebrity owners, including Francis Ford Coppola, Robin Williams, and Robert de Niro (those are his father's oil paintings on the walls), Rubicon has retained its touch of glamour and its chic downtown setting over time. The place is a favorite power-lunch spot for businesspeople in the neighborhood, and Larry Stone, the sommelier, is renowned for his knowledge of wine. Chef Stuart Brioza uses wild anise fronds in several of his dishes, from ice cream to salad; it grows all over San Francisco, including Upper Market Street, near where he lives in Noe Valley. But you can use the fronds reserved from trimming the fennel bulb used to make this subtly flavored soup.

¼ cup grapeseed oil
Cloves from 1 garlic bulb, chopped
4 thyme sprigs and 1 rosemary sprig, tied together with kitchen twine
¼ cup chopped peeled Granny Smith apple
¼ cup chopped fennel bulb
1 cup chopped peeled red potato
Salt to taste
8 cups low-salt chicken broth
4 tablespoons unsalted butter, cut into pieces
2 to 3 tablespoons Chardonnay or other white wine vinegar

GARNISH

2 tablespoons unsalted butter
8 ounces fresh lump Dungeness crabmeat, picked over for shell
18 thin slices unpeeled Granny Smith apple
½ cup julienned prosciutto

Salt and freshly ground pepper to taste
Thin baguette slices brushed with garlic oil and baked
Wild anise or fennel fronds or fresh chervil sprigs

- In a 1-gallon soup pot, heat the grapeseed oil over very low heat and add the garlic and herb bundle. Cook, stirring occasionally, for 20 minutes, or until the garlic just barely begins to turn golden and the raw aroma is gone. Add the chopped apple, fennel, and potato. Cook, stirring once or twice, for 5 to 8 minutes. Season with salt. Add the chicken broth and bring to a boil, then reduce heat to a simmer and cook for 15 minutes. Remove and reserve the herb bundle. In a blender, purée the soup in batches, adding the butter as you go. Transfer the soup back to the pot. Squeeze the herb bundle as hard as you can into the soup. Add the vinegar. Taste and adjust the seasoning.

- To prepare the garnish: In a medium sauté pan or skillet, melt the 2 tablespoons butter over medium heat. Add the crabmeat, apple, and prosciutto. Season with salt and pepper. Stir until heated through.

- Divide the garnish mixture among 6 warmed bowls. Pour 1¼ cups soup into each bowl. Garnish with the croutons and the anise or fennel fronds, or chervil sprigs.

Hangtown Fry

SERVES 1 AS A MAIN COURSE

Tadich Grill
240 California
(between Battery and Front)

The oldest restaurant in town, Tadich Grill started life in a tent on the waterfront in 1849. In its current location since 1967, it remains an authentic taste of Old San Francisco, with its aproned waiters, wooden booths, and dark wood paneling. You owe it to yourself, in a time when new restaurants seem to spring up almost every day, to come here periodically and dine on history with one of the city's classic dishes, like this oyster and bacon frittata that dates from the Gold Rush. This recipe is for one serving, but you could multiply it as needed, using a larger skillet. (For a large frittata, don't try to turn it to cook the second side; instead, use a flameproof skillet and place the pan under a preheated broiler.) It's a great Sunday brunch dish to serve with fried potatoes and fresh fruit.

4 large or 6 medium oysters, shucked
Salt and freshly ground pepper to taste
Fine dried bread crumbs or flour for dredging
2 bacon slices
1 tablespoon unsalted butter
3 eggs, lightly beaten with salt and freshly ground pepper to taste
Herb sprigs for garnish
Tabasco sauce for serving

- Sprinkle the oysters with salt and pepper. Dredge the oysters in the bread crumbs or flour. Set aside on a plate.

- In a 6-inch omelette pan or cast-iron skillet, fry the bacon until lightly crisped, 3 to 5 minutes. Using tongs, transfer the bacon to paper towels to drain.

- Pour off all the fat in the pan. In the same pan, melt the butter over medium heat and fry the oysters just until lightly browned, about 2 minutes on each side. Reduce heat to low and pour the eggs over the oysters. Let the eggs begin to set, then use a spoon to push the cooked edge of the eggs back so the uncooked portion runs underneath, tilting the pan as necessary. When the bottom is golden brown, lay the bacon strips over the top of the frittata. Using a metal spatula, turn the frittata and finish cooking until set on the second side. Serve at once on a warmed plate, garnished with herb sprigs and with Tabasco sauce alongside.

Old San Francisco

They're still there, the old restaurants and cafes of San Francisco, mixed in among all the trendy new places. You won't find much confit or coulis or many balsamic reductions in their kitchens, and the furnishings might be a little the worse for wear, but the patina of time and custom can't be reproduced by any team of designers. Seek out these tried-and-true San Francisco places; each one defines the word unique.

- *Original Joe's*
- *Louis' Restaurant*
- *Red's Java House*
- *Schroeder's*
- *Swan Oyster Depot*
- *Caffè Trieste*
- *The Old Clam House*
- *Tadich Grill (above)*

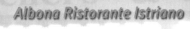

North Beach / Chinatown

CITY LIGHTS Booksellers & B

Albona Ristorante Istriano

Café Jacqueline

Da Flora

Enrico's Sidewalk Cafe

Great Eastern

Helmand

L'Osteria del Forno

Moose's

Rose Pistola

THERE IS NO BEACH IN NORTH BEACH, though there was one once, reaching up to what is today Francisco Street. The beach is hidden now, along with North Point Cove, beneath rubble from the Great Earthquake, including the broken bricks and stones from the original Palace and St. Francis Hotels. Juana Briones's adobe farmhouse, which stood near the northwest corner of what is

today Washington Square (and was then her cow pasture), disappeared long ago, before the streets were platted and paved. — MANY OTHER THINGS HAVE VANISHED FROM THIS PART OF SAN FRANCISCO. The foosball machine has disappeared from Mario's Bohemian Cigar Store; the model ship no longer sinks in the window of Graffeo's Coffee; and Mr. Figoni is gone forever, along with his hardware store on Grant Avenue, lined floor to ceiling with wooden drawers and shelves. — BUT OTHER THINGS REMAIN. You can still smell garlic in the streets, sometimes mingled with the smell of roasting coffee from Graffeo's, or Caffè Roma, or Caffè Trieste. In the middle of the night, the smell of baking bread wafts out into the streets, and if you happen to be walking home after a late evening just then, the bakers at the Italian-French Bakery might hand you a warm sourdough loaf right out of the oven when you knock on their door. Early in the morning, when almost no one else is out, walking down Grant Avenue you can smell wine in the air, mingled with the salt-and-iodine fragrance of the bay. — THE GHOSTS OF OTHER REVELERS WALK HERE, TOO, from the early bohemians who took the Clay and Sacramento cable cars up to their aeries on Russian Hill, to their descendants, the Beats, who lived in once-cheap North Beach apartments and drank dark coffee and cheap red wine in the cafes. — THE ITALIAN PRESENCE

IN NORTH BEACH dates to the earliest days of the town, when Italians built shanties on the slopes of Telegraph Hill, and red wine was made in the basements of the houses meandering down to Columbus Avenue, once the beginning of the road to the Presidio. People who love North Beach worry that it's changing too much and losing its European flavor, and it's true that many of the old family-style Italian restaurants of North Beach have closed, along with the Basque restaurants, originally dining rooms for the hotels where sheepherders stayed when they came down from the Sierra. BUT WONDER OF WONDERS, some things go away only to come back again. Washington Square Bar and Grill was turned into the Cobalt Tavern, then turned back into the "Washbag" again. The U.S. Restaurant went out of business, then reappeared a little later in a different location. Even Clown Alley, famed for its giant burgers, morphed into another restaurant and then came back. And though Panelli's and the Florence Delicatessen have closed, an authentic new Italian deli, Palermo, has opened catty-corner from the square, so now you can buy a huge deli sandwich and picnic on the grass in the sun. THE COFFEEHOUSES ARE STILL GOING STRONG, TOO, and each one is unique, not a clone of some other coffeehouse in town. In early 2005, the San Francisco Board of Supervisors passed legislation banning chain stores in North Beach, so every business here is one of a kind, embodying all the personality and eccentricities of its owners. You can still buy Italian bread in the bakeries, and coffee that's been roasted on site in the coffeehouses. And a few excellent Italian restaurants have open in the last few years in among North Beach's non-Italian places, which range from Persian to Asian fusion and from Irish to Bolivian. SLIPPING OVER BROADWAY and centered around

OTHER
NEIGHBORHOOD
STARS

Café Niebaum-Coppola

Caffè Macaroni

The House

Jai Yun

Mama's

Maykedah

Mo's

North Beach Restaurant

R & G Lounge

Tommaso's

Venticello

Yuet Lee

North Beach / Chinatown

49

Grant Avenue and Stockton Street is Chinatown, a neighborhood where the sidewalks overflow with shoppers. On the edge of Chinatown is Portsmouth

Square, the oldest part of San Francisco after the Presidio and Mission Dolores. It was in this square that the Stars and Stripes was first raised in 1847, and Yerba Buena was changed instantly from a small Mexican pueblo to an American town. Soon after, in 1848, the first Chinese restaurant opened nearby, and the Chinese began doing one of the things they do best: bringing their ancient, complex cuisine to the table. STOREFRONT RESTAURANTS FILL CHINATOWN THESE DAYS. Little or no attempt at decor is made in most of them; Formica tables, paper napkins, and an Asian calendar or painting is usually the extent of the design. Almost always there is a shrine to the Kitchen God, with lighted candles and a pyramid of oranges, usually high up on a wall or perhaps on top of the refrigerator, which may be in the dining room. But the food that you eat there, cooked and served quickly and cheaply, will be the result of centuries of an gastronomic art that blends and balances hot and cold, sweet and sour, taste and texture. INTERSPERSED BETWEEN THE CHINESE RESTAURANTS and dim sum parlors are a few other ethnic restaurants, such as Vietnamese pho houses, and the many food markets that illustrate the Chinese obsession with freshness: Empty wooden boxes stood on end in front of markets support open boxes of fruit and vegetables both familiar and exotic, from spinach and oranges to gai choy, lo bok, and durian. In the fish markets, some of the fish are still alive and swimming in tanks, a feature also found in the best fish restaurants of Chinatown. The markets along Stockton Street, the main shopping street of the neighborhood, are the place to buy some of the freshest and lowest-priced duck, chicken, fish, and crab in town. It seems that everyone in Chinatown is carrying a pink plastic bag, for people shop for food here every day.   THIS NORTHEAST AREA OF THE CITY IS A FOG-FREE ZONE and a food heaven, where two different cultures and cuisines are juxtaposed just a street or a storefront apart. Back in the heart of North Beach, the sidewalks overflow with more tables and chairs than produce stands. A few years ago, a city ordinance was changed (thanks to a challenge by Hanna Suleiman, the owner of Caffè Greco in the Beach), permitting food to be served at sidewalk tables, and North Beach was suddenly transformed into a scene from an Italian movie. If you walk through this neighborhood on a sunny day or on a warm—or even cool—night, you automatically become part of a big outdoor party, no longer just an observer but an active participant in the sweet life of San Francisco.

Coniglio in Agrodolce

(Braised Rabbit in a Sweet and Sour Glaze)

SERVES 6 AS A MAIN COURSE

Albona Ristorante Istriano

545 Francisco Street
(between Mason and Taylor)

Albona is unique in San Francisco and the entire West Coast, for it serves the cuisine of Istria, the homeland of Albona's owner, Bruno Viscovi. Near Trieste, on the Adriatic Coast, today it is part of Croatia, but for much of its long history, it belonged to Italy. Viscovi is passionate about Istrian food, which combines the cooking of northern Italy and Central Europe. On the menu of this intimate restaurant on a quiet street, you'll find such dishes as *braciole di maiale,* pork loin cutlets stuffed with sauerkraut, apples, prunes, and prosciutto, along with this brilliant Istrian dish of braised rabbit served over polenta.

3 rabbits, 2$\frac{1}{2}$ to 3 pounds each, dressed

2 cups chicken broth

4 tablespoons unsalted butter

2 onions, very finely chopped

1 tablespoon juniper berries

3 tablespoons packed brown sugar

1 tablespoon honey

1 tablespoon minced fresh flat-leaf parsley, plus more for garnish

5 tablespoons peanut or canola oil

1 teaspoon salt

$\frac{1}{4}$ teaspoon freshly ground pepper

2 tablespoons flour

$\frac{1}{2}$ cup dry white wine

$\frac{1}{4}$ cup balsamic vinegar

$\frac{1}{4}$ cup red wine vinegar

2 rosemary sprigs, plus more for garnish

Polenta for serving (page 54)

- Preheat the oven to 450°F. Disjoint each rabbit and cut it into 6 pieces. Put the backbones and other trimmings in a saucepan with the chicken broth. Bring to a boil, then reduce the heat to a simmer and cook until reduced by half, about 25 minutes Strain through a fine-meshed sieve and discard solids. Set the rabbit stock aside.

- In a large ovenproof sauté pan or skillet, melt the butter over medium heat and sauté the onions over medium heat until golden brown, 8 to 10 minutes. Reduce the heat to low and add the juniper berries, brown sugar, honey, and the 1 tablespoon parsley. Cook and stir for 2 more minutes, then remove from heat and set aside.

- Place a large roasting pan in the oven to heat. In another large sauté pan or skillet, heat 4 tablespoons of the oil over medium-high heat. Add the rabbit in batches and brown on all sides, 6 to 8 minutes per batch. Add the remaining 1 tablespoon oil to the roasting pan and tilt to coat. Add the rabbit to the roasting pan in one layer.

- Roast the rabbit for 20 minutes, turning the pieces occasionally. Sprinkle the salt, pepper, and flour evenly over the rabbit and roast for 5 minutes. Turn and roast on the second side for 5 minutes. Add the wine and cook to evaporate the alcohol. Add the balsamic and red wine vinegars and roast for 10 more minutes.

- Reduce the oven temperature to 375°F. Coat the rabbit with the onion mixture (reserving the pan used to cook the onions) and roast for 10 minutes. Strain the rabbit stock through a fine-meshed sieve and add one fourth of it to the roasting pan. Roast for 5 minutes. Repeat, adding the stock in one-fourth increments and roasting for 5 minutes after each addition. Remove the roasting pan from the oven and turn off the oven. Transfer the rabbit pieces to the reserved pan and place it in the still-hot oven.

- Strain the contents of the roasting pan into a heavy, medium saucepan. Bring to a boil over medium heat, add the 2 rosemary sprigs, and cook to reduce to a glaze, 3 to 4 minutes.

Make a bed of polenta or place slices on each of 6 warmed plates. Place 3 pieces of rabbit on top of each bed of polenta. Discard the rosemary and pour the glaze over each serving of rabbit. Sprinkle with parsley, garnish with a rosemary sprig, and serve.

Polenta

SERVES 6 AS A SIDE DISH

4 cups water
$^1/_2$ tablespoon salt
1 cup coarse-ground polenta
1 tablespoon unsalted butter
$^1/_4$ teaspoon freshly ground white pepper

In a large, heavy saucepan, preferably enameled cast iron, bring the water to a boil. Add the salt and reduce heat to a rapid simmer. Add the polenta in a very thin stream while stirring constantly with a wooden spoon. Cook, stirring constantly, until the polenta no longer sticks to the spoon, 20 to 25 minutes. Stir in the butter and pepper. Serve warm, poured onto plates. Or, pour onto a wooden surface and let cool until you can shape it with a rubber spatula into a loaf 3 inches thick; cover with a damp towel. To serve, cut into 6 sections.

Lemon Soufflé

SERVES 2 TO 4 AS A DESSERT

The only soufflé restaurant in San Francisco—and in the entire country, as far as owner Jacqueline Margulis knows—is a charming French cafe on Grant Avenue, with lace curtains in the windows, high ceilings, and a dark wood floor. There are salads and soups also, but an unlikely menu featuring only savory soufflés for the main course and sweet soufflés for dessert has kept this tiny place in business since 1979.

Café Jacqueline
1454 Grant Avenue
(between Green and Union)

Jacqueline, who came here from the South of France, still does all the cooking herself. Her soufflés are *baveau,* or moist, in the French style, which means that they are not cooked through. That's why, although you could serve this lemon soufflé with a raspberry coulis or other sauce, its creamy center is really all the sauce you need.

Unlike some soufflés made with a heavy béchamel-sauce base, Jacqueline's soufflés cannot be made ahead. But you can make the base and prepare the soufflé dish before dinner, then serve your guests the salad and/or cheese course while you beat the egg whites and fold in the base. Then, 15 minutes later, bring your soufflé to the table in all its elevated glory.

¹/₂ cup heavy cream
4 tablespoons sugar
1 teaspoon flour
Grated zest and juice of 2 lemons (about ¹/₄ cup juice)
4 large eggs, separated
Pinch of cream of tartar

- Preheat the oven to 450°F. Position a rack in the lower third of the oven. Generously butter the sides and bottom of a 6-cup soufflé dish. Sprinkle sugar evenly over the bottom and sides of the dish.

- In a small, heavy saucepan, combine the cream, sugar, and flour. Whisk over low heat until the mixture comes to a boil and is thickened. Remove from heat and whisk in the egg yolks, one at a time. Whisk in the lemon zest and juice. Set aside and cover to keep warm.

- In a large bowl, beat the egg whites with the cream of tartar until stiff, glossy peaks form. (A lemon soufflé needs cream of tartar, even if you are using a copper bowl.) Spoon ¼ cup of the cream base into the bottom of the prepared dish. Gently fold the remaining cream base into the whites. Spoon the batter into the dish. Bake in the lower third of the oven until the soufflé has risen and is golden brown on top, about 15 minutes.

- Bring the soufflé to the table at once. Insert a serving spoon and fork into the top of the soufflé and remove a section for each guest. Serve on warmed dessert plates.

Meyer Lemons

If you're lucky enough to have a lemon tree in your backyard, it's probably a Meyer lemon, and the fruits it produces will be smaller, rounder, and softer than the Eureka lemon found in every supermarket. In California, Meyers are available in natural foods stores and specialty produce stores; when you find them, snap them up for making a subtly perfumed lemon mousse or soufflé, lemon meringue pie or lemon tart, lemon curd, or lemon sorbet or ice cream. Because their golden yellow skin is much thinner than the bright, cold-yellow rind of the Eureka, Meyers are more delicate and won't keep as long; plan on using them within a few days of purchase. They are also sweeter and juicier than Eurekas, and the thin skin of the Meyer is harder to grate, but this sweet, tangy lemon with a faint whiff of—roses, is it?—is well worth seeking out. It will transform an ordinary lemon dessert into something evocative and memorable.

Portobello Mushroom Pasta

SERVES 4 AS A MAIN COURSE

This classy little Venetian restaurant in a corner storefront on Columbus is one of North Beach's best-kept secrets. Its decor is quirky and charming, and everything about the enterprise is the expression of individual taste, including the consistently excellent and interesting food and even the dinner checks, which are written by hand on the backs of pieces of old menus. Flora Gaspar lived in Venice for five years, and runs this place with her partner, Mary Beth Marks, who makes the fine desserts and focaccia, and her chef, Jen McMahon. Everything about this restaurant is satisfying, beginning with the wonderful, warm focaccia brought to the table almost as soon as you are seated. Here is one of McMahon's pasta dishes. It's so quick that you can make the sauce while the pasta is cooking.

Da Flora
701 Columbus Avenue
(at Greenwich)

1 pound penne pasta

MUSHROOM SAUCE
¹/₄ cup olive oil
5 medium-to-large portobello mushrooms, stemmed and sliced ¹/₂ inch thick
2 garlic cloves, minced
1 tablespoon sweet Hungarian paprika
1 teaspoon minced fresh thyme
1 tablespoon minced fresh flat-leaf parsley
¹/₄ cup dry sherry
¹/₂ cup heavy cream
Salt and freshly ground pepper to taste

In a large pot of boiling water, cook the pasta until al dente (cooked through but slightly chewy), about 10 minutes.

Meanwhile, prepare the sauce: In a large skillet, heat the olive oil over high heat and sauté the mushrooms until tender, about 3 minutes. Add the garlic and sauté for about 30 seconds, then add the paprika, thyme, and parsley. Turn off the heat (so the sherry doesn't catch fire). Add the sherry and cook over medium heat for about 2 minutes. Stir in the cream and cook until slightly thickened, about 2 minutes. Season with salt and pepper.

Drain the pasta and add it to the sauce. Stir to coat evenly, and serve at once in warmed pasta bowls.

Roasted Pork Loin
with Figs and Marsala

SERVES 6 AS A MAIN COURSE

One of the few restaurants to take over a popular establishment and improve it while maintaining the original ambiance, Enrico's is a great North Beach meeting space and people pleaser, as it was under its namesake, Enrico Banducci. People flock here for lunch, after-dinner drinks, early suppers, and late dinners, drawn by the protected outdoor tables, the jazz, the convivial atmosphere—and, not least, the California-Mediterranean food, like this pork loin with a sweet and savory fig sauce. Chef Luis Olvera serves it with roasted potatoes and sautéed spinach.

Enrico's Sidewalk Cafe
504 Broadway (at Kearny)

Note: You will need to begin brining the pork 24 to 36 hours before cooking. If fresh figs are not in season, substitute 2 cups dried figs. Halve the figs and soak them in a mixture of ½ cup dry Marsala and ½ cup water for 30 minutes, then drain. After adding them to the sauce, simmer until tender, about 10 minutes.

BRINE

8 cups water
½ cup sugar
⅓ cup salt
1 rosemary sprig
½ bunch thyme, tied with a string
½ cup garlic cloves
2 star anise pods
2 tablespoons red pepper flakes
2 tablespoons fennel seeds
1 cinnamon stick, broken into pieces
4 bay leaves
2 tablespoons peppercorns
2 tablespoons chopped fresh ginger

One 4-pound center-cut boneless pork loin
Olive oil for coating
¼ cup dry white wine or vermouth

FIG SAUCE WITH MINT AND MARSALA

2 tablespoons unsalted butter
¼ cup diced shallots
1½ teaspoons minced garlic
½ cup dry Marsala wine
1 tablespoon fresh lemon juice
1 tablespoon sherry vinegar
1 tablespoon honey
2 cups chicken stock or canned low-salt chicken broth
3 cups fresh Black Mission figs, cut into large chunks (½ inch to ¾ inch)
Salt and freshly ground pepper to taste
6 fresh mint leaves, chopped

To make the brine: Combine all the ingredients in a nonreactive pot large enough to hold the liquid and the pork. Bring to a boil, reduce heat to a simmer, and cook, uncovered, for 15 minutes. Remove from heat and let cool to room temperature. Add the pork loin to the brine, cover, and refrigerate for at least 24 hours or up to 36 hours.

Preheat the oven to 325°F. Remove the pork loin from the brine, drain, and pat dry with paper towels. Coat the roast with olive oil. In a large skillet over medium heat, brown the roast on all sides.

Transfer the pork to a roasting pan with a roasting rack and roast until an instant-read thermometer inserted in the pork registers 135°F, about 45 minutes. Remove from the oven, cover loosely with aluminum foil, and let rest for 10 minutes. Meanwhile, pour off all the fat from the roasting pan, add the white wine, and stir over medium heat to scrape up the browned bits from the bottom of the pan. Set aside.

- While the roast is cooking, make the sauce: In a large saucepan, melt the butter over medium heat and sauté the shallots until translucent, about 3 minutes. Add the garlic and sauté until fragrant, about 2 minutes. Add the Marsala, raise heat to high, bring to a boil, and cook to reduce the liquid by half. Add the lemon juice, vinegar, honey, stock or broth, and pan drippings. Simmer for 5 minutes to blend the flavors, then add the figs and simmer to heat them through and soften them slightly, about 5 minutes. Season with salt and pepper. Stir in the mint leaves. Set aside and cover to keep warm.

- To serve, cut the loin into ½-inch-thick slices. Serve with the warm sauce spooned over.

Coffeehouses

Long before there was a Starbucks or even a Peet's, coffee roasters were filling the air with the scent of the bean, and fantastical brass espresso machines were shooting out jets of steam in North Beach. This neighborhood still makes some of the best espresso drinks in town. Whether you live here or are just passing through, a cappuccino or latte and a brioche is the perfect way to start the day. Midafternoon, you'll find the coffeehouses quiet, good places to catch up on reading the paper or writing letters, journal entries, or anything else. After five, they start filling up with people dropping by after work, and one of the delights of dining in Chinatown or North Beach is an espresso or dessert in one of these cafes, which are lively and packed at night.

The coffeehouses of North Beach are real coffeehouses, where your coffee is served in a thick Italian-roast-colored china cup with a white interior, not a paper cup, and an actual metal spoon is placed on the saucer for stirring in sugar, which is often set right out on the tables, along with a shaker of powdered cocoa. (If you'd like something extra in your coffee, ask for a shot of VOV, the Italian zabaglione liqueur in the opaque white bottle.)

You can find real coffeehouses in other parts of town, of course. Every neighborhood has at least one or more, like Farley's on Potrero Hill or Jumpin' Java in the Castro. Search one out and make it your home away from home. The decor will be refreshingly noncorporate if not eccentric, and sometimes a little worn around the edges from the countless coffee drinkers who were here before you, taking a break, pouring out their heart, feeding their soul, or meditating on time, being, nothingness, and the joy of caffeine.

Crab in Black Bean Sauce

SERVES 4 AS A FIRST COURSE

If you're hankering for any kind of seafood, the newly remodeled Great Eastern is one of the best places to go in Chinatown. The back of the restaurant is filled with tanks of live fish and shellfish, guaranteeing you the freshest of the fresh. This is a good restaurant to come to with a group, commandeer one of the big round tables, and indulge in a tableful of fish dishes, including some hard-to-find ones such as abalone. Here is chef Shek Wo Lee's classic rendition of crab in black bean sauce, a must-have dish during crab season.

Great Eastern
649 Jackson Street
(between Grant and Kearny)

2 live Dungeness crabs
$^{1}/_{2}$ to $^{3}/_{4}$ cup peanut oil
1 cup chopped green bell pepper
1 cup chopped yellow onion
4 green onions, cut into $1^{1}/_{2}$-inch pieces, including green parts
3 tablespoons fermented black beans, rinsed and mashed
3 tablespoons dark soy sauce
Salt to taste
$^{1}/_{2}$ teaspoon sugar
2 teaspoons cornstarch mixed with 2 tablespoons water
Steamed rice or Chinese noodles for serving

With the back of the crab toward you, grasp 4 legs and a claw in each hand. Sharply strike the center of the bottom of the shell against the edge of a table or counter (this stuns the crab). Working over a tray to catch the juices, pull off the top shell and the small triangular piece from the bottom of the crab. Pull off and discard the gills (small white protuberances) on each side of the body, then set the body aside. Spoon out and reserve the soft white or yellow crab butter in the corners of the shell, taking care not to disturb the intestine (in the center of the top shell, right behind the mouth). Remove the mouth parts from the body and discard them.

- Using a large chef's knife or a cleaver, cut each crab body into 6 pieces, each including one leg.

- In a wok over high heat, heat the peanut oil until it shimmers and stir-fry the crab pieces for 3 to 4 minutes, or until the shell turns red. Using tongs, transfer the crab pieces to a plate. Add the bell pepper, yellow onions, green onions, black beans, soy sauce, salt, sugar, and reserved crab butter and stir-fry until fragrant, about 3 minutes. Return the crab pieces to the wok and stir-fry until well coated, about 2 minutes. Stir in the cornstarch mixture, then cover and cook until the sauce thickens, 4 to 5 minutes.

- Serve at once, with steamed rice or Chinese noodles.

Chowpan

(Grilled Marinated Rack of Lamb with Sautéed Eggplant and Pallow)

SERVES 4 AS A MAIN COURSE

The only Afghan restaurant in San Francisco, Helmand's soulful food and low prices have kept it busy on Broadway since the late eighties. Named after a river in Afghanistan, Helmand is owned by the Karzai family, one of whose members is currently the president of Afghanistan. Everything is made fresh from scratch here, including the Afghan bread, and the chef, Jamilla Karzai, is a woman.

Helmand
430 Broadway (between Kearny and Montgomery)

Chowpan, a classic of the Afghan kitchen, is one of Helmand's signature dishes. The grilled lamb, sautéed eggplant, and rice pilaf are served on top of a traditional flat bread called *nan,* though it is not a raised bread like Indian nan. Use lavosh as a substitute, or simply serve the lamb and its accompaniments directly on plates.

2 large onions, chopped
4 garlic cloves
$^1/_4$ cup canola oil
$^3/_4$ teaspoon salt
$^3/_4$ teaspoon ground pepper
2 racks of lamb (6 ribs each)

PALLOW

2 cups basmati rice
$^1/_2$ cup sugar
$7^1/_2$ cups water
3 tablespoons canola oil
1 teaspoon salt
$^1/_8$ teaspoon each ground cardamom, nutmeg, cumin, and pepper

SAUTÉED EGGPLANT

$1/2$ cup canola oil
1 small onion, thinly sliced
2 large tomatoes, chopped
3 garlic cloves, minced
Salt and freshly ground pepper to taste
1 globe eggplant, peeled and cut into $1/2$-inch dice
$3/4$ cup water

Afghan flat bread or lavosh for serving (optional)

● In a blender, combine the onions, garlic, oil, salt, and pepper. Purée until smooth. Place the lamb in a small glass baking dish and pour the onion purée over it. Cover and refrigerate for 4 to 5 hours, turning the lamb once or twice.

● About 2 hours before serving, make the pallow: Rinse the rice in several changes of water until the water runs clear. Soak the rice in water to cover for 1 hour.

● Preheat the oven to 350°F. In a medium, heavy saucepan, combine the sugar and 1 cup of the water. Bring to a boil over medium heat and cook, swirling the pan occasionally, until the caramel is amber in color. Remove from heat and set aside.

● In a medium ovenproof saucepan, bring 6 cups of the water to a boil. Stir in the rice and boil for exactly 6 minutes. Drain well in a fine-meshed sieve. Heat the caramel over low heat until warm. Return the rice to the pan and stir in the oil, salt, spices, and caramel. Stir until the rice grains are evenly coated with the caramel. Stir in the remaining $1/2$ cup water. Cover and bake until tender, about 40 minutes.

● Meanwhile, prepare a fire in a charcoal grill, remove the lamb from the refrigerator, and cook the eggplant.

To cook the eggplant: In a medium, heavy saucepan over medium heat, heat the oil and sauté the onion until golden brown, about 5 minutes. Add the tomatoes, garlic, salt, and pepper; sauté for 1 minute. Stir in the eggplant, cover, and reduce heat to low. Cook, stirring occasionally and gradually adding the water to prevent sticking, until the eggplant is tender, about 35 minutes. Uncover, increase heat to medium, and cook to reduce the juices until thickened. Set aside and cover to keep warm.

Grill the lamb over white-hot coals for 4 to 5 minutes on each side for medium-rare. Cut each rack in half (3 ribs per serving).

To serve, place a large piece of bread, if using, on each of 4 heated plates. Place ½ rack of lamb on each plate, and add an equal amount of the pallow and eggplant to each plate. Serve at once.

Crespelle alla Boscaiola

(Crêpes with Porcini, Ham, and Béchamel Sauce)

SERVES 4 AS A MAIN COURSE

L'Osteria del Forno
519 Columbus Avenue
(between Green and Union)

Although it's not much bigger than an oven itself, this "inn of the oven" turns out some of the best Italian food in North Beach. Owned by two women, Susanna Borgatti (from Bologna) and Wally Tattamanti (from Varese), the tiny space, with windows on Columbus Avenue, may remind you of one of the many small, unpretentious restaurants in Rome, it's that authentic. Everything is good here, from the soup and salad to the crème caramel, including these rich, savory mushroom crêpes. Serve them with a light appetizer, followed by a green salad or roasted vegetables.

CRESPELLE
2 eggs
1 cup unbleached flour
2 cups milk
Olive oil or melted butter for brushing pan

MUSHROOMS
1 1/2 ounces dried porcini
2 teaspoons olive oil
1 garlic clove
2 tablespoons minced fresh flat-leaf parsley
Salt and freshly ground pepper to taste
1/2 cup dry white wine
1 pound fresh white mushrooms, thinly sliced

BÉCHAMEL SAUCE
2/3 cup (1 1/3 sticks) unsalted butter
5 tablespoons unbleached all-purpose flour
1 teaspoon salt
4 cups milk
1 level teaspoon ground nutmeg

12 thin slices cooked Italian or Canadian ham
2 cups (8 ounces) grated Parmigiano-Reggiano cheese

To make the crespelle: In a medium bowl, whisk the eggs together until just mixed. Whisk in the flour, then the milk, to make a smooth batter. Pour the batter through a sieve into a large measuring cup with a spout. Spoon off any foam on top.

Brush a seasoned or nonstick 8-inch skillet lightly with oil and heat over medium heat until almost smoking. Pour 3 tablespoons batter into the center and rotate the pan in a circle to cover the bottom completely. Cook until lightly browned on the bottom, about 60 seconds. Turn and cook on the second side for about 30 seconds, or until lightly browned. The thinner you can make the crespelle, the lighter the dish will be, so if the first one is too thick, add 1 tablespoon more milk to the mixture. Repeat the process, stacking the crespelle on a plate, until you have used all the batter; you should have 10 to 12, a few more than you need.

To cook the mushrooms: In a bowl, soak the dried porcini in hot water to cover for 30 minutes. Drain the porcini and squeeze them dry into the bowl, reserving the soaking liquid for another use. Chop the porcini finely.

In a large skillet, heat the oil and sauté the garlic until it begins to turn golden. Stir in the porcini, parsley, salt, and pepper and sauté for 4 to 5 minutes. Add the wine and cook until almost evaporated. Stir in the white mushrooms, cover, and reduce heat to low. Cook until tender, about 15 minutes. Uncover the pan and cook until all the liquid evaporates. Set aside.

To make the béchamel: In a medium, heavy saucepan, melt the butter over medium-low heat; take care that it does not brown. Add all the flour at once, stirring constantly with a whisk and making sure not to leave any flour on the bottom of the pan. Stir constantly for 10 minutes to cook away the flour taste. Gradually whisk in half of the milk and continue to cook, stirring frequently, until the sauce begins to thicken. Gradually whisk in the remaining milk, the salt, and the nutmeg and cook, stirring frequently, until you have a smooth, thick sauce, about 5 more minutes.

To assemble: Preheat the oven to 475°F. On a work surface, slightly overlap 2 crespelle so that they equal about 12 inches in length. Place 1 slice of ham on each crespella. Spoon 2 tablespoonfuls of the béchamel the length of the 2 crespelle, then spoon ¼ cup of the mushrooms the length as well. Make sure the filling is evenly thick the whole length, with no gaps. Sprinkle the filling evenly with 2 tablespoons of the cheese. Fold ½ inch of side of the crespelle over lengthwise, then continue to roll gently to make a cylinder. Cut the cylinder into three 4-inch pieces. Repeat to make a total of 4 cylinders and 12 pieces. Place these in a single layer in a buttered large baking dish, or put 3 each in buttered individual oven-resistant dishes for individual servings.

Pour the remaining béchamel sauce over the crespelle and bake until golden brown on top, 20 to 25 minutes. Remove from the oven and let stand for about 2 minutes. Sprinkle with the remaining cheese and serve. *Buon appetito!*

Marinated Shrimp
with Peach and Cucumber Salad

SERVES 6 AS AN *AMUSE-BOUCHE*, 2 AS A FIRST COURSE

A blue neon moose glowing through the cypress trees of Washington Square will guide you to Ed and Mary Etta Moose's elegant, convivial restaurant in the heart of North Beach. Live jazz, a long bar, a small counter, an open kitchen, and a private banquet room are some of the amenities available here, along with weekend brunch and a large, warm dining room good for both small and large parties. The food, too, is both elegant and satisfying, like this *amuse-bouche* from chef Morgen Jacobson, little forkfuls to "amuse the mouth" before the meal begins. You could also serve 3 whole shrimp per person, on a bed of the peach and cucumber salad, as a refreshing first course on a warm summer day.

Moose's
1652 Stockton Street
(between Filbert and Union)

1 garlic clove, thinly sliced
One 2-inch piece fresh ginger, peeled and thinly sliced
4 tablespoons best-quality Spanish extra-virgin olive oil, preferably l'Estornel
Grated zest and juice of 1 lemon
4 basil sprigs
6 jumbo shrimp (15 per pound), shelled and deveined
Salt and freshly ground pepper to taste
1 ripe peach, peeled, halved, pitted, and cut into ¹/₂-inch dice
¹/₂ English (hothouse) cucumber peeled and cut into ¹/₂-inch dice
1 tomato, peeled, seeded (see page 12), and cut into ¹/₂-inch dice
1 shallot, minced

● Using the side of a knife or the bottom of a saucepan, smash the garlic and ginger. Transfer the garlic and ginger to a medium baking dish. Add 2 tablespoons of the olive oil and the lemon zest. Add half of the lemon juice. Pick the basil leaves off the stems. Add the basil stems and half of the leaves to the ginger mixture. Stir well to combine and to slightly bruise the basil leaves and stems. Set aside in a cool place.

In a heavy sauté pan or skillet, heat 1 tablespoon of the olive oil over medium-high heat until a wisp of smoke appears. Generously season the shrimp with salt and pepper and add them to the pan, making certain that each shrimp lies flat.

Cook the shrimp until evenly pink, about 2 minutes, then turn them over and reduce the heat to medium. Cook about 1 minute more, or just until there is a thin translucent stripe along the back of the shrimp. Using a slotted spoon, transfer the shrimp to the ginger marinade. Set the container in the refrigerator to cool for at least 15 minutes.

In a small bowl, combine the peach, cucumber, tomato, and shallot. Add the remaining 1 tablespoon olive oil and salt and pepper to taste. Cut the remaining basil leaves into fine strips and stir them into the mixture. Cover and refrigerate for at least 15 minutes but no longer than 1 hour (or the acid from the tomato will turn the other components mushy).

Remove the shrimp from the marinade and set them on a cutting board. Using a sharp, thin knife, cut each shrimp in half lengthwise, working from head to tail. Stick each halved shrimp onto the end of a cocktail fork.

Add 1 teaspoon of the remaining lemon juice to the peach mixture, or to taste. Taste and adjust the seasoning. Using a slotted spoon or fork, place a small amount of the salad behind the shrimp on each cocktail fork. Arrange the forks on a plate or tray and serve.

Local Favorites

Restaurants are not the only source for memorable food. The city's delicatessens, bakeries, and food stores offer several San Francisco specialties or best-of-kind northern California foods (see also Artisan Breads, page 98). Here is a partial list—in both senses of the word partial.

- Ghirardelli chocolate (at Ghirardelli Square, the Cannery, and many other outlets)
- Scharffen Berger chocolate (at Whole Foods and Real Food stores, Peet's Coffee shops, and elsewhere)
- Anchor Steam Beer (from the brewery at 1705 Mariposa on Potrero Hill, and many other outlets)
- Fortune cookies from Chinatown (Mee Mee Bakery, 1328 Stockton Street)
- Sacripantina and Danish pastries from Stella's Pastry and Caffè in North Beach (446 Columbus Avenue)
- Almond torte and St. Honoré cake from Victoria Bakery and Pastry Company (1362 Stockton) in North Beach and Dianda's in the Mission (2883 Mission Street)
- Hobbs applewood-smoked bacon, prosciutto, and ham, at A. G. Ferrari (468 Castro Street, 3490 California in Laurel Village, and 688 Mission Street)
- Italian sausages and vitellone (older, non-milk-fed veal) from Little City Market in North Beach (1400 Stockton Street)
- Whole-bean and ground coffee from Graffeo Coffee Company in North Beach (735 Columbus Avenue)
- Sheet pasta, ravioli, and tortellini from Molinari Delicatessen in North Beach (373 Columbus Avenue)
- Straus Family Organic Farms milk, cream, yogurt, and cheese from Sonoma County (at Whole Foods, Real Food, and other grocery stores)
- Joseph Schmidt chocolates (3489 Sixteenth Street)
- XOX Truffles in North Beach (754 Columbus Avenue)

Cioppino

SERVES 4 AS A MAIN COURSE

Rose Pistola

532 Columbus Avenue
(between Green and Union)

A San Francisco original, cioppino was created when Italian fishermen used the local Dungeness crab in their native fish soup, *cacciucco*. One of the best versions in town is from Armando Paniagua, executive chef at Rose Pistola. This large, sleek restaurant was named for Rose Evangelista, a famous North Beach cook (her nickname was Pistola, because her husband carried a pistol—and occasionally fired it). Rose's namesake bar and restaurant—with a pool table in the front—was where Washington Square Bar and Grill is today. Her new namesake has garnered numerous awards since it began revitalizing North Beach with its northern Italian cuisine, specializing in dishes from Liguria. This crescent-shaped region on Italy's west coast—the Italian Riviera—includes Genoa and Portofino, and was the homeland for many of the early Italian immigrants in the neighborhood.

Note: Paniagua points out that this fisherman's soup was originally made with crab and whatever other fish or shellfish was available that day, so feel free to make substitutions, including clams or even oysters. Serve this with lots of warm crusty Italian bread (and napkins, and little forks for retrieving the crabmeat) and follow it with finger bowls and a big green salad—maybe a Caesar.

2 live Dungeness crabs
¹/₂ cup olive oil, plus more for drizzling
¹/₂ cup finely chopped white onion, rinsed
2 tablespoons chopped green (spring) garlic or white part of a leek
2 or 3 fresh marjoram or oregano sprigs
2 bay leaves
1 garlic clove, minced
¹/₂ cup chopped fresh flat-leaf parsley
1 teaspoon harissa or red pepper flakes
3 anchovy fillets, chopped
10 ounces rockfish fillets

1 cup dry white wine
4 cups fish stock (page 17) or chicken broth
2 cups tomato sauce
16 black mussels, scrubbed and debearded
8 to 12 ounces cleaned squid, bodies cut into rings
6 ounces rock shrimp, shelled and deveined or left unshelled

With the back of the crab toward you, grasp 4 legs and a claw in each hand. Strike the center part of the bottom of the shell a sharp blow against the edge of a table or counter (this stuns the crab). Working over a tray to catch the juices, pull off the top shell and the small triangular piece from the bottom of the crab. Pull off and discard the gills (small white protuberances) on each side of the body, then set the body aside. Spoon out and reserve the soft white or yellow crab butter in the corners of the shell, taking care not to disturb the intestine (in the center of the top shell, right behind the mouth). Remove the mouth parts from the body and discard them. With a large knife, cut off the legs and claws. Cut the body in half crosswise, then cut each piece in half again. Crack the legs and claws with a hammer or the back of a large chef's knife.

In a large, heavy sauté pan or skillet over high heat, heat the ½ cup olive oil and sauté the onion, green garlic or leek, marjoram or oregano, and bay leaves until the onion is translucent, about 5 minutes. Stir in the garlic, parsley, harissa or pepper flakes, and anchovies. Add the crab and rockfish and stir until the rockfish turns opaque and begins to break up. Add the wine and cook to reduce slightly. Add the reserved crab butter and juice, then the stock or broth and tomato sauce. Bring to a boil and reduce heat to a simmer. Taste and adjust the seasoning. Add the mussels, squid, shrimp, and a healthy drizzle of olive oil. Cover and cook for 3 to 4 minutes, or until the mussels open. Turn off the heat and discard any mussels that have not opened. Serve in a warmed tureen or warmed shallow soup bowls.

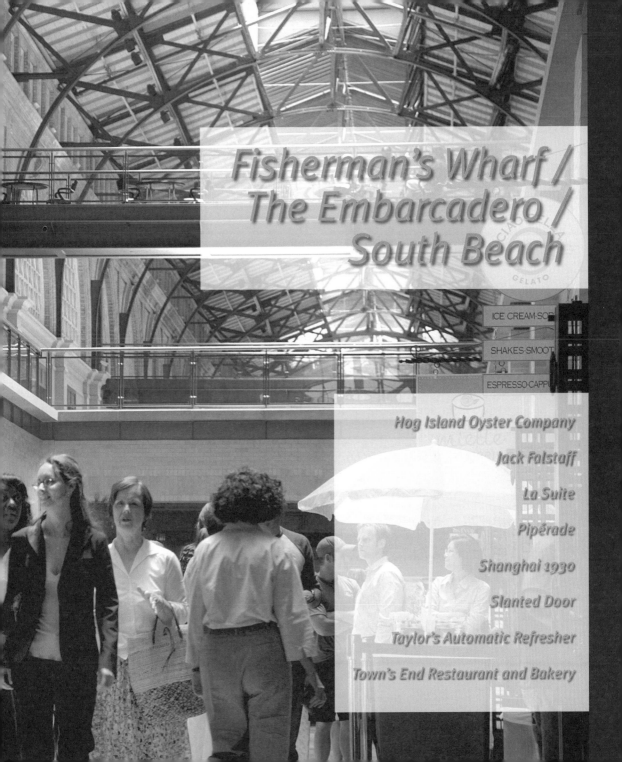

Fisherman's Wharf / The Embarcadero / South Beach

Hog Island Oyster Company

Jack Falstaff

La Suite

Pipérade

Shanghai 1930

Slanted Door

Taylor's Automatic Refresher

Town's End Restaurant and Bakery

A RIM OF LAND, held in by retaining walls and made from earthquake rubble, sunken ships, discarded ships' ballasts, and rocks quarried from the back of Telegraph Hill, rings the north and east of the city, beginning with Fisherman's Wharf, a one-time fishing village that has become a tourist mecca. You can buy crab cocktails and cioppino on the street here, or dine in one of the many fish

restaurants with spectacular bay views but mostly unspectacular food. And, if you look hard enough among the souvenir shops and T-shirt stores, you can find traces of the old fishing village, where the Chinese first sailed their junks and the Italians their feluccas. ⟶ PIER 45, on Jefferson between Jones and Taylor, is the pier for the day boats; you can rent a boat with a group here, catch your own salmon out by the Farallons, and bring it home right away to make some of the freshest sashimi you will ever eat. (Some boats will also arrange to have your salmon smoked for you.) Or, buy a sandwich from the Boudin Bakery cafe (160 Jefferson) and come here to sit and watch the boats tie up and the seagulls patrol the wharf. (If you go down a narrow walkway at the foot of Jones Street—follow the sign to Scoma's—you can walk out almost to the end of Pier 47 and be right on the bay.) ⟶ TO BUY FRESH SEAFOOD, go to Pier 45, Shed B (all the way at the end), where you'll find several wholesale fish outlets and one retail outlet (Pacific American Fish). If the catch was good and the skipper's in a good mood, you can buy fresh fish and crab right off the boat. Or, go to Alioto's Fish Company at 360 Jefferson Street. Along with Chinatown, these wharf sites are your best sources for live Dungeness crab in season. ⟶ IF YOU WALK EAST AND SOUTH, you'll pass Pier 39, a tourists' shopping mall that juts out into the bay, then the long curve of Embarcadero (from the Spanish for "wharf," or "pier"), lined with gray piers. (The piers are odd-numbered north of the Ferry Building, and even-numbered to the south.) Or, you could take a vintage streetcar on the F-Market line, which runs from the Anchorage on Fisherman's Wharf to just past the Ferry Building before it turns to go up Steuart Street and return to Market. On your right is a cluster of reclaimed old red brick warehouses and Levi's Plaza, built to blend in with its surroundings. During the Loma Prieta earthquake of 1989, the elevated freeway exit from the Bay Bridge onto Battery Street sustained terminal damage and was eventually torn down (an event presaged by the much-maligned Vaillancourt Fountain at Embarcadero Four, which looks like rubble). While the city lost a looping, curving thrill ride, it gained a transformed waterfront of open land and unobstructed views. ⎯ THE CITY RUSHED TO CAPITALIZE ON ITS BAD/GOOD FORTUNE, and today the Embarcadero is a glorious swath of space beloved of skate-

boarders, bikers, runners, and strollers, anchored with magnificent Canary palms. Once, these piers bustled with shipping activity, but most of the container ships outgrew the facilities and now dock in Oakland. The Bryant Street Pier Project, a state-of-the-art cruise-ship terminal, hotel, and office/retail complex, is in development at Piers 30–32, just south of the Bay Bridge (and right next to Red's Java House, one of the remnants of the Embarcadero's blue-collar past), while some of the old piers will be developed for sports facilities and open space. ⎯ AT THE END OF MARKET STREET lies the jewel of the Embarcadero: the Ferry Plaza Farmer's Market. The entire Ferry Building has

OTHER NEIGHBORHOOD STARS

Boulevard

Chaya Brasserie

Harbor Village

Hunan

One Market

Ozumo

Scoma's

been transformed into a series of shops dedicated to food, ranging from a caviar cafe to a Chinese teahouse, and including a culinary antiques shop and a Japanese cafeteria. Here are some of San Francisco's finest restaurants, right on the water. And on Saturday, a lively farmers' market, with stands and umbrellas on three sides of the Ferry Building, draws hordes of shoppers looking for the freshest foods of the season direct from northern California growers and vendors. The ferries to Marin County and the East Bay embark and disembark here, so visitors can come to the market for the morning or stop by the food shops on their way home from working in San Francisco. The Ferry Building is both a portal to the city and a celebration of the best food the Bay Area has to offer. ⟶ IF YOU CAN TEAR YOURSELF AWAY from the fresh produce and the seductive prepared foods and restaurants here, walk south now past the Embarcadero Center, four high-rises housing shops and restaurants on their lower floors and built on the former site of San Francisco's produce market. ⟶ SOUTH OF MARKET STREET IS STEUART STREET, a classy little island of buildings with a clear view of the bay that emerged when the freeway came down. Farther on is the Audiffred Building, an architectural jewel built in 1889 and once threatened with destruction, now refurbished and housing Boulevard, one of the city's top high-end restaurants. ⟶ NOW YOU ARE IN SOUTH BEACH, one of San Francisco's newest neighborhoods, constructed among old warehouses and a magnet for new restaurants because of the new Giants baseball stadium nearby. Town's End Restaurant and Bakery, with a patio and a view of the bay, is a good spot to stop. Farther south still, another new community, Mission Bay, is rising along the inlet of Mission Creek. This complex of bio-tech firms and other businesses, apartment buildings, and the campus of the University of California at San Francisco will also soon, without a doubt, feature fine new restaurants basking in the sun and the saltwater fragrance of the bay.

Hog Island
Oysters Rockefeller

SERVES 4 AS A FIRST COURSE

Visiting the Hog Island oyster farm on Highway One at Marshall has long
been a favorite weekend outing, whether to picnic and barbecue on the
grounds (after reserving ahead) or to pick up a clanking batch of
oysters to take home. But now all San Francisco residents have to do
is to wait in line at the Ferry Building for a seat at the open-kitchen
counter or an outside table overlooking the bay. The restaurant is
as simple in decor as most of its preparations, which highlight the
absolute freshness of their own oysters, direct from the salty waters of
Tomales Bay. This dish is made with Sweetwaters, medium in size and
sweet and briny in taste.

Hog Island
Oyster Company
One Ferry Building, 11A

½ cup (1 stick) unsalted butter
1 organic onion, finely chopped
2 organic garlic cloves, minced
1 pound organic baby spinach leaves, rinsed and drained
1 cup heavy cream
3 tablespoons Pernod liqueur
16 Hog Island Sweetwater oysters, shucked and returned to bottom (deeper) shells
Rock salt for baking
Lemon wedges for serving

- In a saucepan, melt the butter over medium heat and sauté the onion
  and garlic until translucent, about 3 minutes. Remove from heat and
  set aside.

- In a large saucepan, cook the spinach, covered, over medium heat, stirring once or twice, until wilted, about 3 minutes. Transfer to a colander and let drain until cool to the touch. Chop the spinach finely. Add
  the spinach to the pan with the onion mixture. Add the cream and cook

over low heat until heated through, about 10 minutes. Remove from heat and stir in the Pernod.

- Preheat the broiler. Fill a flameproof baking dish or cast-iron skillet half full of rock salt. Nestle the oysters in the rock salt so they will not tip. Place the oysters under the broiler about 5 inches from the heat source and broil for about 5 minutes, or until they start to curl. Top each oyster with a spoonful of the spinach mixture (just enough to cover the surface of the oyster) and broil for 3 more minutes, or until lightly browned. Serve at once, with wedges of lemon.

Kale-Wrapped Wild Salmon
with Red Bell Pepper, Almond, and Garlic Sauce

SERVES 4 AS A MAIN COURSE

Jack Falstaff is a study in contrasts: Its decor (by Stanlee Gatti) is high style and high end, but it's right across the street from the Giants baseball stadium. And though the restaurant is named for a famously large Shakespeare character who overindulged in both food and drink, the dishes that come out of chef James Ormsby's kitchen emphasize healthfulness more than almost any other restaurant in the city. Ormsby uses only whole grains and organic ingredients, and chooses his fruits and vegetables with their high-oxidant qualities in mind, such as the kale and bell pepper that complement this dish of wild salmon. The chef suggests serving this with a rice and almond pilaf and buttered lima beans.

Jack Falstaff
300 Brannan Street
(at Second Street)

RED BELL PEPPER, ALMOND, AND GARLIC SAUCE

¹/₂ cup olive oil
2 large red bell peppers, seeded, deribbed, and chopped
4 garlic cloves, sliced
¹/₂ cup sliced almonds
Salt to taste
1 tablespoon sherry vinegar
1 tablespoon sweet Hungarian paprika
Freshly ground pepper to taste

1 large bunch green kale
Extra-virgin olive oil for brushing and whisking
Salt and freshly ground pepper to taste
Four 6-ounce wild salmon fillets, skin and pinbones removed

To make the sauce: In a medium sauté pan or skillet, heat the oil over medium heat. Add the bell peppers, garlic, almonds, and a little salt and cook, stirring frequently, for 15 to 20 minutes, or until the peppers have softened. Add the sherry vinegar and the paprika. Season with salt and pepper to taste.

Remove from heat and transfer to a blender. Blend on high speed until very smooth. Strain the sauce through a coarse-meshed sieve and set aside.

Preheat the oven to 400°F. Cut out the thick central core of the kale leaves, leaving the leaves whole. Blanch in boiling water for 2 minutes, drain, and rinse under cold water. Dry the leaves on paper towels. On a work surface, lay out a square of leaves large enough to wrap a salmon fillet. Brush the leaves with olive oil and season with salt and pepper. Place a fillet in the center, season it with salt and pepper, and drizzle with olive oil. Wrap the salmon in the leaves like a package. Repeat to wrap the remaining fillets. Wrap each packet in aluminum foil.

Place the packets on a baking sheet pan and bake for 15 minutes. Remove from the oven and let rest for about 3 minutes. The salmon will be extremely moist, and opaque throughout.

Pool one-fourth of the sauce in the center of each of 4 warmed plates. Unwrap the salmon from the foil, reserving the juices. Pour the juices into a small bowl and whisk in a little olive oil. Pour this over the salmon to moisten. Place the kale-wrapped salmon on the pools of sauce and serve at once.

Ferry Plaza Farmers' Market

Sometimes you can go home again, or at least sometimes beloved things can return in a new guise: The lost lagoon by the bay at what is now Crissy Field has been reborn; the Embarcadero has reemerged from the shadow of the Embarcadero Freeway; and a produce market is thriving on the water, very near the site of the original San Francisco produce market (where the Embarcadero towers rise). For years, it was only a gleam in the eyes of a group of food-lovers. Its first incarnation was in a parking lot at the foot of Green Street, where it bloomed every Saturday in a thicket of umbrellas. Meanwhile, that ambitious group of true believers was helping to ensure that the market would eventually move to the refurbished Ferry Building at the foot of Market.

The Ferry Building, which dates to 1898, was the terminus for ferries to Marin and the East Bay before the Golden Gate and Bay Bridges were built. Once they were constructed, the building lost its original purpose. In the 1950s, much of it was converted into office space, then hidden behind the Embarcadero Freeway. The Loma Prieta earthquake that stopped the building's clock in 1989 also terminally damaged the freeway, and liberated the Embarcadero from its double-decker shadow. Almost the entire Ferry Building is now given over to food, drink, and food-related goods, with farmers' market stands outside on given days, and permanent shops and restaurants inside the building that include everything from a caviar cafe and a Japanese cafeteria to a culinary antiques store.

The Ferry Building Marketplace is run by the Center for Urban Education about Sustainable Agriculture (CUESA), which is devoted to encouraging northern California farmers to grow organic, sustainable foods. Not all the vegetables and fruits at the market are certified

(continued)

organic, but most of them are; each stand will have a sign specifying if its produce is organically grown.

The range of goods available at the Ferry Plaza market is nothing short of amazing, from prepared foods to flowers to produce to culinary herbs in pots. The list of vendors is like an honor roll of the finest suppliers in northern California, from Cowgirl Creamery and June Taylor (jams and conserves) to Bruce Aidells (sausages) and Frog Hollow Farm (glorious fruit and prepared foods, including jams). The entire place is like an apotheosis of the California idea of good food: locally grown or produced, and fresh from the farm or kitchen.

A visit to the Saturday outdoor market at the height of summer can be almost overwhelming: The crowds are thick, there are lines for the restaurants inside and the food stands outside, and the abundance of foods, both unusual (wild arugula, miniature bell peppers, cardoons) and familiar (ears of corn just picked that morning, almost any fresh herb you can think of, newly bottled honey) is enough to give you sensory overload.

Come to the farmers' market for breakfast (several wonderful bakeries sell just-baked sweet rolls) or lunch on Saturday and eat inside the Ferry Building at one of the restaurants (which range from Vietnamese to Mexican, some facing the bay with tables outside), or buy crêpes or Mexican food or sausages or a salmon BLT at one of the outdoor stands and sit at a picnic table right by the water. You won't believe how good your food will taste.

Most of the indoor shops and restaurants in the Ferry Building Marketplace are open every day; the Saturday market runs from 8 A.M. to 2 P.M. A smaller farmers' market (with stands only in front of the building) runs from 10 A.M. to 2 P.M. year-round on Tuesdays, while the Thursday market (4 to 8 P.M.) and Sunday market (10 A.M. to 2 P.M.) are seasonal (spring to fall).

Duck à l'Orange Provençale

SERVES 6 AS A MAIN COURSE

Who knew that what San Francisco really needed and wanted was a spacious brasserie on the Embarcadero, serving such classic French dishes as roasted bone marrow, sliced pig trotters, escargots, and floating island? Jocelyn Bulow just keeps extending his restaurant empire (Plouf, Chez Papa, Chez Maman, Baraka). This one is all gleaming surfaces and tableside carts, and the food from chef Bruno Chemel and the service from the wait staff are imbued with those special Gallic skills of knowing just how to prepare and present excellent food. Come here for this classic French dish with a Provençal twist, served just a few feet from the bay.

La Suite
100 Brannan Street
(at Embarcadero)

Note: You will need to start this recipe 1 day before serving.

One 3-pound duck, cut into 8 serving pieces

3 tablespoons olive oil

1 1/2 cups dry white wine

1 garlic clove, minced

3 fresh sage leaves

1 slice thick-cut bacon, cut crosswise into pieces 1/2 inch wide

2 onions, chopped

2 carrots, peeled and sliced

1 turnip, peeled and cut into large dice

1 cup chicken stock

1/2 cup fresh orange juice

Zest stripped from 4 oranges

1/2 celery stalk, cut into 4 equal pieces

Bouquet garni: 2 or 3 thyme sprigs, parsley sprigs, and sage leaves, plus 1 bay leaf, tied together with kitchen twine

5 ounces fresh white mushrooms, brushed clean and sliced

1/2 cup niçoise olives, pitted

Sea salt and freshly ground pepper to taste
4 tablespoons unsalted butter
Chervil sprigs and orange segments (see page 7) for garnish

- Prick the duck pieces all over with a fork. In a Dutch oven or flame-proof casserole, heat 1 tablespoon of the olive oil over high heat and brown the duck on all sides, 10 to 15 minutes. Transfer the duck to a cutting board. Pour off the duck fat from the pan and reserve it for another use. Set the pan aside without washing it. Lay the duck pieces in a baking dish just large enough to hold them and add the wine, garlic, and sage. Let cool, then cover and refrigerate for 24 hours.

- After refrigerating the duck, fry the bacon in the reserved duck pan over medium heat until crisp, about 1 minute. Add the onions, carrots, and turnip to the pan and fry for about 2 minutes, or until the onions are translucent. Add the stock and orange juice and bring to a boil. Stir to scrape up the browned bits from the bottom of the pan. Reduce heat to low and simmer to reduce until thickened, about 10 minutes. Strain the liquid in the pan into a bowl (discard the vegetables). Let the liquid cool, cover, and refrigerate overnight. Set the duck pan aside without washing.

- The next day, to finish cooking the duck, preheat the oven to 350°F. Return the duck pieces, slightly overlapping, to the reserved pan, then pour in the liquid from the cooked vegetables and the marinade from the duck. Add the orange zest, celery, bouquet garni, mushrooms, and olives and season with salt and pepper. Cover, place in the oven, and cook until the duck is tender, about 45 minutes.

- Transfer the pan to the stove top. Using a slotted spoon, transfer the duck pieces and vegetables to a warmed platter and discard the bouquet garni and orange zest. Cook the pan juices over medium-high heat to reduce to a sauce consistency. Taste and adjust the seasoning. Whisk in the butter. Spoon the sauce over the duck, garnish with the chervil and orange segments, and serve immediately.

Pipérade

SERVES 4 AS A LIGHT MAIN COURSE, 6 AS A FIRST COURSE OR SIDE DISH

Gerald Hirigoyen's Basque restaurant near Levi's Plaza is named for this traditional Basque dish of peppers, tomatoes, and eggs. In this eatery at the foot of Telegraph Hill you will find rustic dishes that are served nowhere else in town (except for Bocadillos, Hirigoyen's offshoot in the Financial District; see page 31). Try this colorful, easy dish for lunch, or serve it as a first course or side dish with roasted meats.

Pipérade
1015 Battery Street
(at Green)

¹/₂ cup olive oil
8 red Anaheim chilies or 6 red bell peppers, seeded, deribbed, and finely julienned
1 onion, finely sliced
6 garlic cloves, crushed
6 large vine-ripened tomatoes, peeled (see page 12) and coarsely chopped
1 teaspoon sugar
¹/₈ teaspoon piment d'Espelette (Basque chili powder), or
a pinch of cayenne pepper and a pinch of sweet Hungarian paprika
1 bay leaf
Kosher salt to taste
¹/₂ teaspoon freshly ground white pepper
6 large eggs

- In a large sauté pan or skillet, heat the olive oil over medium-high heat. Add the chilies or bell peppers, onion, and garlic. Sauté for 5 minutes, or until the vegetables are beginning to soften. Stir in the tomatoes, sugar, piment d'Espelette or cayenne and paprika, and bay leaf. Season with the salt and pepper. Bring to a boil and cook for 5 minutes, stirring occasionally. Reduce the heat to a simmer, cover, and cook for 25 to 30 minutes, or until the vegetables are very soft but not disintegrated.

- Remove and discard the bay leaf. Break the eggs directly into the pan and, using a wooden spoon, stir the whites gently into the pepper mixture, leaving the yolks whole. Cover and cook for 5 minutes, or until the eggs are just set. Spoon onto warmed plates to serve.

Minced Duck in Lettuce Petals

SERVES 8 AS AN APPETIZER

Shanghai 1930
133 Steuart Street
(between Howard and Mission)

One of the stylish restaurants adding excitement to this short street south of Market is Shanghai 1930, a restaurant and cabaret featuring live jazz. The large space, down a long flight of stairs, also features a bar area and two spacious dining rooms, one with curtained booths. If you've ever imagined yourself lounging in a swanky dinner club straight out of a thirties movie, this is the place to fulfill that fantasy. The cuisine of chef Jason Xu is the icing on the cake. Here is his version of a classic Asian dish, with roast duck replacing minced chicken. To make this quick appetizer at home, buy roast duck in a Chinatown deli.

SAUCE

3 tablespoons hoisin sauce

3 tablespoons plum sauce

^{1}/$_3$ cup finely chopped roast duck

^{1}/$_3$ cup finely chopped stemmed shiitake mushrooms

^{1}/$_3$ cup finely chopped water chestnuts

^{1}/$_3$ cup finely chopped celery

^{1}/$_3$ cup finely chopped pitted kalamata olives

^{1}/$_2$ teaspoon canola oil

^{1}/$_2$ teaspoon Shaoxing wine or dry sherry

1 teaspoon light soy sauce

1 teaspoon black mushroom soy sauce

1 teaspoon sugar

^{1}/$_2$ teaspoon oyster sauce

1 tablespoon minced green onion

^{1}/$_2$ teaspoon minced fresh ginger

^{1}/$_4$ teaspoon minced garlic

16 inner iceberg lettuce leaves

- In a small bowl, mix the hoisin sauce and plum sauce together; set aside.

- In a medium saucepan, combine all the remaining ingredients except the lettuce leaves. Cook over medium heat, stirring constantly, until hot, about 2 minutes. Form the mixture into a mound in the center of a serving plate and surround with the lettuce leaves.

- Serve at once, with a small bowl of the sauce alongside. Each guest spoons about ½ teaspoon of the sauce on a lettuce leaf, then tops it with a spoonful of the duck mixture.

Grapefruit Salad with Jicama

SERVES 4 AS A FIRST COURSE

Slanted Door

Ferry Building
(One Ferry Plaza)

A prime example of creative second-generation ethnic cuisine, chef-owner Charles Phan's Slanted Door became one of the biggest draws in town when it opened in the Mission in the late nineties, in a building with a metal front door that angled inward. The food stayed just as good and the size of the clientele increased when the restaurant moved to the Embarcadero so the Mission Street address could be remodeled. Now, the restaurant is in its third incarnation in a gorgeous big space in the Ferry Building, with a view of the ferry boats arriving and departing on the bay, and even more people crowd in for a taste of the Door's flavor-layered food, like this refreshing salad of grapefruit, jicama, and red cabbage, tossed with a sweet-hot dressing, candied pecans, and fresh herbs. Serve it at home with grilled meat, fish, or chicken.

Note: Rau ram, an aromatic herb with long, pointed leaves, is available in Southeast Asian markets.

DRESSING

5 garlic cloves
2 green Thai chilies, or ¹/₂ small jalapeño chili
³/₄ cup sugar
¹/₂ cup rice vinegar
1 cup soy sauce
1 cup water

1 pound red cabbage, cored and shredded (about 4 cups)
¹/₂ jicama, peeled and shredded (about 3 cups)
1 large pink grapefruit, peeled and sectioned (see page 7)
¹/₂ cup Candied Pecans (recipe follows)
1 tablespoon olive oil
2 tablespoons chopped fresh rau ram or cilantro
2 tablespoons chopped fresh mint

- To make the dressing: In a large mortar, pound the garlic, chilies or chili, and sugar to a paste. Stir in the vinegar, soy sauce, and water.

- In a large bowl, combine the cabbage, jicama, grapefruit, pecans, olive oil, rau ram or cilantro, and mint. Add the dressing. Toss well and serve.

Candied Pecans

MAKES 2 CUPS

This recipe makes 4 times more than you will need for the above salad. Although you can cut the recipe, the pecans will keep for up to 1 month and are great to have on hand to garnish salads or desserts, for serving with cheese and/or fruit, or for snacking. They also make a good gift.

4 egg whites
$1/2$ cup sugar
$1/4$ teaspoon salt
2 cups (8 ounces) pecan halves

- Preheat the oven to 325°F. Line a rimmed baking sheet (jelly-roll pan) with parchment paper. In a large bowl, beat the egg whites until soft peaks form. Gradually beat in the sugar and salt until stiff, glossy peaks form. Fold the pecans into the egg whites and spread them out on the prepared pan. Bake until the egg whites are puffed and golden brown, about 15 minutes. Remove the pan from the oven and toss the pecans to deflate the whites. Return to the oven and toast for another 15 minutes. Remove from the oven and toss again. Let cool completely. Store in an airtight container at room temperature for up to 1 month.

Ahi Burgers
with Ginger-Wasabi Mayo

SERVES 4 AS A MAIN COURSE

Taylor's
Automatic Refresher

One Ferry Building

The first thing you see at the Ferry Building if you approach from the south is the vast space of Taylor's Automatic Refresher, and the long lines of people waiting to get in. What started in 1949 in St. Helena as a roadside burger stand has turned out to be a major crowd-pleaser in San Francisco. The mood is casual; the food is classic American with a gourmet twist, like these amazingly good ahi burgers; and the place is especially popular with families for its kid- and family-friendly menu. At Taylor's, these burgers are usually served with sweet potato fries or onion rings.

Note: To make your own wasabi paste, use 2 parts wasabi powder to 1 part water.

> Four 4-ounce No. 1–grade ahi (yellowfin) tuna steaks
> ½ cup soy sauce
> 1 cup shredded napa cabbage
> 1 cup shredded red cabbage
> 1 cup shredded carrots
> ¼ cup fresh lime juice
> 4 egg-bread buns
> 4 tablespoons unsalted butter, melted
> Ginger-Wasabi Mayo (recipe follows)

● Prepare a hot fire in a charcoal grill, or plan to use a grill pan. Place the ahi steaks in a baking dish that will just fit them and pour the soy sauce over them. Let stand for 5 minutes, turning once.

● In a medium bowl, combine the cabbages and carrots. Toss with the lime juice and set aside.

- Brush the cut side of each bun with the melted butter and toast in a large skillet or on a griddle over medium heat until light brown, 2 or 3 minutes. Spread the ginger-wasabi mayo on the toasted half of each bun. Top the toasted half of each bun with some of the cabbage mixture.

- If using a charcoal grill, coat the grill grate with oil using wadded-up paper towels. Or, heat a grill pan over high heat for about 1 minute and coat with oil in the same way. Sear the ahi for about 1 minute on each side for rare. Serve at once on the dressed buns, with any leftover slaw alongside.

Ginger-Wasabi Mayo

MAKES ABOUT ³/₄ CUP

¹/₂ cup mayonnaise
¹/₃ cup pickled ginger, drained
2 tablespoons wasabi paste
1 tablespoon Asian sesame oil
2 tablespoons fresh lime juice
1 tablespoon soy sauce

- Combine all the ingredients in blender or food processor and process to make a smooth sauce.

Swedish Oatmeal Pancakes
with Pears and Almonds

SERVES 4 TO 6

Town's End Restaurant and Bakery

2 Townsend Street (at Embarcadero)

Town's End is the best of several worlds: It's a great brunch spot, it's a bay-view restaurant with a patio, and it's home to one of the best bakeries in town. The dinners are good, but this place really shines when the sun is out. Come here on a bright Sunday morning with the *New York Times* and feast on pastries, eggs Benedict, or other brunchy things, like these nutty-tasting oatmeal pancakes—they're even good for you. You can order them on their own, or as part of Mary's Special, along with eggs scrambled with mushrooms, green onions, garlic, and white Cheddar.

Note: Soak the oatmeal overnight if you want to make these first thing in the morning.

2 cups old-fashioned rolled oats
2 cups buttermilk, plus more as needed
1/2 cup unbleached all-purpose flour
2 tablespoons sugar
1 teaspoon baking powder
1 teaspoon baking soda
2 eggs, lightly beaten
4 tablespoons unsalted butter, melted, plus unsalted butter for serving
Canola oil for cooking
1 pear, cored, peeled, and thinly sliced
1/4 cup sliced almonds
Warm maple syrup for serving

In a large bowl, combine the oats and the 2 cups buttermilk and let soak for at least 30 minutes or as long as overnight.

- In a medium bowl, stir the flour, sugar, baking powder, and baking soda together with a whisk. Stir the dry ingredients into the oat mixture. Stir in the eggs and melted butter. The batter should be thick, but add 1 or 2 tablespoons more buttermilk if it seems too thick to pour.

- Heat a nonstick or well-seasoned griddle or large skillet over medium heat. Coat lightly with oil. Pour the batter by ¼-cup portions onto the griddle or skillet. Distribute 3 or 4 slices of pears and about 1 teaspoon of sliced almonds over each pancake. Cook until nicely browned on the bottom, 2 or 3 minutes. Flip and cook on the other side until evenly browned, 2 or 3 minutes (these will need to cook a little longer than regular buttermilk pancakes, to allow the oats to cook thoroughly). Keep warm in a low oven. Repeat until all the batter is used. Serve at once on warmed plates, topped with a little butter and some maple syrup.

Artisan Breads

First, there was sourdough and only sourdough. It was made from the "mother," a thick paste redolent with the aroma of fermented yeast, which bubbled in crocks in the mining camps. It was the elemental artisan, or handmade, bread, baked in a Dutch oven over a wood fire. With its sour fragrance and coarse texture honeycombed with bubbles, it kept many a miner fed and many a mining claim afloat.

In the city, bakers turned out bread in wood-fired ovens, each loaf golden brown, shiny, and blistered on top, and each one slightly different from every other because it had been shaped by human hands. And soon it was said that the sourdough made in San Francisco had a special flavor like no other, one compounded of fog and fresh sea air with the smell of saltwater on it.

One company, Boudin, has been making sourdough in the city since 1849, and today, they have bakeries all over town. Factory-made white sandwich loaves with soft crusts and an insubstantial crumb eventually came along to compete with the chewy, thick-crusted sourdough. But 150 years after the first sourdough loaves were made here, handmade breads baked in wood-fired ovens are the height of food fashion, and bakeries around the bay, such as Acme, Grace Baking, La Farine, and Semifreddi's are turning out a wide variety of loaves, from walnut sourdough to Italian pugliese and focaccia to French pain levain and fougasse.

Exceptional sweet baguettes and sour baguettes, made from dough shipped up from La Brea Bakery in Los Angeles, are available hot out of the oven at the two Whole Foods Markets in San Francisco. The impeccable loaves from Della Fattoria in Petaluma are sold at the Ferry Plaza Farmers' Market every Saturday, as are bread and pastries from Downtown Bakery in Healdsburg and the glorious fruit-filled breads from the Noe Valley Bakery on Twenty-fourth Street.

Pascal Rigo's Bay Breads came to town a few years ago and upped the ante with a selection of French breads made from organic flours. Boulangerie, their blue storefront on Pine Street just off Fillmore, has a line out the door almost every morning, and they have two other shops in the city (La Boulange de Polk on Polk Street and La Boulange de Cole in Cole Valley). Tartine Bakery (600 Guerrero), the latest bakery to draw people desperately looking for parking places so they can line up for the country bread, which comes out of the oven around 4 P.M.

And many of the oldest bakeries in town have been baking handmade old-country breads for years, long before the phrase "artisan bread" was ever thought of. In North Beach, Danilo Bakery (516 Green Street) continues to make authentic Italian breads, including anise-flavored buccellato *and breads shaped like hands. At Eastertime they make* colombe di Pasqua, *egg breads in the shape of doves, and* buccellato *wreaths and bread men with colored Easter eggs embedded in the dough. The Italian-French Baking Company (1501 Grant Avenue) makes smooth, oval-shaped St. Francis rolls and huge crunchy bread sticks. Victoria Bakery and Pastry Company (1362 Stockton Street) makes* brioche, *airy, golden Italian versions of croissants. The Liguria Bakery (1700 Stockton Street) still makes focaccia in the back of its bare-bones store. (People have tried to make their focaccia elsewhere, but Mr. Sorocco says it never tastes the same.) Pick out your focaccia (plain, or topped with chopped green onions, raisins, garlic, or a smear of tomato paste) and one of the Soroccos behind the counter will wrap it in paper for you and tie it with string. (They bake all morning and early afternoon; the doors open at 8 A.M. and close at 4 P.M., or whenever they run out of focaccia, which can be three o' clock or earlier.) Call ahead to order focaccia for a party.) And in bakeries all over town, the sourdough mother is still breathing in the San Francisco air, still bubbling, still exhaling its faintly sour, inimitable, only–in–San Francisco fragrance.*

POWELL &
28
HOME OF THE MOST FOCUSED REAL ESTATE PROFESSIONALS IN THE WORLD.
SOLD
COLDWELL BANKER
Expect the best
SAN FRANCISCO MUNICIPAL RAILWAY

Russian Hill / Nob Hill / Polk Street

HYDE Sts.

Antica Trattoria

1550 Hyde Cafe and Wine Bar

La Folie

Le Petit Robert

Pesce Seafoof Bar

Ristorante Milano

Tablespoon

Zarzuela

RUSSIAN HILL SITS LIKE AN ISLAND OF FRANCISCAN BEDROCK on the northern tip of San Francisco. To the east, it looks down over Chinatown and  North Beach, and across to Telegraph Hill; to the south is Nob Hill. To the west, at the foot of the hill, is Polk Street, and to the north, the hill looks out over the bay. Here is where the cable cars really do seem to climb toward the stars, as they labor up Hyde Street to the crest of Russian Hill; or, going the other way, seem, for one breath-stopping moment, to shoot off into space before they thunder precipitously down toward Aquatic Park. THERE ARE NO RUSSIAN RESTAURANTS ON RUSSIAN HILL, and probably not all that many Russians; the name was given to it because some Russian sailors were buried there in the days when San Francisco was Yerba Buena, and Russia had a fur-trading foothold on the coast. But it does have some of the oldest houses in the city, the crookedest street in the world, one of the two steepest streets in town (Filbert Street between Leavenworth and Hyde), secret stairway walks, and—restaurants. The restaurants range the cuisines of the world, from hole-in-the-wall Indian and Thai restaurants to the latest California/fusion/Mediterranean/New American/New French hybrids. ONCE, RUSSIAN HILL WAS AN ENCLAVE OF BOHEMIAN ARTISTS and the perch of poets; the only parks on the hill are small, hidden away, and named for nineteenth-century poets George Sterling and Ina Coolbrith. Their bohemian legacy was revived in the fifties by the Beats: Jack Kerouac, Neal Cassady, and Carolyn Cassady lived together in a little house that still stands on Russell Place. Today, the hill is a quiet neighborhood of corner stores, apartment houses, and a few single-family dwellings. AT THE FOOT OF THE HILL IS POLK STREET, which runs from the Maritime Museum to Market Street. The central blocks are one of the oldest gay communities in the city, while those closer to Market verge onto the Tenderloin. The part of the street toward the bay, however, is a burgeoning restaurant row, with several coffeehouses and a Real Food natural foods store. The cuisines offered here include Mexican, Indian, Vietnamese, Thai, Italian, and Japanese; you'll also find a cluster of charming French shops and eating places, among them La Folie, one of the city's few four-star restaurants. ⟶ FROM RUSSIAN HILL, you can walk over rolling streets of apartment buildings to the summit of Nob Hill, once crowned with the mansions of the silver and railroad kings, now crowned with luxury hotels, luxury apartment buildings, and Grace Cathedral. ⟶ IF YOU'RE WALKING BACK TOWARD RUSSIAN HILL on one of the winter nights when fog reaches this far east, you might easily imagine that you're in a novel by Dashiell Hammett, who lived at various locations in this neighborhood—the houses and streets haven't changed much since his day. Or maybe it's one of those occasional warm summer nights when the restaurants on Hyde Street put a quarter of their tables out on the sidewalk. In either case, have a seat, order a glass of wine, and enjoy this neighborhood's unique dinner music: the rumble of passing cable cars and the clanging of their bells.

OTHER NEIGHBORHOOD STARS

Acquarello

Ana Mandara

Frascati

Gary Danko

Hyde Street Bistro

Luella

Mandarin

Matterhorn

Nob Hill Café

Shalimar

Sushi Groove

Swan Oyster Depot

Yabbie's Coastal Kitchen

Gnocchi al Tartufo
(Potato Dumplings with Truffle Sauce)

SERVES 6 AS A FIRST COURSE, 4 AS A MAIN COURSE

Antica Trattoria
2400 Polk Street (at Union)

When Antica opened in 1996, it quickly established a reputation as one of the best of San Francisco's many small Italian restaurants. Today, the restaurant has maintained its high standards. The high-ceilinged room with windows on Polk and Union Streets is restrained and somewhat formal in decor, but the food that comes out of the kitchen is rustic and full of flavor. When in season, truffles are featured in several of Antica's dishes, such as these gnocchi. If truffles are not in your budget, truffle oil will give your gnocchi just enough of that desirable earthy fragrance.

TRUFFLE SAUCE
1 cup (4 ounces) shredded fontina cheese
1 cup dry white wine
1 cup heavy cream
1 egg yolk
$^1/_2$ ounce fresh white truffle, sliced paper thin on a mandoline or with a vegetable peeler, or 1 tablespoon white truffle oil
Salt and freshly ground pepper to taste

POTATO GNOCCHI
2 pounds russet (baking) potatoes
$5^2/_3$ cups sifted unbleached all-purpose flour
$^1/_4$ cup grated Parmigiano-Reggiano cheese
1 egg yolk
1 egg, beaten lightly
Salt and freshly grated nutmeg to taste

$^1/_2$ ounce fresh white truffle, sliced paper thin with a mandoline or a vegetable peeler, or 1 tablespoon white truffle oil, for garnish

Savoring San Francisco

104

To make the sauce: In a large stainless-steel bowl, combine the fontina and white wine. Set aside and let soak for about 1 hour, then drain off the wine (reserve it for another use). In a small saucepan, bring the cream to a boil. At the same time, add 2 inches of water to a medium saucepan and bring to a simmer to use as a double boiler. Add the hot cream to the cheese mixture. Place the bowl over the pan of simmering water. With a wooden spoon, stir the mixture until the cheese is melted. Stir in the egg yolk and sliced white truffle or truffle oil. Season with salt and pepper. Set aside in a warm place and cover to keep warm.

While the cheese is soaking for the sauce, make the gnocchi: Preheat the oven to 450°F. Pierce the potatoes with a fork and bake them until tender when pierced with a knife, about 45 minutes. Remove the potatoes and peel them while hot. Pass the flesh through a potato ricer or food mill onto a marble or wooden board and let cool.

Add the flour, cheese, egg yolk, egg, salt, and nutmeg to the potatoes. Mix and knead with your hands to make a smooth dough. Let the dough rest for 10 minutes.

Divide the dough into 4 pieces. On a lightly floured board, roll each piece into a log about ¾ inch in diameter. Cut each log into ¾-inch-long pieces. Press one long side of each piece against the inner curve of a fork's tines to leave ridges on the dough, and press your thumb into the center of the other side to leave a hollow (these indentations catch the sauce). Place the gnocchi on a lightly floured baking sheet.

In a large pot of salted boiling water, cook the gnocchi until they rise to the surface, about 2 minutes. Using a wire skimmer, transfer the gnocchi to the pan of warm sauce. Dish the gnocchi and sauce into a warmed pasta bowl or individual bowls. Garnish with the sliced truffle or truffle oil and serve *presto*.

Tuna Confit
with Fennel-Rucola Salad
and Anchovy Vinaigrette

MAKES 6 FIRST-COURSE SERVINGS

1550 Hyde Cafe and Wine Bar
1550 Hyde Street (at Pacific)

1550 Hyde seems to sum up one of the things San Francisco does best: It's an amazingly accomplished restaurant opened in a tiny storefront by two consummate professionals. The decor is simple but pleasing, and the cuisine has the kind of personality that is present only when people truly know and understand food. Come to this restaurant to enjoy their California-Mediterranean cooking and to hear the cable cars clanging by outside on the Hyde Street line.

1 pound albacore tuna (tombo) or yellowfin (ahi) tuna,
skinned and bloodline removed if necessary
Kosher salt and freshly ground pepper to taste
1 rosemary sprig
3 thyme sprigs
2 bay leaves, torn in half
3 garlic cloves, halved lengthwise
Extra-virgin olive oil to cover

ANCHOVY VINAIGRETTE
2 salt-packed anchovies, rinsed, boned, and minced
1 garlic clove, minced
1 tablespoon minced fresh flat-leaf parsley
2 teaspoons minced fresh chives
1 teaspoon grated lemon zest
Juice of 1 lemon
1 tablespoon Champagne vinegar
Salt and freshly ground pepper to taste
About ¹/₂ cup extra-virgin olive oil

1 fennel bulb, trimmed, cored, and very finely sliced, on a mandoline if possible
8 ounces rucola (wild arugula) or baby arugula leaves
Crostini (page 279) for serving

- Season the tuna generously with salt and pepper. Place the tuna in a glass or ceramic baking dish just large enough to hold it and refrigerate for at least 4 hours or as long as overnight.

- Preheat the oven to 250°F. Add the herbs and garlic to the dish and pour in olive oil to cover the tuna. Cover the dish with aluminum foil. Roast in the oven for about 1 hour, or until firm to the touch. The tuna will be opaque throughout. Let cool to room temperature. Use now, or refrigerate for up to 2 weeks.

- To serve, bring the tuna to room temperature if refrigerated. Remove the fish from the oil and gently flake it with your fingers.

- To make the vinaigrette: In a bowl, combine all the ingredients except the olive oil. Gradually whisk in the olive oil. Put the fennel and rucola or arugula in a bowl, add some of the vinaigrette, and toss to coat. Divide the mixture among 6 salad plates. Divide the tuna on top of the salad. Spoon 1 teaspoon of the remaining vinaigrette over each serving of tuna and accompany with crostini.

Coconut Tapioca
with Passion Fruit Sorbet, Basil Infusion, and Coconut Tuiles

SERVES 6 AS A DESSERT

La Folie
2316 Polk Street (between Green and Union)

One of the few four-star restaurants in San Francisco is a small but elegant storefront on Polk Street. Roland Passot creates some of the most exquisite French food in San Francisco at the recently remodeled La Folie. The mirrored and curtained walls and the muted colors give this space all the stylish ambiance of a luxurious Parisian restaurant. Passot's menus change with the seasons, combining the best of California foods with fresh variations on classic French techniques, and his food is lyrical and imaginative, like this dessert built on exotic flavors and unexpected ingredients.

Note: Make your own fruit purée from fresh fruit (you will need about 2 pounds of fruit), or order frozen passion fruit and mango purées from Perfect Puree at www. perfectpuree.com. To simplify this recipe, use all mango or passion fruit purée, or buy a commercial fruit sorbet.

PASSION FRUIT SORBET
$^1/_4$ cup granulated sugar
1 tablespoon fresh lemon juice
1 teaspoon corn syrup
1 cup mango purée or pulp
1 cup passion fruit purée or pulp

COCONUT TAPIOCA
$^2/_3$ cup small-pearl tapioca
One 13 $^1/_2$-ounce can coconut milk
2 cups whole milk
3 tablespoons honey
1 $^1/_2$ tablespoons sugar

COCONUT TUILES
1 large egg white
$^1/_4$ cup granulated sugar
$^1/_3$ cup unsweetened shredded dried coconut
2 tablespoons unsalted butter, melted

BASIL SYRUP
1 bunch basil, stemmed
$^1/_2$ cup granulated sugar
$^1/_4$ cup corn syrup
$^1/_2$ cup water

Mint sprigs and fresh raspberries or strawberries for garnish
Confectioners' sugar for dusting

- To make the sorbet: In a medium bowl, stir the sugar, lemon juice, and corn syrup together. Gradually stir in the purées or pulp until blended. Cover and refrigerate for at least 2 hours or overnight. Freeze in an ice cream maker according to the manufacturer's instructions. Transfer to a stainless-steel container and place in the freezer.

- To make the tapioca: In a heavy, medium saucepan, combine all the ingredients and bring to a boil over medium heat. Reduce heat to medium-low and cook, stirring constantly to keep the mixture from sticking, for 35 to 45 minutes, or until the pearls become translucent. Remove from heat and let cool.

- To make the tuiles: Preheat the oven to 350°F. In a medium bowl, stir the egg whites, sugar, and coconut together until blended. Gradually stir in the melted butter to make a paste. Refrigerate until thickened, about 1 hour.

- Line a baking sheet with parchment paper. Space 6 heaping tablespoon-fuls of tuile batter about 5 inches apart on the prepared pan. With an offset spatula, spread the batter into rounds 3$^1/_2$ to 4 inches in diameter. Bake for about 15 minutes, or until golden brown. Remove from the oven and let rest on the pan for about 1 minute. Using a thin metal spatula, carefully transfer each tuile to a wire rack to harden and cool completely. (If the tuiles are too hard to remove from the pan, replace the pan in the warm oven for about 1 minute to soften them.) Store in an airtight container.

To make the basil syrup: Blanch the basil in a large pot of salted boiling water for 60 seconds. Using a wire skimmer, transfer to an ice bath. Drain, squeeze dry, and coarsely chop. Transfer to a blender.

In a deep, heavy saucepan with a candy thermometer attached, combine the sugar, corn syrup, and water. Bring to a boil over high heat and cook to the soft-ball stage; the candy thermometer should register 235°F. Pour the hot syrup over the basil in the blender and purée on low speed until smooth.

Strain through a fine-meshed sieve into a stainless-steel bowl. Place the bowl in an ice bath to cool to room temperature quickly; this will allow the purée to retain its bright green color. Pour into a plastic squirt bottle and refrigerate until ready to use.

To serve, divide the tapioca among 6 shallow soup bowls. Place a quenelle of sorbet on top. Drizzle a ring of basil syrup around the edges of the tapioca. Top with a coconut tuile placed at an angle on the sorbet and garnish with mint sprigs and berries. Dust with confectioners' sugar and serve at once.

Fava Bean Tartines

SERVES 6 AS A FIRST COURSE, 3 AS A LIGHT MAIN COURSE

With La Folie, Boulange de Polk, and Le Petit Robert (not to mention several French decor/antiques shops) clustered within one block of Polk Street, this area is a miniature French enclave. Another of Pascal Rigo's enterprises, as is the next-door bakery, Le Petit Robert (known to some of the locals as Little Bob's) opened with a simple white interior, only to close for a week and emerge as a sort of Moroccan nightclub on the inside while remaining an unpretentious bistro on the outside. The food is carefully prepared, the flavors are bright and fresh, and you can bet that almost anything you order here will be good.

Le Petit Robert
2300 Polk Street (at Green)

FAVA BEAN PURÉE
2 pounds fava beans, shelled
$^{1}/_{2}$ cup extra-virgin olive oil
2 tablespoons minced shallots
Salt and freshly ground pepper to taste
2 tablespoons fresh lemon juice
6 slices levain bread
4 ounces fresh goat cheese

LEMON VINAIGRETTE
1 tablespoon fresh lemon juice
3 tablespoons extra-virgin oil
Salt and freshly ground pepper to taste

2 teaspoons minced shallots
2 tablespoons finely shredded fresh basil
2 tablespoons finely shredded fresh mint
3 cups arugula
6 slices prosciutto

- To make the purée: Blanch the fava beans in a pot of salted boiling water for 2 minutes. Transfer to a bowl of ice water. Drain and pop off the skins by pinching each bean between your thumb and forefinger.

- In a sauté pan or skillet, heat the olive oil over medium heat and sauté the shallots until translucent, about 3 minutes. Add the fava beans and cook to heat through, about 2 minutes. In a blender, combine the beans, salt, pepper, and lemon juice. Taste and adjust the seasoning. Set aside.

- Preheat the broiler. Place the bread on a broiler pan and toast about 5 inches from the heat source until lightly golden, 30 to 45 seconds on each side. Remove from the broiler, leaving the broiler on. Spread the fava purée on one side of the grilled bread, dot with the goat cheese, and place on the broiler pan. Broil about 5 inches from the heat source just until the cheese is heated through, 1 to 2 minutes.

- Meanwhile, make the vinaigrette: Combine the lemon juice and oil in a small bowl and whisk to blend. Season with salt and pepper. In a medium bowl, combine the shallots, basil, mint, and arugula. Add the vinaigrette and toss to coat the arugula.

- Place each toasted tartine on a plate and top with a slice of prosciutto, then a portion of the arugula salad. Serve at once.

Sicilian Swordfish Rolls

SERVES 6 AS A FIRST COURSE, 3 TO 4 AS A MAIN COURSE

In the trend of chef/owners opening simpler, smaller places not far from their original location, Ruggero Gadaldi debuted this narrow space just down the street from his Antica Trattoria (page 104). Pesce serves both small plates, Venetian *cicchetti* style, and large plates, and the choices range from raw oysters or cioppino to pasta with lobster. The specials change often, and the kitchen's Caesar salad is one of the best around. A long bar takes up half of the front room, making this a good place for single diners and couples drawn by skillfully prepared food tasting of the sea.

Pesce Seafood Bar

2227 Polk Street
(between Green and Vallejo)

FILLING

$^{1}/_{2}$ cup extra-virgin olive oil

1 tablespoon minced garlic

1 tablespoon minced fresh thyme

1 tablespoon fennel seeds

1 tablespoon dried oregano

1 cup fresh bread crumbs

$^{1}/_{4}$ cup pine nuts

3 tablespoons dried currants, soaked in water for 30 minutes and drained

Salt and freshly ground pepper to taste

OLIVE-CAPER SAUCE

2 tablespoons (1 ounce) salt-packed Sicilian capers,
rinsed, soaked in water for 1 hour, rinsed again, and drained

$^{1}/_{2}$ cup pitted Cerignola or other mild green olives, finely chopped,
plus 2 tablespoons of their liquid

2 tablespoons water

$^{1}/_{4}$ cup extra-virgin olive oil

Salt and freshly ground pepper to taste

24 ounces swordfish, cut vertically into twelve 2-ounce slices
(ask your butcher to do this for you)
6 fresh bay leaves, or 6 dried bay leaves soaked in water for 15 minutes
Flour for dusting
¼ cup extra-virgin olive oil
½ cup dry white wine
Juice of 2 lemons
1 tablespoon minced fresh flat-leaf parsley

To make the filling: In a medium sauté pan or skillet, heat the extra-virgin olive oil over medium heat. Add the garlic, thyme, fennel seeds, and oregano and sauté for 30 seconds, or until fragrant. Add the bread crumbs and sauté until light brown, about 3 minutes. Add the pine nuts and sauté for 1 minute, then stir in the drained currants. Season with salt and pepper. Remove from the heat and set aside to cool.

To make the sauce: In a small bowl, combine all the ingredients. Stir to blend, then set aside.

Place each swordfish slice between two sheets of plastic wrap and gently pound with a flat meat pounder or the bottom of a small skillet to an even ⅛ inch. Remove the top sheet of plastic and place a heaping tablespoonful of filling in a line the length of each slice and roll the slice lengthwise. Pair 2 rolls side by side with a bay leaf between them and secure with two short wooden skewers. Dust the swordfish rolls with flour.

In a large sauté pan or skillet, heat the oil over medium heat and sauté the rolls for 1 minute, or just until opaque, turning to cook all sides. Add the wine, cover, and cook for 2 to 3 minutes.

Transfer each pair of rolls to a warmed plate and remove the skewers. Drizzle with the lemon juice and top with the olive-caper sauce. Sprinkle with parsley and serve at once. *Mangia, mangia!*

Polenta alla Coda di Rospo

(Stewed Monkfish, Clams, and Mussels over Soft Polenta)

SERVES 4 AS A MAIN COURSE

One of Nob Hill's secret treasures is this unassuming restaurant on a quiet block of Pacific. For years Aldo Blasi and Nicola Viti have brightened the neighborhood with their authentic northern Italian food. Their gnocchi is famous among gnocchi-lovers, and their risotto is impeccable. Here is their Venetian version of fish stew, based on monkfish and served over soft polenta, perfect for a foggy night on the hill.

Ristorante Milano
1448 Pacific Avenue
(between Hyde and Larkin)

SOFT POLENTA

About 10 cups water
1 tablespoon salt
1 1/4 cups polenta

FISH STEW

3 tablespoons olive oil
1 garlic clove, crushed
1 small dried red pepper, seeded
12 ounces baby Manila clams, scrubbed
12 ounces black mussels, scrubbed and debearded
32 ounces canned diced Italian tomatoes with juice (preferably Muir Glen organic tomatoes)
3/4 cup fish stock (page 17) or bottled clam juice
1/4 cup dry white wine
1 1/2 pounds monkfish fillets, cut into 1-inch cubes
1/2 cup minced fresh flat-leaf parsley

To make the polenta: In a large pot, bring 8 cups of the water to a boil and add the salt. While stirring constantly with one hand, repeatedly pick up the polenta by the fistful with the other hand and let it gradually pour out of your hand into the water. Continue to cook, stirring constantly, until the grains of polenta are tender to the bite, about 45 minutes. Gradually add up to 2 cups more water as needed during cooking to make a soft, pourable polenta.

About 10 minutes before the polenta is done, make the fish stew: In a soup pot, heat the olive oil over medium heat and sauté the garlic and red pepper until fragrant, about 1 minute. Add the mussels and clams, cover, and cook until the shellfish open, 3 to 4 minutes. Using a slotted spoon, transfer the shellfish to a bowl. Discard any shellfish that have not opened.

Add the tomatoes and juice, fish stock or clam juice, and white wine to the soup pot. Bring to a boil over high heat, reduce heat to a simmer, and cook for about 5 minutes. Add the monkfish. Cook, uncovered, until the fish is just opaque throughout, about 5 minutes. Turn off heat and return the shellfish and any juices to the soup pot. Stir in the parsley.

Divide the polenta among 4 warmed shallow soup bowls. Arrange the shellfish in a crown on top of the polenta. Add the fish and some of the pan liquid to the middle of the crown, letting the yellow of the polenta show around the edges. Serve at once.

Asian Pear Ajo Blanco

SERVES 4 AS A FIRST COURSE

A streamlined restaurant with the aura of a supper club, Tablespoon serves unfailingly interesting food, and its service is exemplary. Many of the dishes here are classics that have been transformed by inspired variations, like this traditional cold Spanish almond soup given a California twist with the addition of Asian pears. Serve it on a hot summer night, with a light main course and a Spanish rosado wine.

Tablespoon
2209 Polk Street (at Vallejo)

Note: This soup is best when made 8 to 24 hours before serving.

1 slice country bread, crust removed, toasted

2 very ripe Asian pears or ripe Bosc pears, peeled, cored, and chopped

1 1/2 cups vegetable broth or water

1 garlic clove

1/2 cup whole blanched almonds

3/4 cup olive oil

2 tablespoons sherry vinegar

2 teaspoons salt

- Break the toasted bread into small pieces and set aside. In a blender, combine the pears and 1/2 cup of the vegetable broth and purée until smooth. With the machine running, add the garlic and the almonds and blend well. Add the pieces of toast, one at a time, and continue puréeing to make a paste. Gradually add the olive oil in a slow, steady stream. Gradually add the rest of the vegetable broth and all of the vinegar. Stir in the salt and pass through a fine-meshed sieve.

- Cover and refrigerate for at least 8 hours or preferably overnight so that the flavors are well blended. Serve very cold.

Gazpacho Andaluz

SERVES 6 AS A FIRST COURSE

Zarzuela

2000 Hyde Street
(at Union)

One of the first of several fine Spanish restaurants in San Francisco, Zarzuela debuted with crowds of people waiting to get in, and it remains a huge draw today. High ceilings, white walls decorated with Spanish plates, and arched windows looking out on Union and Hyde streets (where the cable cars go by) are the setting for their specialties of tapas and paella. The wait staff is charming, and many have been with the restaurant since it opened. (If you're lucky, someone in the restaurant will be celebrating a birthday, and Arturo will serenade them with a Spanish song that translates as "On the day you were born, all the flowers bloomed in Spain.") On a rare hot summer day in San Francisco, begin your meal at Zarzuela with this velvety gazpacho, or make it yourself at home when tomatoes are at their peak.

Note: This is a simpler version of the gazpacho in the first edition of *Savoring San Francisco*.

2½ slices (4 ounces) day-old French or Italian bread, crust removed

4 cups ice water

⅓ large English (hothouse) cucumber

½ small white onion

1 small sweet apple, such as a Fuji, peeled and cored

1 small green bell pepper, seeded and deribbed

1 small red bell pepper, seeded and deribbed

4 very ripe vine-ripened tomatoes

Pinch of ground cumin

Pinch of sweet pimentón (Spanish smoked paprika)

1 tablespoon plus ¾ teaspoon salt

2 peeled garlic cloves

3 tablespoons sherry vinegar

¼ cup Spanish extra-virgin olive oil

1 small white onion, finely diced
1 very ripe vine-ripened tomato, peeled, seeded, and finely diced (see page 12)
1 small seedless cucumber, finely diced
1½ slices (2 ounces) day-old French or Italian bread, crust removed,
cut into ½-inch cubes and sautéed in olive oil until golden brown

- Tear the 2½ slices bread into pieces and soak in a bowl with the water for at least 2 hours or as long as overnight. Coarsely chop all the vegetables. Put the bread and water in a blender and purée. Add the vegetables and all the remaining ingredients, except the garnishes, ending with the oil. (You may have to do this in batches.) Strain the soup though a medium-meshed sieve, forcing it through with the back or a soup ladle or large spoon. Cover and refrigerate for at least 2 hours or up to 2 days.

- Divide the soup among 6 soup bowls and serve with the garnishes on the side or sprinkled on top.

The Marina /Cow Hollow/ Pacific Heights

A 16 Restaurant and Wine Bar

Betelnut Pejui Wu

Cafe Kati

Chez Nous

Greens Restaurant

Isa

Plumpjack Café

Quince

Rose's Café

Sociale Caffè and Wine Bar

Vivande Porta Via

ON THE NORTHERN EDGE OF THE CITY, two streets, Chestnut and Union, head westward to the Presidio Wall, each the center of its respective neighborhood, the Marina and Cow Hollow. Both are shopping streets, lined with

mostly one- and two-story buildings. Cow Hollow is the older neighborhood, with a stock of Victorian houses that predate the 1906 earthquake and fire. Once, this stretch of land at the foot of Pacific Heights was the site of San Francisco's dairy industry. The fire that followed the quake was stopped at Van Ness, so many signs of the past remain here, such as the original Cow Hollow farmhouse (2040 Union Street). If you look closely on Union Street and its side streets, you'll see the hitching posts and metal rings that were used for tying up horses.   THE MARINA, a newer residential neighborhood, is built partly on earthquake fill but mostly on sand, much of it dredged up from the bay to form the site of the Panama-Pacific International Exposition of 1915. This fantasy of the future, past, and present was ostensibly held to celebrate the completion of the Panama Canal, but its real mission was to announce to the world that San Francisco had recovered from the Great Quake. (The only building remaining from it is the Palace of Fine Arts, designed by Barnard Maybeck to resemble Roman ruins.) In 1989, the Loma Prieta earthquake set the Marina fill wobbling like a bowl of Jell-0, making it the site of some of the worst destruction in the city.   YET AGAIN, San Francisco showed its phoenixlike ability to reinvent itself, and the once-quiet, conservative neighborhood became instead the epicenter of a youth movement, thanks to young people moving into the area's newly reinforced and rebuilt apartment buildings. Now, on weekends, San Franciscans from all over the city join them in the eclectic restaurants along the street. A few of the old Marina hangouts remain, like Bechelli's, a classic, unreconstructed coffee shop from the fifties, but most places are new, and a few, like A 16 and Isa, are cutting edge. ⟶ THIS CLOSE TO THE WATER, you can walk to the Marina Green for a picnic lunch after buying huge deli sandwiches at Lucca Delicatessen (2120 Chestnut); this is also the place to pick up a great wedge of spinach frittata to serve for parties, and handmade ravioli on Tuesdays and Fridays for a quick dinner at home. On the Green, you can watch the fog as it snakes through the Gate in summer and stretches out over the bay, or see the sailboats flying by if the day is clear. At the east end of the Green are the Fort Mason piers, site of the famed Greens Restaurant, a perfect place to dine while watching the sun set over the Golden Gate. ⟶ LOOKING OUT OVER COW HOLLOW and the Marina is Pacific Heights, home to another treasure trove of Victorians and the city's most elegant mansions. Fillmore Street runs north and south through the center of the area, changing from an eclectic and sophisticated street of restaurants and shops on the hill, to a formerly vibrant black neighborhood on the flats, now in the process of being revitalized from the destruction wrought by urban "renewal." Running across it at a right angle is Sacramento Street, finishing its journey from downtown and up the fearsome Sacramento Street hill to lead you into Presidio Heights, an area with some of the city's finest antiques stores, dress shops, home decorating shops, and small restaurants.

OTHER NEIGHBORHOOD STARS

Alegrías, Food from Spain

Baker Street Bistro

Bistro Aix

Desirée

Dragon Well

E' Angelo

Florio

Jackson Fillmore Trattoria

La Mediterranée

Nectar Wine Lounge

Pacific Catch

Pane e Vino

Parma

Three Seasons

Yukol Place Thai Cuisine

Cranberry Bean and Dandelion Soup

MAKES 8 FIRST-COURSE SERVINGS

A 16 Restaurant and Wine Bar

2355 Chestnut Street (between Divisadero and Scott)

Named after the mother road that runs from Naples across Italy to the Adriatic Coast, A 16 is an outpost of southern Italian cuisine on the coast of California. The food here is as authentic as it can be outside of the region of Campania, down to chef Christophe Hille's certification as a *pizzaiolo* (pizza maker) by the Verace Pizza Napoletana Association, which trains chefs in the exacting art of making true Neapolitan pizza. Walk through the narrow bar to the inner room of the restaurant and indulge in A 16's robust regional specialties, like this earthy summer soup.

Note: If you can't find fresh shell beans, dried cranberry beans or chickpeas are equally satisfying in this dish (see the variation).

2 pounds fresh cranberry beans, shelled

4 cups water

Salt to taste

2 bunches dandelion greens

¹/₂ cup olive oil

6 slices guanciale (cured pig's cheek) or pancetta

1 bay leaf, preferably fresh

1 small onion, diced

1 celery stalk, diced

Chili olive oil or extra-virgin olive oil for drizzling

Bruschetta for serving (recipe follows)

In a soup pot, combine the beans and water. Bring to a boil, then reduce heat to a simmer and cook gently until just tender, about 15 minutes. (Add water as needed if the level drops below the surface of the beans.) Remove from heat and add salt to taste. Let stand for at least 30 minutes or as long as overnight.

Bring a large pot of water to a boil, salt it generously (as for pasta), and add the dandelion greens. Let the water return to a boil and cook the greens for 5 minutes. Using a wire skimmer, quickly transfer the greens to a bowl of ice water and let cool for 1 to 2 minutes, but no longer. Remove from the ice water and squeeze out the excess water with your hands (in batches). Chop coarsely into 1-inch pieces and set aside.

In a large stockpot, heat the olive oil over medium heat. Add the guanciale or pancetta and the bay leaf and sauté until the meat just begins to brown. Add the onion and celery and continue cooking until tender, about 5 minutes. Add the cooked beans and enough of their liquid to cover the ingredients. Bring to a boil, add the dandelion greens, and cook at a high simmer until the greens are tender, about 10 minutes. Remove from heat. Taste and adjust the seasoning. Divide among warmed soup bowls, drizzle with oil, and serve with bruschetta.

Bruschetta: Cut Italian bread into thick slices, toast or grill until nicely browned on each side, then rub with the cut side of a garlic clove and drizzle with oil.

Variation: The fresh cranberry beans can be replaced with 1½ cups dried cranberry beans or chickpeas, which should be soaked overnight in water to cover, then cooked in water to cover by 4 inches (cook cranberry beans 1 to 1½ hours, chickpeas 2 to 2½ hours).

Emerald Fire Noodles

SERVES 3 OR 4 AS A MAIN COURSE

Betelnut Pejui Wu

2030 Union Street
(at Buchanan)

This hip eatery, a stylized Asian beer house (*pejui wu*), is always jammed with people who love the small plates of Southeast Asian street food, like minced chicken in lettuce cups and these spicy green noodles; another draw is the house-brewed beers and large selection of Asian brews. You can dine downstairs at the high-energy bar, upstairs in the dining room, or outside at sidewalk tables under heat lamps. Go early, before catching a movie across the street perhaps, when the restaurant is a little less crowded.

Note: If you can't find spinach chow mein, use regular fresh chow mein noodles. Your dish won't be as emerald, but it will be fiery and delicious.

SAUCE

1 tablespoon canola oil
$^1/_2$ tablespoon minced fresh ginger
$^1/_2$ tablespoon minced garlic
2 tablespoons Thai red curry paste
2 tablespoons fish sauce
2 tablespoons oyster sauce
3 tablespoons sugar
$^1/_4$ cup water
1 cup coconut milk

1 pound fresh Chinese spinach egg noodles
(chow mein, available in Asian markets)
2 tablespoons canola oil
1 teaspoon minced ginger
1 teaspoon minced garlic
1 cup bean sprouts
1 tablespoon red Fresno or jalapeño chili rings
$^1/_4$ cup fresh mint or rau ram (Vietnamese mint) leaves

¹/₄ cup fresh basil leaves
¹/₄ cup snipped garlic chives (2 inches long)
¹/₄ cup fresh cilantro leaves
1 tablespoon chopped unsalted skinned roasted peanuts

- To make the sauce: In a medium saucepan, heat the oil over medium heat and add the ginger, garlic, and red curry paste. Stir-fry for 3 to 4 minutes, or until fragrant. Add the fish sauce, oyster sauce, sugar, water, and coconut milk. Bring to a boil, then reduce heat to a bare simmer and cook for 10 minutes. Remove from heat and cover to keep warm.

- In a large pot of boiling water, cook the noodles until just tender, about 4 minutes. Drain and toss with a little oil to prevent sticking.

- In a large wok or skillet, heat the oil and stir-fry the ginger, garlic, sprouts, and chili until fragrant, about 30 seconds. Add the noodles and stir-fry for about 2 minutes, then stir in the sprouts. Ladle in the sauce. Add the herbs and toss until just wilted. Serve at once, preferably in a green bowl, with the peanuts sprinkled over.

Three-Mustard-Crusted Pork Tenderloin
with Soy-Braised Cabbage

SERVES 4 AS A MAIN COURSE

Cafe Kati
1963 Sutter Street (between Fillmore and Webster)

Tucked away in lower Pacific Heights, far from any other dining places of its caliber, tiny Cafe Kati turns out the kind of sophisticated dishes found in world-class restaurants. The witty architectural presentations mirror the food, which is an innovative blend of East, West, and the culinary imagination of chef Kirk Webber. This is the food of a chef who loves what he does.

MARINADE

¼ cup Dijon mustard

3 tablespoons whole-grain mustard

2 tablespoons black mustard seeds, toasted (see note)

3 tablespoons honey

1 tablespoon red wine vinegar

¼ cup soy sauce

2 garlic cloves, minced

1 teaspoon ground pepper

Dash of Tabasco sauce (optional)

Four 5-ounce pieces pork tenderloin

2 tablespoons canola oil

SOY-BRAISED CABBAGE

1 tablespoon canola oil

½ small red onion, thinly sliced

1 garlic clove, minced

2 tablespoons soy sauce

¼ cup red wine vinegar

¼ cup dry white wine

Pinch of ground cloves
1 tablespoon sugar
$^{1}/_{8}$ teaspoon caraway seeds
1 apple, peeled, cored, and chopped
3 cups shredded cabbage (about $^{1}/_{2}$ small cabbage)

$^{3}/_{4}$ cup chicken stock or canned low-salt chicken broth
3 tablespoons unsalted butter

- Preheat the oven to 425°F. In a medium bowl, combine all the marinade ingredients and mix well. Add the pork, cover, and refrigerate for 2 to 3 hours.

- Remove the pork from the refrigerator 30 minutes before cooking. Drain the pork, reserving the marinade. Pat the pork dry.

- In an ovenproof nonstick pan or a well-seasoned cast-iron skillet, heat the oil over medium-high heat and sear the pork until browned on all sides, about 4 minutes. Transfer the pan to the oven and roast the pork for 10 minutes, or until just cooked through. Remove from the oven and loosely cover with aluminum foil.

- To make the braised cabbage: In a large skillet, heat the oil over medium-high heat and sauté the onion and garlic until the onion is translucent, 2 or 3 minutes. Add all the remaining ingredients and cook until the liquid is slightly reduced and the cabbage is wilted, about 10 minutes. Set aside and cover to keep warm.

- Pour the marinade into a small saucepan, add the stock or broth, bring to a boil, and cook for about 3 minutes. Stir in the butter. Cut the meat into $^{1}/_{4}$-inch-thick slices. Make a bed of the cabbage on 4 warmed plates. Place equal amounts of the pork on top of the cabbage. Spoon a little of the sauce on top of the pork and serve at once, with the remaining sauce alongside.

Toasting Seeds: In a dry small skillet over medium heat, stir seeds just until they are fragrant, about 3 minutes. Empty them into a bowl to stop the cooking process.

Grilled Herbes de Provence Lamb Chops
with Lavender Salt

SERVES 4 AS A MAIN COURSE

Chez Nous
1911 Fillmore Street
(between Bush and Pine)

This true neighborhood spot serves breakfast, lunch, and dinner, and features little plates from Greece, Spain, Northern Africa, France, and Italy. The French blue facade and pumpkin-colored awning are a clue that this restaurant is connected with Pascal Rigo, whose Boulangerie is just around the corner on Pine Street. The breads and pastries are from that wildly popular bakery, and many of the cheeses come from Artisan Cheeses on California Street. Here is a typical Chez Nous dish, this one from Provence. Serve it with couscous and ratatouille or seasonal vegetables.

HERB PASTE

¹/₂ teaspoon dried lavender buds
1 tablespoon herbes de Provence
Cloves from ¹/₂ whole head of garlic, peeled and coarsely chopped
¹/₄ cup olive oil

8 lamb chops

LAVENDER SALT

1 tablespoon dried lavender buds
¹/₂ cup coarse gray sea salt (sel gris)

Fresh lavender sprigs for garnish

To make the herb paste: In a mortar, crush the lavender with a pestle until coarsely ground. In a small bowl, combine the lavender, herbes de Provence, garlic, and olive oil. Place the chops in a baking dish and rub on both sides with the lavender mixture. Cover with plastic wrap and refrigerate overnight.

To make the lavender salt: In an electric coffee grinder, process the lavender until coarsely ground. In a small bowl, combine the lavender and sea salt; stir to blend. Set aside.

Drain the chops in a colander to remove the excess oil. Heat a grill pan over medium heat for 2 minutes. Add the chops and cook for 2 to 3 minutes on each side for medium-rare. Transfer the chops to a platter and let rest for 2 to 3 minutes.

Transfer the chops to warmed plates and garnish with a sprig of lavender. Accompany each serving with a small dish of lavender salt for sprinkling over the chops.

Apricot-Cherry Crisp

SERVES 6 AS A DESSERT

Greens Restaurant

Fort Mason Center,
Building A (at Laguna)

Since the late seventies, this celebrated vegetarian restaurant has been delighting meat-eaters and non-meat-eaters with its fresh seasonal dishes based on organic produce. All the courses are inspired and inventive here, including the popular weekend brunch and the desserts. This early-summer crisp is served during that brief window when California apricots and cherries are at the height of their season. The colors are beautiful, and the flavor of ginger highlights the taste of the fruit. This recipe is adapted from chef Annie Somerville's landmark cookbook, *Field of Greens* (Bantam, 1993).

CRISP TOPPING

1 cup unbleached all-purpose flour
¹/₄ cup granulated sugar
¹/₄ cup packed light brown sugar
¹/₂ teaspoon ground cinnamon
¹/₄ teaspoon freshly grated nutmeg
¹/₂ cup (1 stick) cold unsalted butter, cut into ¹/₄-inch cubes
¹/₄ cup chopped walnuts

1¹/₂ pounds fresh apricots, quartered and pitted (about 6 cups)
8 ounces fresh Bing cherries, pitted (about 2 cups)
Zest of 1 lemon, minced
1 generous teaspoon grated fresh ginger
¹/₂ cup granulated sugar
2 tablespoons unbleached all-purpose flour
Lightly whipped cream for serving

Preheat the oven to 375°F. To make the topping: In a medium bowl, stir the flours, sugars, salt, cinnamon, and nutmeg together. Using your fingers, work in the butter until the mixture is crumbly and begins to hold together. Add the nuts and quickly mix them in.

- In a large bowl, toss the apricots, cherries, lemon zest, ginger, sugar, and flour together. Put the fruit mixture in a 9-inch square baking dish, a 9-inch round cake pan, or 6 individual ovenproof dishes. Level the fruit and cover evenly with the topping.

- Bake until the topping is golden brown and the juices bubble around the sides of the dish, 45 to 50 minutes for a large crisp, and 25 to 30 minutes for individual crisps. Serve warm, with a dollop of whipped cream.

Potato-Wrapped Bluenose Sea Bass

SERVES 4 AS A MAIN COURSE

Isa

3324 Steiner Street (between Chestnut and Lombard)

One of the early small-plate places, but with a twist: *haute* French food in small portions. Isa (named for chef/owner Luke Sung's daughter) is a small, family-run hideaway in the Marina district, with an open kitchen and a heated patio in back, but the food is sophisticated and masterfully executed. Chef Sung suggests serving this dish with potatoes and asparagus.

2 large russet potatoes
Four 6-ounce bluenose sea bass fillets, skinned and deboned
(ask your fishmonger to do this)
Salt and freshly ground pepper to taste
4 tablespoons extra-virgin olive oil
4 tablespoons unsalted butter
2 tablespoons diced tomato
1 tablespoon brine-packed capers, rinsed and lightly chopped
2 tablespoons fresh lemon juice
1 tablespoon minced fresh flat-leaf parsley
1 tablespoon sliced seeded red Fresno or jalapeño chili

● Preheat the oven to 400°F. Peel and slice the potatoes lengthwise as thinly as possible, using a mandoline if available, or a large chef's knife. In a pot of boiling water, blanch the potatoes for about 30 seconds. Drain and transfer to an ice-water bath to stop the cooking. Drain again and transfer to paper towels to dry.

● Season the fish with salt and pepper. Overlap the potato slices on the fish to tightly and completely cover each fillet.

In a large ovenproof nonstick sauté pan or skillet, heat the oil over medium heat until fragrant and sear the fish until the potatoes are lightly browned, about 2 minutes on each side. Place the pan in the oven and cook until opaque throughout, 6 to 8 minutes. Transfer the fish to a platter and cover to keep warm.

Pour off all the fat from the pan and wipe it clean with paper towels. In the same pan, melt the butter over medium-high heat and let it brown. Stir in the tomato, capers, lemon juice, parsley, chili, and salt and pepper to taste. Place the fish on warmed plates, pour the butter sauce over, and serve at once.

Spring Asparagus Soup
with Mint and Red Radishes

MAKES 8 FIRST-COURSE SERVINGS

Plumpjack Café
2137 Fillmore Street (between Filbert and Greenwich)

High in style, yet with the intimacy of a private club, Plumpjack attracts food-lovers who adore the kitchen's California-Mediterranean food. With Mayor Gavin Newsom as a former owner and with the Getty family still part of the mix, this is a favorite lunch and dinner spot for politicos and members of San Francisco high society. The menu changes seasonally but is consistently intriguing, with dishes like chef James Ormsby's bright green spring soup.

½ cup (1 stick) unsalted butter
½ cup diced onion
1 large russet potato, peeled and diced
2 tablespoons salt
1 tablespoon sugar
½ cup dry white wine
8 cups water
2 bunches asparagus, trimmed
¼ cup heavy cream
Freshly ground pepper to taste
Freshly grated nutmeg to taste

RADISH AND MINT SALAD
1 cup finely diced red radishes
1 tablespoon minced fresh mint
1 teaspoon salt
1 tablespoon extra-virgin olive oil

● In a soup pot, melt the butter over medium heat. Add the onion, potato, 1 tablespoon of the salt, and the sugar. Sauté for about 5 minutes, or until the onion is translucent. Add the white wine, then the water. Stir and increase heat to high; bring to a boil and cook for 10 minutes.

- Cut the top 2 inches off the asparagus. Blanch the tips in the boiling soup base for 2 to 4 minutes, or until crisp-tender. Using a wire skimmer, cool them under cold running water, then spread them out on a plate. Chop the remaining asparagus stalks and add them to the boiling soup base. Cook for 3 minutes. Remove from heat. In batches, transfer the mixture to a blender and purée until very smooth. Strain through a fine-meshed sieve into a clean soup pot. Add the cream, the remaining 1 tablespoon salt, and the pepper and nutmeg. Taste and adjust the seasoning, adding more salt if necessary.

- To make the radish and mint salad: In a small bowl, combine all the ingredients and stir to blend.

- Heat the soup and ladle into warmed bowls. Divide the asparagus tips among the bowls, then garnish each with a spoonful of the radish and mint salad.

Huckleberry Soufflés

SERVES 8 AS A DESSERT

A prized Pacific Heights location houses this restaurant, which is small in size but large in savoir faire. The chef/owners have sterling credentials:

Quince
1701 Octavia Street
(at Bush)

Lindsay and Michael Tusk are graduates of Chez Panisse and Oliveto, and their food is a blend of the best of French and Italian traditions as transformed by a California sensibility. These brightly flavored soufflés from pastry chef Jehnee Rains are an adaptation of Michel Guérard's raspberry soufflé, which doesn't use a pastry cream, allowing the flavor of the fruit to dominate. Chef Rains says that raspberries or passion fruit may be used in place of the huckleberries.

HUCKLEBERRY PURÉE

1 cup fresh or thawed frozen huckleberries
1 tablespoon water
1 tablespoon sugar

FOR RAMEKINS

2 tablespoons unsalted butter, softened
¹/₄ cup sugar

3 egg yolks, beaten
8 large egg whites
Pinch of salt
¹/₂ teaspoon cream of tartar (optional)
1 tablespoon cornstarch
¹/₂ cup sugar
Confectioners' sugar for dusting

- Preheat the oven to 425°F, with a baking stone, if you have one, on the center shelf.

- To make the huckleberry purée: In a nonreactive saucepan, combine the berries, water, and sugar. Cook over medium heat for about 5 minutes, or until the berries release their juices. Using a potato masher, crush the berries. Strain through a fine-meshed sieve, pushing on the berries with the back of a ladle or large spoon to extract as much juice as possible. (You can also put the berries through a food mill first, to help break up the berries, but you'll still have to press them hard through a fine-meshed sieve.)

Choose eight 4-inch-diameter ramekins and butter just the sides. Avoid brushing the bottom, to limit unwanted melted butter at the bottom of your soufflé. Now, make a thin lip of butter all around the inside of the top rim of the ramekins. Once you put the soufflé in the oven, this extra lip of butter will melt down the inside of the ramekin, allowing the batter to rise straight up. Sprinkle sugar inside the ramekin to coat all the butter.

Taste the huckleberry purée and add a little more sugar if it seems too tart. In a medium bowl, combine the purée and the egg yolks. Whisk to blend well.

In a large bowl, beat the egg whites until foamy. Add the salt, cream of tartar (if you are not using a copper bowl to beat the whites), and cornstarch. Beat until soft peaks form. Gradually beat in the granulated sugar, 1 tablespoon at a time. Keep beating until stiff, glossy peaks form.

In thirds, gently fold the egg whites into the huckleberry mixture. Fill the ramekins to ½ inch from the top. Once the batter is in the ramekins, they can sit for up to 30 minutes, but it's best to bake them right away. Set the ramekins on a baking sheet and place in the oven on the baking stone, if using one. Bake until risen and lightly golden, about 8 minutes. Remove from the oven. Place each ramekin on a small serving plate. Dust the soufflés with confectioners' sugar and serve at once.

Salmon Salad Cozies
with Arugula, Tomatoes, and Aioli

SERVES 4 AS A LIGHT MAIN COURSE

Rose's Café
2298 Union Street
(at Steiner)

Rose's Café, on a quiet corner at the end of Union Street's shopping area, is a real neighborhood place where you can stop by for breakfast, lunch, dinner, or afternoon coffee. People come early for the breakfast or soft polenta or one of the house-made pastries, and the stream of customers continues through dinner. The food here, like that at Rose's sister restaurant, Rose Pistola (page 74), is Ligurian in flavor, and the specialties include focaccia and pizza cooked in the wood-fired oven. You can sit outside under the heat lamps in all but the coldest weather, and the cafe will provide a water bowl and a complimentary dog biscuit for your dog.

Try these outrageously good salmon cozies for lunch; they're warm pizza-dough ovals stuffed with a salad of salmon, arugula, and aioli. The pizza dough is made with a biga, or sponge, and you will need to start the dough 4 to 6 hours before you plan to bake it. If you don't have time to make your own dough, use frozen bread dough, or pita breads—or just serve the salad on its own.

Four 4-ounce salmon fillets, pinbones removed
Olive oil for coating
Sea salt and freshly ground pepper to taste
Pizza Dough (recipe follows)
Cornmeal for sprinkling
1 fennel bulb, trimmed, cored, and cut into paper-thin lengthwise slices
24 niçoise olives, pitted
4 handfuls arugula
24 cherry tomatoes, stemmed and halved
8 red onion slices
$^1/_2$ cup aioli (see note)
$^1/_4$ cup red wine vinegar

- Preheat the oven to 500°F with a pizza stone, if you have one, on the center rack.

- Lightly coat each salmon fillet with olive oil and season with salt and pepper. Place the fillets in a roasting pan or ovenproof skillet and roast in the oven for 4 to 8 minutes, or until still slightly translucent in the center. Remove from the oven and cover to keep warm.

- On a lightly floured board, roll out each ball of dough into an oval about 8 inches long, 6 inches wide, and ¼ inch thick. Lightly flour the bottom of each oval. If using a pizza stone, sprinkle a baker's peel or a rimless baking sheet with cornmeal, place an oval or dough on top, and slide onto the stone in the oven; repeat with the remaining ovals. If not using a stone, place all the ovals on a baking sheet sprinkled with cornmeal. Bake until the dough has puffed and is slightly golden underneath, 7 to 8 minutes. Remove from the oven and cut each oval open lengthwise along one side.

- Quickly remove and discard the skin from the salmon. Break the salmon into bite-sized chunks. In a medium bowl, combine the salmon, fennel, olives, arugula, tomatoes, and onion slices. Season with salt and pepper to taste. Add the aioli and vinegar. Toss lightly with a fork to flake the salmon and dress the salad. Place one fourth of the salad inside each warm oval and serve at once.

Pizza Dough

MAKES ABOUT 8 OUNCES

BIGA

⅛ teaspoon active dry yeast
¼ cup warm (105° to 115°F) water
⅓ cup unbleached all-purpose flour

DOUGH

½ teaspoon active dry yeast
¼ cup warm (105° to 115°F) water
Biga, above
1 cup unbleached all-purpose flour

- To make the biga: In a medium bowl, whisk all the ingredients together until smooth. Cover tightly with plastic wrap and let rise at room temperature for 2 to 3 hours, or until doubled.

- To make the dough: In the bowl of a heavy-duty mixer fitted with a dough hook, stir the yeast into the water until dissolved. Let stand until foamy, about 5 minutes. Add the biga and flour and mix on low speed until the dough pulls away from the sides of the bowl and is smooth and elastic, 8 to 10 minutes. Form the dough into a ball. Or, to make by hand, stir the yeast into the water in a large bowl. Let stand until foamy, about 5 minutes. Add the biga and mix it into the yeast mixture with a wooden spoon. Stir in the flour ½ cup at a time, then stir until the dough is well mixed. Turn out onto a lightly floured board and knead until the dough is smooth and elastic, about 8 minutes; when you make an indentation in the dough with your finger, the hole should fill in again.

- Rinse a large bowl with warm water, then dry it. Coat the bowl well with olive oil. Add the dough ball and turn it to coat all the surfaces with oil. Cover the bowl with plastic wrap or a damp kitchen towel and let the dough rise in a warm place until doubled in size, 2 to 3 hours.

- On a lightly floured board, divide the dough into 4 equal pieces. Form each into a ball. Cover with a kitchen towel and let sit for 10 minutes before rolling out.

Aioli: In a blender, combine 1 egg, ½ teaspoon salt, 1 tablespoon fresh lemon juice, and 2 chopped garlic cloves. Cover and blend for about 30 seconds. With the machine running, gradually add 1 cup light olive oil very slowly, drop by drop at first, then in a thin stream after the mixture begins to thicken to a mayonnaise. Taste and adjust the seasoning. Cover and store leftover sauce in the refrigerator for up to 3 days. Makes about 1 cup.

Salmon

The Native Americans worshiped the salmon, believing that by consuming the flesh of this fish they would take on its characteristics: courage, determination, strength, and beauty. Today, science actually confirms this belief, for salmon has been found to be one of the most healthful of all foods because of the omega-3 fats it contains.

Salmon is a favorite food for restaurants, as you can see by the number of recipes for it in this book. Chefs adore it for its sweet, firm, colorful flesh, which stands up well to assertive sauces and flavorings, and also shines when paired with a mild sauce. Salmon can be prepared in so many different ways, from raw in sashimi or carpaccio to baked, sautéed, or grilled, either whole or in chunks, steaks, or fillets. It can also be served in soups, salads, pastas, sandwiches, and casseroles.

Salmon is available year-round, thanks to fish farms, while the season for wild salmon runs from spring to fall. There is a marked difference, however, between farmed salmon and wild salmon; the latter is darker in color, chewier in texture, and more flavorful. It is also free of the pollutants that are due to fish-farming practices, although some fish farms, such as those in Scotland, follow high standards that prevent pollutants from affecting the fish. Restaurant menus will usually say so if their salmon is wild, while in fish stores you may need to ask. Most wild salmon on the West Coast comes from Alaska, though as California slowly begins to restore salmon habitat, more wild California salmon will be available. Be sure to partake in the seasonal bounty of this fish, thereby making yourself stronger, braver, and more beautiful.

Sausage Ravioli
in a Red Bell Pepper Sauce

SERVES 4 AS A MAIN COURSE (4 RAVIOLI PER PERSON)

Sociale

3665 Sacramento Street
(between Locust and Spruce)

is romantic restaurant tucked away down a passageway off Sacramento Street, you will find a menu filled with robust Italian dishes, like David Nichol and Tia Harrison's sausage ravioli. Come for lunch or dinner on a warm day or evening and dine in the little garden, or tuck into the finely seasoned fare in the cozy, low-ceilinged interior. You will be well cared for and well fed.

FILLING
3 sweet Italian sausages, meat removed from casings
1 cup grated Parmesan cheese
2 eggs, beaten
1 tablespoon minced fresh marjoram
1 tablespoon minced fresh tarragon
1 tablespoon minced fresh thyme
1 teaspoon freshly ground pepper
$^1/_4$ cup heavy cream
3 tablespoons tomato paste

4 fresh pasta sheets, each 11 by 14 inches (about 1 pound)
1 egg, beaten

RED BELL PEPPER SAUCE
3 red bell peppers, roasted, seeded, and peeled (see page 40)
1 cup chicken broth
$^1/_2$ cup plus 1 tablespoon tomato paste
$1^1/_2$ tablespoons sugar
$^1/_2$ tablespoon salt

1 tablespoon unsalted butter
2 handfuls arugula
Lemon Vinaigrette (page 111) for dressing
¹/₂ cup crumbled fresh goat cheese

- To make the filling: In a large sauté pan or skillet over medium heat, sauté the sausage, stirring and breaking up the meat frequently, until browned, about 8 minutes. Pulse the sausage in a food processor until ground. In a medium bowl, combine the sausage, Parmesan, eggs, herbs, pepper, cream, and tomato paste. Stir until well combined and set aside.

- Lay a pasta sheet on a work surface. Place 1 tablespoonful of the filling on the pasta, leaving a border of about 2 inches all around. Repeat until you have filled the sheet. Brush the pasta surrounding the filling mounds with the remaining egg, place another pasta sheet on top, and press down around the mounds to seal the two sheets. Using a 3-inch round ravioli cutter, cut out the ravioli. Check the seal on the edges of the ravioli, making sure there are no holes to let water in when cooking. Repeat to make 16 ravioli. Place them on a baking sheet lined with parchment paper and dusted with semolina flour, and separate the layers with more parchment paper dusted with semolina flour so they won't stick. The ravioli can be made several hours ahead of cooking.

- To make the sauce: In a blender, combine the peppers, broth, tomato paste, sugar, and salt. Process until smooth. Cover and refrigerate until ready to serve.

- In a large pot of salted, slowly boiling water, cook the ravioli until they rise to the top, 3 to 4 minutes. Meanwhile, in a saucepan, melt the butter over low heat. Add the bell pepper sauce and heat. Taste and adjust the seasoning.

- Using a wire skimmer, carefully transfer the ravioli to warmed bowls, placing 4 in each bowl. Spoon a generous portion of the sauce on top. Serve at once, with a side salad of the arugula tossed with a little vinaigrette and sprinkled with a little goat cheese.

Melanzane al Forno

(Baked Herbed Eggplant with Capers and Olives)

SERVES 6 AS A SIDE DISH OR FIRST COURSE

Vivande Porta Via

2125 Fillmore Street (between California and Sacramento)

Carlo Middione's Vivande Porta Via is both a sit-down restaurant and a take-out spot, with a range of prepared Italian foods at the counter along one wall. Middione, the author of several cookbooks on Southern Italian cuisine, says: "These eggplants can be eaten hot, but in most parts of southern Italy and especially in Sicily, they are enjoyed at room temperature, and are often included in an antipasto. Serve with good crusty, Italian bread. They are also a good accompaniment to broiled fish, or chicken or pork. Served with cannellini beans, lentils, fresh or baked polenta, they make a tasty vegetarian meal."

$^1/_4$ cup salted capers, preferably from Pantelleria (see note)
6 Japanese eggplants, halved lengthwise
Extra-virgin olive oil for coating, plus $^1/_4$ cup for cooking and more for drizzling
$^1/_3$ cup pitted black and Sicilian green olives, finely chopped
Leaves from 6 or 7 mint sprigs, minced
Leaves from 6 or 7 basil sprigs
3 garlic cloves, minced
Salt and freshly ground pepper to taste
$^1/_3$ cup grated caciocavallo or pecorino romano cheese

- Soak the capers in cold water for 1 hour before using, changing the water 2 or 3 times. Drain, rinse, and squeeze dry. (You can use bottled vinegar-packed capers if necessary, but be sure to rinse them well many times to get rid the vinegar and let the caper taste come out.)

- Preheat the oven to 400°F, with the rack placed in the upper third of the oven. Make a series of deep crosshatches in the cut sides of the eggplants, but don't cut through the skin. Coat the cut surfaces liberally with extra-virgin olive oil. In a large sauté pan or skillet, heat the

¼ cup olive oil over high heat until shimmering. Fry the eggplants, cut side down, until golden on the bottom, 1 or 2 minutes. Turn them over and fry for about 2 minutes on the skin side. They will look slightly softened. Using a slotted metal spatula, transfer to a baking sheet, cut sides up, and let cool.

In a medium bowl, combine the olives, capers, mint, basil, and garlic, and mash lightly with a fork to make a coarse paste. Stir in the salt and pepper. Add the grated cheese and mix well. Press the mixture into the cuts in each eggplant and drizzle with a little more oil.

Bake the eggplant for about 25 minutes, or until the eggplant is soft and the topping is gilded here and there. Be careful not to burn them. The tops should be bubbling and look moist and tempting.

Note: Pantelleria, a tiny island off Sicily, is famous the world over for its capers.

Civic Center / Hayes Valley

Absinthe

Bistro Clovis

Citizen Cake

Suppenküche

JUST OFF MARKET STREET, BETWEEN VAN NESS AND POLK, a cluster of gray granite Beaux Arts–style buildings are home to the city's opera house, symphony hall, main library, Veterans Building, Asian art museum, state and  federal buildings, and city hall. The dome of City Hall, bright with gold leaf that matches the gates between the opera house and the Veterans Building, towers over all. (The first city hall, built on the site of today's library, collapsed during the 1906 quake, which was when San Franciscans learned that, thanks to wide-spread graft among the city administration and certain building contractors, the building's foundations were substandard.) ⸺ THE POST-QUAKE CIVIC CENTER COMPLEX was constructed during the same flush of civic pride and faith in the future as the 1915 Panama-Pacific International Exposition in the newly created Marina, and was the work of a local architectural firm, Bakewell and Brown. Later buildings, such as the library, mirror the French baroque shapes, materials, and some architectural elements, but are more modern and stylized in design. ⸺ SOME PEOPLE ARE COMMITTED URBAN DWELLERS because they love both food and art, and can think of nothing better than combining an early dinner with a concert or an opera or a ballet performance. Fortunately, you don't have to be wealthy to be a patron of the arts: open rehearsals, stage seating, standing-room-only tickets, and ushering gigs will give you access to many venues, and eating places serving inexpensive Vietnamese food, pizza, and sandwiches will feed the body. There's even a "symphony bus" that stops on the corner of Van Ness and Hayes after the concerts. ⸺ MANY OF SAN FRANCISCO'S BEST RESTAURANTS are also found in the Civic Center area, catering to office holders and office workers, and patrons of the symphony, opera, San Francisco Ballet (which performs in the Opera House), and Herbst Hall in the Veterans Building. They range from the large and glittery (Jardinère) to the small and charming (Bistro Clovis). THE AREA SURROUNDING THE CIVIC CENTER IS TRANSITIONAL, with the east merging into the Tenderloin and the west into the edges of the Fillmore, a neighborhood of pre-Earthquake Victorians. The southern end runs into Market Street just before it turns into Upper Market, the site of the Warfield Theatre, a concert and musical venue. RUNNING PERPENDICULAR TO VAN NESS is Hayes Valley, clustered around one of the city's newer shopping streets and one of the most interesting. The earthquake of 1989 liberated Hayes Valley from the elevated freeway that once marred this neighborhood, giving this thoroughfare new life. The shops and restaurants here are a combination of the offbeat and the upscale, with an ambiance reminiscent of New York's West Side. Art galleries, a rare-book store, a wine bar, a watch repair shop, antiques shops, and cutting-edge clothing stores are part of the mix, and the restaurants range from Hayes Street Grill (minimalist seafood) to Espetus Churrascaria (Brazilian steakhouse). This little street of urban pleasures is an ideal place to spend an afternoon browsing, to have a drink after work, or to dine before or after the symphony or opera.

OTHER NEIGHBORHOOD STARS

Espetus Churrascaria

Hayes Street Grill

Indigo

Jardinère

Pissaladière

MAKES EIGHT 6-INCH PIZZAS; SERVES 8 AS AN APPETIZER

Absinthe

398 Hayes Street (at Gough)

This beautiful corner restaurant brings a touch of Art Nouveau Paris to Hayes Valley. The two long rooms, one with a bar, have windows on Hayes Street, making Absinthe a colorful and pleasant place for a long lunch, or dinner before or after the opera. Topped with braised onions, anchovies, and olives, this Provençal pizza is a savory appetizer to serve with pastis, or you could make 4 pizzas to serve with salad for lunch.

Note: The dough rises in the refrigerator and can be made 12 hours to 2½ days ahead; the braised onions can be made 1 day ahead and refrigerated as well. Roll out and assemble the pizzas just before baking. To simplify this dish, use frozen pizza dough.

PIZZA DOUGH
1 teaspoon active dry yeast
1½ cups warm (105° to 115°F) water
3½ cups all-purpose unbleached bread flour
½ tablespoon kosher salt

BRAISED ONIONS
3 yellow onions, halved crosswise and sliced lengthwise
1 bay leaf
Leaves from 4 thyme sprigs
2 tablespoons olive oil
3 tablespoons red wine vinegar
1 garlic clove, slivered
Kosher salt and freshly ground pepper to taste

6 paper-thin lemon slices, cut into quarters
Extra-virgin olive oil for brushing, plus more for sprinkling
8 anchovy fillets
24 niçoise olives, pitted and chopped
Fresh flat-leaf parsley or tarragon leaves for sprinkling

- To make the dough: In the bowl of a heavy-duty mixer fitted with a paddle, stir the yeast into the water until dissolved. Let stand until foamy, about 5 minutes. On low speed, gradually mix in about one third of the flour. Gradually add the remaining flour and the salt to make a smooth dough. Or, to make by hand, whisk ½ cup of the flour and the salt into the yeast mixture, then whisk in the remaining flour ½ cup at a time until the dough is too thick to whisk; switch to a wooden spoon to stir in the remaining flour.

- On a lightly floured board, knead the dough until smooth and elastic, 8 to 10 minutes; add more flour 1 tablespoon at a time if the dough is too sticky.

- Coat a large bowl with olive oil, add the dough, and turn it to coat it with oil. Cover the bowl with plastic wrap and refrigerate for at least 12 hours, or until the dough has risen by at least one third to one half; it does not need to double. The dough may be refrigerated for as long as 2½ days.

- Meanwhile, make the braised onions: In a medium bowl, combine the onions, bay leaf, and thyme; toss to mix. In a large sauté pan or skillet, heat the oil over medium-high heat and sauté the onion mixture, stirring occasionally, until the onions are golden, about 6 minutes. Stir in the vinegar, reduce heat to low, and cook, stirring occasionally, until a deep golden brown, about 20 minutes. Remove from heat and stir in the garlic. Season with salt and pepper. Use now, or cover and refrigerate overnight. Reheat before using to top the pizza dough.

- To assemble and bake the pizzas: Preheat the oven to 500°F with a pizza stone, if you have one, on the middle rack. Remove the dough from the refrigerator about 10 minutes before rolling it out. On a lightly floured board, cut the dough into 8 pieces. Form each into a tight ball with the seam sealed underneath. With floured hands, press each ball into a 6-inch-diameter round; it will be unevenly thick. Transfer the rounds to a floured baker's paddle or a rimless baking sheet. Top each round with one eighth of the braised onions, then with 4 quarter-slices of lemon.

If using a pizza stone, transfer the pizzas to the stone by sliding them off the paddle or baking sheet onto the stone. Without a stone, leave them on the baking sheet. Bake until the edges are golden, about 7 minutes. Remove from the oven and brush the edges of the pizzas with olive oil. Top each pizza with 1 anchovy fillet and 4 olives. Drizzle with olive oil and sprinkle with parsley or tarragon leaves. Serve at once.

Chicken Fricassee
with Glazed Shallots, Garlic, and Sherry Vinegar Sauce

SERVES 4 AS A MAIN COURSE

If you think of Market Street as similar to a Parisian *grand boulevard*, it's not quite such a surprise to find this classic French bistro, complete with lace curtains and French antiques, at the corner of Market and Franklin. The menu is classic as well, including this savory Gallic comfort food: chicken braised in a rich, tangy cream sauce and served with fresh pasta. This quiet, charming spot is a good choice for an early dinner before the opera or symphony.

Bistro Clovis
1596 Market Street
(at Franklin)

1 tablespoon unsalted butter
1 tablespoon canola oil
1 chicken, cut into 8 serving pieces
8 shallots
8 unpeeled garlic cloves
¹/₂ cup sherry vinegar
¹/₄ cup rich chicken stock or broth (see note)
1 cup heavy cream
Salt and freshly ground pepper to taste
8 ounces fresh pasta, such as fettuccine, cooked until al dente for serving

- In a large, heavy skillet or sauté pan, melt the butter with the oil over medium-low heat and brown the chicken pieces on all sides. Using tongs, transfer the chicken to a plate. Add the shallots and garlic and sauté for a few minutes until golden brown. Using a slotted spoon, transfer the shallots and garlic to the plate with the chicken. Pour off all the fat from the pan.

- Add the vinegar to the pan and stir over medium heat to scrape up the browned bits from the bottom. Return the chicken, garlic, and shallots to the pan and cook for a few minutes to reduce the vinegar. Add the stock or broth, cover, and cook over low heat until the chicken is fork-tender, 35 to 45 minutes.

Transfer the chicken, shallots, and garlic to a plate. Spoon off as much fat as possible from the pan juices. Cook the juices over medium heat until reduced to a syrup. Add the cream and cook to reduce to a sauce. Strain the sauce through a fine-meshed sieve. Return the chicken, shallots, and garlic to the pan and simmer for a few minutes until heated through.

On warmed plates, serve 2 pieces of chicken per person, along with 2 glazed shallots, 2 garlic cloves, and one fourth of the pasta. Sprinkle with the parsley.

Rich Chicken Stock or Broth: In a heavy saucepan, cook unsalted chicken stock or canned low-salt chicken broth over medium heat until it is reduced by about a third, or until it is richly flavorful.

Natural Foods Stores

The food revolution that made California restaurants famous wasn't really a revolution so much as a return, a return to the way our grandparents cooked and ate, before agribusiness, factory farms, pesticides, hormone additives, and interstate transport of produce. Basic to this revolution was the belief that any dish is no better than the ingredients that go into it. Along with this fresh respect for what some chefs call "product" came the realization that not only are organically grown foods more healthful, they actually have more flavor. Some chefs insist on organic ingredients for this reason, while others use them simply because many of the best vendors of fruits, vegetables, grains, meats, and poultry happen to be organic.

San Francisco is also home to several natural foods stores: Rainbow Grocery, in the Mission (1745 Folsom), is a counterculture grocery store that has managed to not only stay open into the new century but to grow and prosper. It cleaves closest to the sixties cooperative-grocery sensibility, recycling paper and plastic bags and providing shampoo, body lotion, dish soap, and laundry soap in bulk, as well as a wide variety of bulk staples.

Real Food, with two stores in the city (2140 Polk Street and 3060 Fillmore) is known for its wide selection of excellent produce. Whole Foods, the largest natural foods chain in the United States, now has two San Francisco locations as well (1765 California Street near Pacific Heights, and 399 Fourth Street, in SoMa). Both stores have a fabulous deli counter, and a bakery that features both sweet and sour La Brea baguettes, baked in-house. Another natural foods store, the Harvest Urban Market, now serves SoMa as well (191 Eighth Street).

S'More Brownies

MAKES 16 WEDGES OR RECTANGLES

When Elizabeth Falkner opened Citizen Cake on an obscure side street in the Mission, dessert-lovers all over the city went on alert. So many, in fact, that Falkner moved to a space twice as big in Hayes Valley, where

Citizen Cake

399 Grove Street
(at Gough)

she offers an expanded range of innovative pastries, along with lunch and dinner service. Last year, Elizabeth and crew opened a satellite cafe, Citizen Cupcake, on the third floor of the Virgin Megastore on Union Square, a favorite lunch hideaway where you can decorate your own cupcake.

S'More Brownies, a twist on the old camping favorite, illustrate the kind of wit and imagination that Falkner brings to her confections. At Citizen Cake, they make their own graham crackers and marshmallows, but you can use commercial ones. Natural foods stores are a good source for these.

10 ounces Scharffen Berger or other 70 percent bittersweet chocolate, chopped
1¹/₄ cups (2¹/₂ sticks) unsalted butter
1 cup plus 1 tablespoon granulated sugar
1 cup packed dark brown sugar
5 eggs, lightly beaten
1 cup plus 2 tablespoons unbleached all-purpose flour
¹/₂ teaspoon kosher salt
1¹/₄ teaspoons baking powder
4 rectangular (double squares) honey graham crackers, broken into 1-inch pieces
3 ounces milk chocolate, such as El Rey brand, chopped
12 large marshmallows, cut in half horizontally

● Preheat the oven to 350°F. Grease a 10-inch round cake pan or a 9-by-13-inch baking pan.

● In a medium saucepan, combine the bittersweet chocolate, butter, and sugars and cook over low heat, stirring constantly, until the chocolate and butter are melted. Take care not to burn the mixture. Remove from heat. Add the eggs all at once and stir just to combine.

In a medium bowl, stir the flour, salt, and baking powder together with a whisk to combine. Add the flour mixture to the chocolate mixture and stir just until combined. Fold in the graham crackers and milk chocolate. Pour the batter into the pan and smooth the top. Place the marshmallows, cut-side down, evenly over the top.

Bake for 30 to 40 minutes, or just until the surface begins to crack and the marshmallows turn golden brown. If you want to cut clean pieces, let the brownies cool completely in their pans on wire racks. However, they are irresistible warm and gooey from the oven, though you should let them cool for 10 to 15 minutes first.

Spätzle

SERVES 6 AS A SIDE DISH

Suppenküche

*601 Hayes Street
(at Laguna)*

Although it serves New German (read: less heavy) cuisine and is popular with a young, hip clientele (partly because of its huge selection of German beers), Suppenküche still serves up favorite traditional dishes like these chewy little dumplings. A major comfort food in Germany, Austria, and Hungary, spätzle is quick to make and is eaten in soups and stews, as a side dish, or even sweetened as a dessert. Serve it with gravy, or with a dish cooked in a rich sauce, like chicken paprikash. Or, come to Suppenküche on a cold San Francisco night, sit at one of the long beer-hall tables, and dine on a plate of sauerbraten and spätzle.

6 eggs
2 cups all-purpose unbleached flour
1/2 teaspoon salt, plus salt to taste
1/4 teaspoon freshly grated nutmeg
1/4 to 3/4 cup water
2 tablespoons unsalted butter
Freshly ground pepper to taste

- Choose a large pot and a colander that will rest securely over the top of the pot. Fill the pot with water so that it doesn't touch the bottom of the perforated container. Bring the water to a boil and salt liberally.

- While the water is coming to a boil, make the batter: In a medium bowl, beat the eggs lightly. In a small bowl, stir the flour, the 1/2 teaspoon salt, and the nutmeg together. Gradually whisk the flour mixture into the eggs. Gradually stir in enough water to make a stiff but smooth batter.

- Set the colander over the pot of boiling water. Add about 3/4 cup of the batter to the colander, quickly dip your hand in cold water, and, using the ball of your hand, push the batter through the holes into the boiling water. There should be only one layer of spätzle at a time in the water.

Stir the spätzle with a spoon so that they do not stick together, and cook until they float, 3 to 5 minutes. Using a slotted spoon or a wire-mesh skimmer, transfer the spätzle to a bowl of ice water to stop the cooking process. Repeat until all the batter is cooked.

To reheat the spätzle, drain it well. Melt the butter in a medium sauce-pan, add the spätzle, cover, and cook for about 2 minutes, or until heated through. Season with salt and pepper and serve at once.

South of Market / Potrero Hill

Aperto

bacar restaurant and wine salon

Baraka

Chez Papa Bistrot

Fringale

Koh Samui and the Monkey

Le Charm French Bistro

Maya

Oola Restaurant and Bar

Pazzia Caffè Pizzeria Rosticceria

Restaurant LuLu

South Park Café

Town Hall

Yank Sing

ONCE, IT WAS CALLED SOUTH OF THE SLOT, because a cable car line (with its cable slot) ran on Market Street, but today the vast stretches of streets south of Market are known as SoMa, a coinage modeled after New York's SoHo. The diagonal line of Market Street was built to parallel Mission Street, which followed the old road out to Mission Dolores and runs at an angle to the streets of

the Financial District. The streets below Market were then platted on the same angle (although with blocks twice the size of those to the north), thereby creating endless confusion for both residents and tourists who attempt to navigate the city. ⌐ THE SOUTH SIDE OF MARKET IS LINED WITH LARGE, handsome buildings, many built right after the Great Quake. The Sheraton Palace Hotel, formerly called the Palace and the original jewel of the street, withstood the earthquake, only to be destroyed by the subsequent fire that leveled most of the commercial heart of the city. It was rebuilt with the glass-domed Garden Court, where generations of San Franciscans have taken afternoon tea and celebrated Mother's Day and other special occasions with crab Louis and such S.F. originals as Green Goddess salad. Other important buildings on this side of Market include the Hotel Palomar in a refurbished building that houses the luxurious Fifth Floor restaurant; the Four Seasons Hotel and its high-end Seasons restaurant; the former Emporium department store, which is being converted into a Bloomingdale's; and the San Francisco Centre, a vertical urban shopping mall. ⌐ JUST ONE BLOCK AWAY, on Mission Street at Fourth, the city's arts and convention center keeps on growing. The San Francisco Museum of Modern Art and the Yerba Buena Center (with art galleries and theaters) are at one end of a pleasant park, and the Sony Metreon, a glitzy multistoried urban mall, is at the other, all built to accompany the Moscone Convention Center. ⟶ FOR DECADES, the wide streets south of Market harbored working-class homes and small industries such as printing plants and manufacturing firms. Now, only a few of those industries remain, and many of the old warehouses have been converted to residential lofts. There are also large numbers of newer live-work loft buildings, which proliferated during the dot-com era. ⟶ AT ANGLES TO THE TILTING STREETS (some of the ground here is filled in over lost streams that once ran to the bay, and you can see how some of the older buildings have settled unevenly below the roadway, encouraged by earthquakes) run tiny alleys lined with two-story Victorian houses and small commercial buildings; many of the alleys are named after women, though no one knows just why. ⟶ THE BAYFRONT EDGE OF SOMA has been transformed by the Giants ballpark, built right on the water, accelerating the transition of the neighborhood and providing a venue for several good restaurants. Once, Rincon Hill, also on the bay, was really a hill, studded with nouveau-riche mansions. All of them burned in the days after the Great Quake, and much of the hill was blasted away to

become the footpad for the southern end of the Bay Bridge. But because so many of the buildings here are old and large, and still less expensive per foot than those in other parts of town, SoMa continues to house small businesses and arts groups that flock to the funky buildings and wide thoroughfares of this fog-free neighborhood. ⟶ AMONG THE LONG BLOCKS is a dusting of San Francisco's best restaurants, beginning with the South Park Café,

OTHER NEIGHBORHOOD STARS

Basil Thai

Eliza's

Fifth Floor

Hawthorne Lane

Manora's Thai Cuisine

Seasons

the first French bistro to venture to this side of town. Within a few years it was followed by Fringale, Restaurant LuLu, and Le Charm. A few blocks of Folsom Street are home to a diverse and always changing group of restaurants. Hawthorne Lane, an esteemed restaurant opened by two graduates of Postrio, occupies the ground floor of a building on a small street just a half-block from Third. ⟶ SMACK IN THE MIDDLE BETWEEN THIRD STREET and the Mission is Potrero Hill, the city's version of a perched village, blessed with the same sunny weather as the rest of the eastern part of town, and named for the Spanish word for "meadow," which is what it once was. Now, it is home not to cows and goats but to street after climbing street of small Victorians, a crop of newer houses—some of them quite eccentric—corner groceries, small shops, neighborhood bars, coffeehouses, and storefront restaurants. If you come for lunch or dinner to this laid-back and quiet place, you will be able to look out over the bay and the Mission and the warehouses of Potrero Flats, all the way to the shimmering island of downtown San Francisco.

Tagliolini Pepati

(Tagliolini with Spicy Roasted-Tomato Sauce)

SERVES 4 AS A MAIN COURSE

It's worth standing in line for a table in this cozy Italian restaurant on Potrero Hill. The food is flavorful and satisfying, especially the roast chicken and any of the pastas, such as this dish of tagliolini with a robust and very spicy tomato-and-arugula sauce flavored with bacon. (You will always find this on the menu; chef/owner Chris Shepherd says that he would have to leave town if he ever took it off.) Like many of the best Italian places, they make their own focaccia. Their weekend brunch, featuring panettone French toast, frittatas, and omelets, also draws a crowd, so come early.

Aperto

1434 Eighteenth Street
(at Connecticut)

4 bacon slices, chopped
$^1/_4$ cup olive oil
2 garlic cloves, thinly sliced
2 jalapeño chilies, seeded and sliced
Pinch of red pepper flakes
Tomato Sauce (recipe follows)
$^1/_2$ cup (1 stick) butter
$^1/_2$ cup chicken broth
1 pound fresh tagliolini or linguine
3 cups arugula, stemmed
Salt and freshly ground pepper to taste
2 cups grated Parmigiano-Reggiano cheese

- In a large nonreactive skillet over medium heat, cook the bacon until it renders its fat. Using a slotted spoon, transfer the bacon to paper towels to drain. Pour off the bacon fat and wipe out the pan with paper towels.

- In the same pan over medium heat, heat the oil and sauté the garlic until it begins to brown. Add the bacon and chilies. Add the red pepper flakes, tomato sauce, butter, and chicken broth. Bring to a simmer.

- Meanwhile, add the pasta to a large pot of salted boiling water and stir. Once the water returns to a boil, cook the pasta for 30 to 60 seconds, or until al dente; drain.

- Add the arugula to the tomato mixture and cook until wilted, about 60 seconds. Add the salt and pepper. Add the pasta to the sauce, then add ¾ cup to 1 cup of the cheese. Divide among warmed shallow soup bowls and serve at once, with the remaining cheese alongside.

Tomato Sauce

MAKES ABOUT 1¼ CUPS

16 ounces canned diced Italian tomatoes
Salt and freshly ground pepper to taste
½ cup (4 ounces) canned tomato purée (not paste)
¼ cup olive oil
½ yellow onion, diced
1 garlic clove, sliced

- Preheat the oven to 350°F. Drain the diced tomatoes in a fine-meshed sieve over a saucepan. Leaving the sieve on the pan to continue the draining, bring the tomato juice to a simmer over medium heat and cook until reduced by about two thirds. Transfer the drained tomatoes to an oiled 8-inch square baking dish, season with salt and pepper, and bake for 45 to 60 minutes, stirring frequently. Add the tomato purée and continue to bake, stirring frequently, until thickened, about 1 hour.

- In a medium skillet over medium heat, heat the olive oil and sauté the onion and garlic until golden. Remove the tomato mixture from the oven and add the reduced tomato juice, onion, and garlic. Stir to blend. Set aside and let cool. The sauce should be very thick.

Seared Day-Boat Scallops
with Sunchoke Purée

SERVES 4 AS A FIRST COURSE

Bacar opened with great buzz at the height of the dot-com madness, complete with a series of newspaper articles on every detail of the planning and building stages of the restaurant. Larger and more elaborate by quantum leaps from Eos, Arnold Eric Wong's other well-regarded restaurant, bacar has three levels and a wall of wine that stretches up all three. Perhaps because of its amazing collection of wine, and certainly because of Wong's superlative food, bacar is lively and thriving in SoMa.

bacar restaurant and wine salon
448 Brannan Street (between Third and Fourth Streets)

12 large day boat scallops
4 tablespoons unsalted butter
3 shallots, minced
2 garlic cloves, minced
12 ounces sunchokes (Jerusalem artichokes), peeled and cut into ¹/₂-inch chunks
¹/₂ cup chicken broth, plus more if needed
¹/₂ cup heavy cream, plus more if needed
Salt and freshly ground white pepper to taste
¹/₃ cup clarified butter (see note)
¹/₄ cup extra-virgin olive oil, plus more for drizzling
1 tablespoon fresh lemon juice
3 cups sunflower sprouts or mixed baby salad greens
Toasted sunflower seeds for garnish (see page 129)

- Rinse the scallops under cold water. Pat dry with paper towels and set aside.

- In a heavy, medium saucepan, melt the 4 tablespoons butter over medium heat. Add the shallots and garlic and sauté until the shallots are translucent, about 3 minutes. Add the sunchokes and sauté for 2 to 3 minutes. Add the ¹/₂ cup chicken broth and ¹/₂ cup cream and season with salt and pepper. Cook until the sunchokes are fork-tender, about 8 minutes. Transfer to a blender in batches and purée until very

smooth. Add more chicken broth or cream if necessary to make a very thick sauce. Pour into a saucepan. Taste and adjust the seasoning. Set aside and keep warm.

- In a large, heavy sauté pan or skillet, heat the clarified butter over high heat until it begins to smoke. Season the scallops with salt and white pepper. Sear them until golden brown on the outside and still translucent in the center, about 3 minutes on each side. Do not overcook.

- To serve, whisk ¼ cup oil and the lemon juice together in a large bowl. Season with salt and white pepper to taste. Add the sprouts or greens to the bowl and toss to coat lightly. Pool the sunchoke purée in the center of each warmed plate.

- Arrange the scallops in a ring on top of the purée and mound the dressed greens in the center. Drizzle the entire plate with olive oil. Garnish with toasted sunflower seeds and serve at once.

Clarified Butter: In a heavy saucepan, melt ½ cup (1 stick) unsalted butter over medium-low heat. Remove from heat and let stand until the milk solids settle. Spoon off any foam on the top and carefully pour just the clear yellow liquid into a jar. Use the remaining milk solids in soups or sauces.

Braised Short Ribs
with Celery and Herb Salad

SERVES 6 TO 8 AS A MAIN COURSE

Baraka opened as a small-plates restaurant featuring dishes from around the Mediterranean: Provençal, Italian, Spanish, and Moroccan. When chef David Bazirgan came on board, he added some large plates to the menu, but he kept the exotic spicing that gives Baraka's food its subtle perfumes. The dishes in this small corner spot vary from tagines to a foie gras *au torchon*, and all of them are prepared with attention to contrasting flavors and textures, like these slow-cooked short ribs served with a crunchy, refreshing celery salad. Chef Bazirgan suggests accompanying them with glazed pearl onions, roasted sweet potatoes, mushrooms, or any combination of the three.

Baraka

288 Connecticut Street
(at Eighteenth Street)

Note: You will need to begin this dish 1 day before serving.

Six 9-ounce beef short ribs
Salt and freshly ground pepper to taste
5 tablespoons olive oil
1 onion, cut into $^1/_2$-inch dice
2 celery stalks, cut into $^1/_2$-inch dice
2 carrots, peeled and cut into $^1/_2$-inch dice
2 cups dry red wine
$^1/_2$ cup red wine vinegar
2 tablespoons tomato paste
1 teaspoon ground cumin
2 bay leaves
5 thyme sprigs
5 star anise pods
$^1/_2$ teaspoon ground allspice
1 cinnamon stick
8 cups veal stock, veal demi-glace diluted with water,
or half chicken and half beef broth

CELERY AND HERB SALAD

1 cup fresh flat-leaf parsley leaves
¹/₂ cup 1-inch-long snipped fresh chives
¹/₂ cup fresh tarragon leaves
5 celery stalks, cut into ¹/₈-inch-thick diagonal slices
¹/₂ cup extra-virgin olive oil
Juice of 1 Meyer lemon
Salt and freshly ground pepper to taste

● Preheat the oven to 350°F. Season the ribs generously with salt and pepper on both sides. In a Dutch oven or heavy flameproof casserole, heat 3 tablespoons of the olive oil over medium-high heat. Place the ribs in the pan, meat side down, and cook for about 5 minutes, or until nicely browned. Using tongs, turn the ribs over and cook on the second side for 3 minutes. Transfer the ribs to a platter.

● In a large sauté pan or skillet, heat the remaining 2 tablespoons olive oil over medium heat and sauté the vegetables until they begin to brown, about 5 minutes. Add the wine, vinegar, tomato paste, herbs, and spices. Cook to reduce until the mixture begins to thicken, about 3 minutes. Remove from heat and set aside.

● Add the veal stock or broth to the pan in which the ribs were cooked and stir over medium heat to scrape up the browned bits from the bottom of the pan. Return the ribs to the pan and pour the vegetable mixture over the ribs. Cover and bake for about 3 hours, or until the ribs are very tender. Using tongs, transfer the ribs to a platter. While the ribs are still hot, use the tongs and a fork to remove the meat from the bones, in large pieces if possible. Discard the bones. Strain the meat and reserve both the liquid and the meat. Let both cool, then cover and refrigerate overnight.

The next day, remove any congealed fat from the rib meat, using a paring knife. Cut the meat into 6 to 8 nice portions, if necessary. Remove and discard the congealed fat from the liquid. In a stockpot, bring the sauce to a simmer over medium heat. Add the ribs, cover, reduce heat to low, and simmer until the ribs are heated through and very tender, 15 to 20 minutes. Turn off heat and keep covered.

To make the celery and herb salad: In a medium bowl, combine all the ingredients and toss well. Serve the ribs on warmed plates, with the salad alongside.

Ahi Tuna au Poivre
with Chanterelles, Niçoise Olives, and Artichokes

SERVES 6 AS A MAIN COURSE

Chez Papa Bistrot
*1401 Eighteenth Street
(at Missouri)*

Jocelyn Bulow and his pals branched out from their successful Plouf in the Financial District to open this classy little bistro on Potrero Hill, and the neighborhood has responded with warm support ever since. The decor is high-Parisian red and black, and the Provençal-flavored food is uncompromisingly high in style as well, as is seen in their recipe for rare tuna crusted with crushed peppercorns and topped with a red wine reduction. Note: Their minuscule crêpe restaurant, Chez Maman, is right next door.

RED WINE REDUCTION
2 cups dry red wine
Stems from 1 bunch thyme (leaves stripped off)
1 cup veal stock, chicken broth, or half chicken and half beef broth
1 tablespoon unsalted butter
Salt and freshly ground pepper to taste

1 tablespoon unsalted butter
1 tablespoon minced garlic
5 ounces chanterelle mushrooms, cut into 1-inch pieces
1 cup pitted and halved niçoise olives
6 large artichokes, cooked, trimmed into hearts, and quartered (see note)
1 teaspoon minced fresh thyme
1 cup chicken stock
Salt and freshly ground pepper to taste
4 tablespoons olive oil
Six 6-ounce portions ahi tuna
¹/₂ cup freshly crushed black peppercorns
Fleur de sel for garnish

◉ To make the red wine reduction: In a medium, heavy saucepan, combine the red wine and thyme stems. Bring to a low boil over medium heat and cook to reduce by half. Add the veal stock and cook to reduce by half again. Add the butter and season with salt and pepper. Remove from heat and set aside.

◉ In a medium sauté pan or skillet, melt the 1 tablespoon butter over medium heat. Add the garlic and mushrooms and sauté until they begin to brown slightly, about 3 minutes. Add the olives, artichokes, and minced thyme. Cook for 1 minute, then stir in the chicken stock, scraping the bottom of the pan well. Season with salt and pepper. Remove from heat and keep warm.

◉ In a large cast-iron skillet or heavy sauté pan or skillet, heat 2 tablespoons of the olive oil over high heat until smoking. Season the tuna steaks lightly on all sides with salt. Press the crushed pepper evenly into one side of each steak. Sear 3 of the steaks, pepper side down, for about 30 seconds, then turn and sear on the other side for 30 seconds for rare. Transfer to a plate and keep warm. Repeat with the remaining 3 steaks.

◉ Reheat the mushroom mixture over low heat. Bring the wine reduction to a low boil. Evenly divide the mushroom mixture among 6 warmed plates. Pour the sauce in a circle around the mushrooms, leaving a 2-inch border from the rim. Slice each tuna steak vertically into 3 pieces and fan the slices pepper side up and leaning against the mushrooms. Sprinkle the tuna lightly with fleur de sel and serve at once.

Preparing Artichoke Hearts: Cut a lemon in half and squeeze each half into a large bowl of water. Using a large knife, cut off the top 2 inches of an artichoke. Trim the stem end flush with the bottom. Using kitchen shears, cut off the tip of each leaf. Drop the artichoke into the lemon water and repeat to trim the remaining artichokes.

Fit the artichokes snugly into a large pot, stem ends up. Add the lemon halves and lemon water, plus more water to cover by 2 inches. Bring the water to a boil over hight heat, reduce heat to a simmer, cover, and cook until the stem end is fork-tender, about 30 minutes. Drain upside down until cool to the touch. Pull off each leaf and trim each artichoke heart with a paring knife. Using a teaspoon, dig out the spiny choke.

Artichokes

It may look like a medieval helmet, or a samurai headdress, or an African sculpture of some kind, but this armored vegetable hides a heart with a buttery texture and a subtle, sweet, grassy flavor. Ranging in size from not much bigger than a walnut to larger than a softball, and in color from deep violet to pale avocado, the artichoke is actually a cultivated thistle. A Mediterranean native, it also loves the rich coastal fields and mild weather of the Monterey peninsula, where almost all of the U.S. crop is grown, making it a quintessential Cal-Med vegetable.

Artichokes are in season in spring and again in early fall, and are eaten shaved and raw in salads, fried (a specialty of Salinas, California, next to the artichoke fields), pared into hearts and marinated, stuffed, and in main courses. If you use the baby ones, just cut off the tops and pull off the dark green leaves; the choke doesn't need to be removed. Serve large artichokes whole and boiled, with a sauce for dipping, or cut away all but the heart for use in recipes.

Pear Tarte Tatin

SERVES 8 AS A DESSERT

One of the pioneers of the SoMa dining scene, Fringale is a golden, intimate space out on a wide stretch of Fourth Street. Named for the French word for "hunger pang," Fringale satisfies hunger with food that feeds both body and soul. The Basque-inspired menu also includes such variations on French classics as chef Thierry Clement's dark amber pear tarte Tatin.

Fringale
570 Fourth Street (between Brannan and Bryant)

6 to 8 firm, ripe Comice or Anjou pears
1 star anise pod, ground
1 teaspoon ground cinnamon
1 teaspoon freshly ground pepper
1 cup water
2 cups sugar
1 sheet thawed frozen puff pastry
Vanilla ice cream or pear sorbet for serving

Preheat the oven to 400°F. Peel, halve, and core the pears. Cut each half into 4 crosswise pieces. In a bowl, combine the pears, star anise, cinnamon, and pepper. Stir gently to coat and let stand for 1 hour.

In a large, heavy saucepan, combine the water and sugar. Cook over medium heat until caramelized to golden brown, shaking pan to help dissolve sugar and brushing the sides of the pan with a wet pastry brush once or twice. Add the pears. The caramel will seize up at this point; push the hardened caramel into the center of the pan so it can melt again. Cook, stirring gently, until the pears are tender, 8 to 12 minutes, depending on the ripeness of the pears. Pour the pears and caramel into a heavy 8-inch ovenproof skillet, round gratin dish, or deep pie dish. Cut the puff pastry into a round 9 inches in diameter. Cover the top with the puff pastry and tuck in the dough all around the edges.

- Bake for 30 minutes, or until the dough is golden. Remove from the oven and let cool completely. Refrigerate for 2 hours (this will keep the tart from falling apart when cut).

- To serve, rewarm the tart in a preheated 200°F oven for about 20 minutes. Remove from the oven. Place a serving plate upside down on top of the tart pan. Holding both the plate and the tart pan together, quickly invert them both to unmold the tart. Serve warm, with ice cream or sorbet.

Pumpkin Curry Tofu

SERVES 6 AS A MAIN COURSE

Like their high-style Thai restaurant in a converted warehouse space in SoMa, Aom and Chris Foley are a blend of two cultures: Koh Samui is the island south of Thailand where they met, and Aom was born in the Chinese year of the monkey. Their food is uncomplicated, reasonably priced, and always satisfying. This rich vegetarian dish makes a whole meal when served with steamed jasmine rice and a green vegetable.

Koh Samui and the Monkey

415 Brannan Street (at Ritch)

1 cup $^1/_2$-inch-diced pumpkin or butternut squash

1 tablespoon Thai red curry paste, or more to taste if you like it spicy

One 13 $^1/_2$-ounce can coconut milk

1 pound firm tofu, cut into $^1/_2$-inch dice

Salt to taste

2 tablespoons sugar

$^1/_4$ cup thinly sliced green bell pepper

$^1/_4$ cup thinly sliced red bell pepper

15 fresh Thai basil leaves, plus sprigs for garnish

Steamed jasmine rice for serving

- In a covered steamer over simmering water, cook the pumpkin or squash until tender, about 10 minutes.

- Put the curry paste in a large saucepan and stir in the coconut milk until blended. Bring to a boil over medium-high heat and add the tofu, pumpkin or squash, salt, and sugar. Reduce heat to medium and cook at a low boil for 5 minutes. Stir in the bell peppers and basil leaves. Transfer to a serving bowl, garnish with basil sprigs, and serve at once, with steamed rice.

Orange Crème Brûlée

SERVES 6 AS A DESSERT

Le Charm French Bistro

315 Fifth Street (between Folsom and Harrison)

Aptly named, this bright space brings a touch of Gallic charm to an otherwise bleak stretch of Fifth Street. Le Charm's well-executed dishes and relatively low prices makes it a favorite lunch and early-supper spot for people who work in the area, and it has become a destination restaurant for lovers of French food and savoir faire as well. Specialties of the house include a faultless sautéed chicken liver salad, and this silky crème brûlée enlivened with the flavor and fragrance of oranges.

7 large egg yolks
Grated zest of 2 Valencia oranges
1 1/2 cups sugar
2 cups heavy cream
3/4 cup milk
Orange segments for garnish (optional), see page 7

- In a medium bowl, beat the egg yolks, orange zest, and orange juice until just blended. Stir in 3/4 cup of the sugar. Stir in the cream and milk until blended. Cover and refrigerate for at least 2 hours or, preferably, overnight.

- Preheat the oven to 250°F. Ladle the custard into six 6-ounce shallow ramekins. Bake until set, about 1 hour and 15 minutes. (Check after 1 hour to see if bubbles have appeared in the custards; if so, the oven is too hot. Open the oven door for a few minutes to reduce the oven temperature slightly.) Remove the custards from the oven and let cool to room temperature. Refrigerate for at least 2 hours or up to 6 hours.

- Just before serving, preheat the broiler. Spread 2 tablespoons of the remaining 3/4 cup sugar evenly over the top of each custard. Place the custards under the broiler, 3 to 4 inches from the heat source, and broil until the sugar is caramelized, 3 to 5 minutes. Or, if you have a small blowtorch, use that to caramelize the crème brulée. Let stand for a few moments to cool, then serve, garnished with orange segments, if you like.

Huachinango a la Talla

(Red Snapper with Chipotle Rouille and Warm Cabbage Salad)

SERVES 4 AS A MAIN COURSE

A vividly decorated, upscale Mexican restaurant in an office-complex setting, Maya brings the kind of food to San Francisco usually found only in a few high-end restaurants in Acapulco and Mexico City, and at Maya in New York City, executive chef/owner Richard Sandoval's other well-received restaurant. Combining authentic regional Mexican dishes with touches of European and Californian ingredients and techniques, the Maya kitchen prepares such offerings as this Veracruz-style fried snapper, topped with a rouille made with chipotle chilies.

Maya

303 Second Street (between Folsom and Harrison)

CHILI-SPICE PASTE

1 tablespoon canola oil

1 onion, sliced

2 garlic cloves

¹/₂ guajillo chili

1 cinnamon stick

1 tablespoon cumin seeds

3 cups water

Four 5-ounce red snapper fillets

1 tablespoon canola oil, plus oil for deep-frying

1 cup shredded red cabbage

1 cup shredded napa cabbage

2 teaspoons fresh lemon juice

1 teaspoon honey

Salt and freshly ground pepper to taste

Chipotle Rouille (recipe follows)

4 corn tortillas

1 tomato, cut into 8 slices

- To make the paste: In a heavy, medium saucepan, heat the oil over medium heat and sauté the onion, garlic, and chili until the onion is translucent, about 3 minutes. Add the cinnamon stick and cumin seeds. Add the water, bring to a boil over high heat, reduce heat to a simmer, and cook until the chili is soft, about 15 minutes. Drain, reserving the cooking liquid. In a blender, purée the onion, garlic, and chili with a little of the reserved cooking liquid until smooth. Strain through a fine-meshed sieve into a bowl, pressing on the solids with the back of a large spoon. Add more of the reserved cooking liquid, if necessary, to make a smooth paste.

- Place the fish on a plate and spread the paste on both sides of each fillet. Cover and refrigerate for 30 minutes. Remove from the refrigerator 30 minutes before cooking.

- In a large sauté pan or skillet over medium-high heat, heat the 1 tablespoon oil until smoking. Add the fish and cook until golden brown, about 3 minutes on each side. Transfer to a plate and keep warm in a low oven.

- In a medium bowl, combine the cabbages, lemon juice, honey, salt, and pepper. Toss with about ¼ cup of the rouille, or enough to coat the cabbage. Taste and adjust the seasoning. Set aside.

- In a heavy, large skillet over medium-high heat, heat about ½ inch oil until the surface shimmers and fry a tortilla until it begins to crisp, just a few seconds. Using tongs, transfer to paper towels to drain and blot dry with more paper towels on both sides. Transfer to a plate and keep warm in a very low oven while frying the remaining tortillas.

- Place a tortilla in the center of each of 4 warmed plates. Place one fourth of the cabbage salad on top of each tortilla. Place 2 tomato slices on top of the cabbage. Place a fish fillet on top of the tomatoes. Top with a spoonful of the rouille and serve at once.

Chipotle Rouille

MAKES ABOUT 1¹/₃ CUPS

1 egg yolk
¹/₄ cup chopped chipotle chilies in adobo sauce
1¹/₃ cups canola oil
¹/₂ teaspoon honey, dissolved in 1 teaspoon fresh lime juice
Salt and freshly ground pepper to taste

● In a blender, combine the egg yolk and chilies. Purée to a thick paste. With the machine running, gradually add the oil in a very thin stream to make a smooth sauce. Pour into a bowl. Whisk in the honey and lime juice, salt, and pepper. Taste and adjust the seasoning.

Oven-Dried-Tomato Tarts
with Goat Cheese and Onion Jam

SERVES 4 AS A FIRST COURSE

Oola Restaurant and Bar

860 Folsom Street (between Fourth and Fifth Streets)

After cooking in a number of places around town, from Plouf to Chez Papa to Baraka, chef Ola Fendert opened his own place in SoMa, and named it with the phonetic pronunciation of his Swedish first name. The high, narrow space with banquettes and sheer curtains has a theatrical supper-club ambiance, and the restaurant stays open until midnight Sunday through Monday and until 1 A.M. Tuesday through Saturday, making it a magnet for the late-night crowd. The food is eclectic, ranging from hamburgers to these savory tarts, rich with the flavor of caramelized onions and slowly roasted tomatoes.

OVEN-DRIED TOMATOES
8 Roma (plum) tomatoes, cored
1 tablespoon extra-virgin olive oil
Salt and freshly ground pepper to taste

ONION JAM
1 tablespoon unsalted butter
$1/2$ tablespoon grapeseed or canola oil
2 onions, very thinly sliced
2 tablespoons sugar
1 teaspoon minced fresh thyme

$1/2$ thawed frozen puff pastry sheet
2 tablespoons crème fraîche
4 tablespoons fresh goat cheese
2 cups mixed baby salad greens
Extra-virgin olive oil for drizzling
Aged balsamic vinegar for drizzling

- To make the oven-dried tomatoes: Preheat the oven to 225°F. In a pot of boiling water, blanch the tomatoes for 20 seconds. Using a slotted spoon, transfer to a bowl of ice water. Drain and peel. Cut the tomatoes into quarters and remove the seeds. Line a baking sheet with parchment paper. Place the tomatoes on the paper, cut side down. Drizzle with the oil and season with salt and pepper. Place in the oven and cook for about 2 hours, or until they are shrunken but still moist. Remove from the oven and let cool.

- To make the onion jam: In a medium sauté pan or skillet, melt the butter with the oil over very low heat and add the onions. Cook for about 30 minutes, stirring occasionally, until the onions are soft and golden. Add the sugar and cook, stirring frequently, until the onions are a golden brown, about 10 minutes. Remove from heat and let cool. Stir in the thyme.

- Preheat the oven to 400°F. Cut the puff pastry sheet into four 3½-inch squares. Line a baking sheet with a sheet of parchment paper. Top with a square of puff pastry, then another sheet of parchment paper. Place a baking sheet on top and weigh down the pastries evenly by placing two baking dishes on top. This will make the pastries thin and crisp. Bake for about 25 minutes, or until golden brown. Remove from the oven, remove the weights and top paper, and let cool, leaving the oven on.

- Spread a thin layer of crème fraîche on each puff pastry. Cover this with a thin layer of onion jam. Place the tomatoes on top of this, making sure to cover the whole surface. Put some nice pieces of goat cheese on top of the tomatoes. Put them in the 400°F oven for 2 to 3 minutes to heat slightly. Remove from the oven and transfer each tart to a plate. Top with one fourth of the salad greens, drizzle with olive oil and balsamic, and serve at once.

Seafood Risotto

SERVES 6 AS A FIRST COURSE, 4 AS A MAIN COURSE

Pazzia Caffè
Pizzeria Rosticceria
337 Third Street (between
Folsom and Harrison)

Noisy, crowded, and lively, Pazzia will remind you of trattorias in Italy where everyone is having a wonderful time and eating great food, like this main-course seafood risotto. Make it for company and serve it with a big green salad, crusty bread, and a dessert of fruit and cheese. Or, come to Pazzia before or after visiting MoMa or attending a dance concert at Yerba Buena; it has patio seating, is open for lunch during the week, and it's only a block away from the museum and the center for the arts.

4 cups fish stock (page 17) or chicken broth
1 cup water
6 tablespoons extra-virgin olive oil
12 ounces salmon fillet, skin and pinbones removed, cut into $^1/_2$-inch dice
18 clams, rinsed
18 mussels, rinsed and debearded
18 jumbo shrimp, shelled and deveined
2 garlic cloves, minced
$^1/_4$ cup finely chopped onion
2 cups Arborio rice
1 cup dry white wine
3 Roma tomatoes, finely chopped
Salt and freshly ground white pepper to taste
Minced fresh flat-leaf parsley for garnish

- In a medium saucepan, combine the stock or broth and water. Bring to a simmer over medium heat. Adjust the heat so the liquid maintains a bare simmer.

- In a large sauté pan or skillet, heat 1 tablespoon of the oil over medium heat. Add the salmon and sauté just until opaque on the outside, about 30 seconds. Using a slotted spoon, transfer the salmon to a bowl.

- Add the clams, mussels, shrimp, and garlic to the pan over medium heat. Cover the pan and cook for 3 minutes, or until the shrimp are evenly pink. Remove the shrimp from the pan. If the clams and mussels have not all opened, cover the pan and cook another minute. Turn off the heat and discard any clams and mussels that have not opened. Set the pan aside, uncovered.

- In a heavy, medium saucepan, heat the remaining 5 tablespoons of the oil over medium heat and sauté the onion until translucent, about 3 minutes. Add the rice and stir until the grains are coated well, about 1 minute.

- Add the white wine and stir until it is absorbed. Add ½ cup of the simmering stock or broth and stir constantly until it is absorbed. Continue adding the liquid in ½-cup increments and stirring until absorbed, for about 20 minutes, or until the rice is al dente. You may have some liquid left over. If you have used all the liquid but the risotto is not al dente, add ½ cup water and stir until it is absorbed; repeat if necessary.

- Add the chopped tomatoes, salt, and pepper to the rice and stir until the juice from the tomatoes is absorbed. Add the clams, mussels, shrimp, and salmon to the pan and gently stir them into the risotto. Cover the pan for about 15 seconds to heat the seafood, then spoon at once into warmed bowls. Sprinkle with the parsley and serve.

Whole Fish
with Tomato and Fennel Ragout
à la Niçoise

SERVES 4 AS A MAIN COURSE

Restaurant LuLu

*816 Folsom Street (between
Fourth and Fifth Streets)*

Restaurant LuLu gives energy and life to this stretch of SoMa, just around the corner from the Moscone Convention Center. The great, open space with its high ceiling crackles with energy and noise; people love to congregate here within view of the open kitchen to enjoy the California-French food, which is served family style. Here is chef Jared A. Doob's description of the following recipe: "This dish typifies the cuisine of Provence. A rustic cooking method and presentation, coupled with the traditional ingredients of the region, combine to give all present the feeling of being in southern France."

TOMATO AND FENNEL RAGOUT

2 tablespoons extra-virgin olive oil
3 fennel bulbs, trimmed (fronds reserved), cored, and finely diced
3 white onions, finely diced
4 garlic cloves, minced
2 salt-cured anchovies, rinsed, deboned, and minced
Grated zest of 2 lemons
1 teaspoon red pepper flakes
7 tomatoes, peeled, seeded, and finely diced (see page 12)
¼ cup unpitted niçoise olives
1 tablespoon capers, drained and rinsed
Salt and freshly ground pepper to taste

1 whole fish (about 1¼ pounds), such as branzino, tai snapper, or black bass, scaled and gutted
Salt and freshly ground pepper to taste
6 fennel fronds
6 thyme sprigs

Extra-virgin olive oil for coating
$\frac{1}{2}$ cup Pernod liqueur
$\frac{1}{2}$ cup dry white wine
$\frac{1}{2}$ cup water

To make the ragout: In a medium saucepan, heat the olive oil over medium-high heat and sauté the fennel and onions until translucent, about 10 minutes. Add the garlic, anchovies, lemon zest, and pepper flakes and continue to cook until the vegetables are crisp-tender, about 2 minutes. Reduce the heat to medium and add the tomatoes, olives, and capers. Simmer, stirring occasionally, for 15 to 20 minutes, or until thickened. Season with salt and pepper.

Preheat the oven to 400°F. To prepare the fish, trim off all the fins as well as the tail fin to prevent them from burning. Season the cavity with salt and pepper and stuff it with the fennel fronds and thyme sprigs. Coat the whole fish with olive oil and season with salt and pepper. Lay the fish in a small baking dish. Place in the oven and bake until the skin starts to become opaque, about 6 minutes. Add the Pernod, wine, and water to the dish and return to the oven. Bake for 3 to 4 minutes, or until the skin starts to brown. Add the fennel and tomato ragout to the baking dish and continue to cook until the ragout is heated and fish is golden and soft to the touch, about 6 minutes.

Garnish with the reserved fennel fronds. Serve whole and fillet at the table for your guests.

Macaroni Gratin

SERVES 4 AS A SIDE DISH

South Park Café

108 South Park (between
Second and Third Streets)

South Park, an oval green on the English model once lined with elegant townhouses, is no longer an epicenter of the dot-com era, and the neighborhood has reverted back to a quiet mixture of designers, artists, residents of live-work lofts, and people living in residential hotels. But the centerpiece of the area remains this chic French cafe. Everything about this place is done right, from the zinc bar to the almond tuiles and *citron pressé* to the photographs of Paris park benches.

This rich, creamy French gratin is typical of South Park's fare. Serve it with roasted meats such as lamb, veal, and beef.

8 ounces macaroni
1 1/2 cups milk
1 1/2 cups heavy cream
1/2 tablespoon unsalted butter
1 tablespoon all-purpose flour
1 1/4 cups (5 ounces) shredded Gruyère cheese
Salt and freshly ground white pepper to taste
Pinch of cayenne pepper

In a large pot of salted boiling water, cook the macaroni until al dente, about 10 minutes. Drain but do not rinse. Cover and set aside.

Preheat the oven to 350°F. In a large saucepan, combine the milk and cream. Bring to a bare simmer over medium-low heat. Remove from heat and keep warm.

In another large saucepan, make a roux by melting the butter over medium-low heat and stirring in the flour. Cook and stir for 2 to 3 minutes, but do not let the mixture brown. Gradually whisk the hot milk mixture into the roux. Bring to a low boil, and cook, whisking frequently, for about 10 minutes. Season with the salt, white pepper, and cayenne.

Butter a gratin or baking dish. In a large bowl, combine the warm macaroni and shredded cheese. Stir to blend well. Pour the mixture into the prepared baking dish. Pour the cream sauce over the macaroni and cheese. Bake until lightly golden on top, about 30 minutes.

Artisan Cheeses

When Laura Chenel began raising goats almost thirty-five years ago, she traveled to France to study traditional goat cheese–making methods, then brought that knowledge back to her small farm in the Napa Valley. The thick white logs of sweet, fresh goat cheese she made as a result would spawn goat-cheese companies all across the United States and initiate the artisan cheese movement in northern California. Now, handmade farmhouse California cheeses (made on the same farm where the milk is produced) can be found in San Francisco cheese stores and on the celebrated cheese carts of such restaurants as the Dining Room at the Ritz-Carlton and Gary Danko.

Three of the city's premier creameries are Say Cheese in Cole Valley (856 Cole Street), the 24th Street Cheese Company in Noe Valley (3893 Twenty-fourth Street), and Cowgirl Creamery's Artisan Cheese (2413 California Street and in the Ferry Building). Cheeses to look for include fromage blanc, ricotta, and Crescenza, a meltingly soft cow's milk cheese similar to teleme, from Bellwether Farms (Petaluma); Humboldt Fog, a goat cheese with a gray line of vegetable ash at its heart, from California's north coast; and Mt. Tam, a triple-cream from Cowgirl Creamery.

The three great traditional California cheeses, which have been around for decades, are Monterey jack, teleme, and dry Monterey jack. Both fresh and dry Monterey jack are excellent in Mexican recipes, and teleme is a luxurious after-dinner cheese. Look for fresh, dry, and partially dry (mezzo secco) Monterey jack with the Vella Cheese Company brand, or visit their store in Sonoma.

Aromatic, dense, and ripe with flavor, artisan cheeses are waiting for you in cold cases and on counters throughout San Francisco neighborhoods. Take two or preferably three of them home with you and let them come to room temperature, then serve them with fruit for dessert, or as a separate cheese course with bread following the salad and before dessert, French style. It's a lovely way to prolong dinner and lengthen your guests' stay at the table.

Tuna Tartare
with Fried Green Tomatoes and Tabasco

SERVES 4 AS A FIRST COURSE

Town Hall

342 Howard Street (at Fremont)

The Rosenthal brothers and chefs, Stephen and Mitchell, have managed the difficult act of running two restaurants at the same time: Postrio and the newer Town Hall, in an ornate, historic building in SoMa. Intended as a gathering place for people who live and work in the area, the space is warm and welcoming, and the food, with its Creole and Cajun accents, is the best kind of American cuisine.

RED PEPPER AIOLI
¹/₂ garlic clove
1 egg yolk
³/₄ cup olive oil
¹/₂ red bell pepper, roasted and peeled (see page 40)
Salt and freshly ground pepper to taste
Tabasco sauce to taste

TABASCO VINAIGRETTE
1 garlic clove
¹/₄ cup olive oil
¹/₂ shallot, minced
¹/₂ green onion, finely chopped, including green parts
4 teaspoons Champagne vinegar
Tabasco sauce to taste

Canola oil or peanut oil for deep-frying
¹/₂ cup cornmeal
¹/₂ cup all-purpose flour
¹/₄ teaspoon salt, plus salt to taste

Freshly ground pepper to taste
1 large green (unripe) tomato, cut into 4 crosswise slices
1 cup buttermilk
8 to 12 ounces sushi-quality ahi tuna, finely chopped

To make the aioli: In a mortar or a bowl, crush the garlic clove to a paste. Add the egg yolk and mix with the garlic, using a pestle or wooden spoon, until sticky. Whisk in the olive oil a few drops at a time, gradually increasing the flow to a thin stream as the mixture emulsifies. In a blender, purée the roasted pepper until smooth. Stir the purée into the aioli. Add the salt, pepper, and Tabasco. Set aside.

To make the vinaigrette: Combine the garlic clove and olive oil in a sauté pan or skillet and bring to a simmer over medium heat. Cook for 1 minute, then remove from heat and let cool. Strain, reserving the oil and discarding the garlic. Combine the shallot and green onion in a bowl. Stir in the garlic oil, Champagne vinegar, and Tabasco.

In a Dutch oven or deep fryer, heat 2 inches of oil to 350°F. In a shallow bowl, combine the cornmeal, flour, ¼ teaspoon salt, and pepper. Stir to blend. In a bowl, soak the tomato slices in the buttermilk for 20 seconds. Dredge each slice in the cornmeal mixture to coat evenly. Carefully add to the hot oil and cook until golden brown, about 2 minutes. Using a wire skimmer, transfer to paper towels to drain.

Put the tuna in a bowl and add 2 or 3 tablespoons of the Tabasco vinaigrette. Stir well and add salt and pepper to taste. Divide the tartare among 4 salad plates. Cut the fried tomatoes in half and place around the tuna. Drizzle some of the aioli on the tomatoes and serve.

Shrimp Goldfish

Yank Sing

Rincon Center, 101 Spear Street
(between Howard and Mission)
and 49 Stevenson Street
(between First and Second Streets)

There's no culinary experience quite like sitting at your table and having cart after silver dim-sum cart go by, with the waitperson lifting metal domes to show you a selection of savory steamed and fried morsels to choose at your pleasure. It's a favorite Sunday brunch, weekend afternoon, and lunch pastime, especially at either of Yank Sing's downtown restaurants. Their dim sum are exemplary, not to mention addictive, like these cunning dumplings shaped to look like goldfish.

Note: The goldfish are made with har gow wrappers, which become transparent when cooked and must be made at home, as they are not available commercially. However, you can also make these with wonton (siu mai) wrappers, available in any Chinese market and many supermarkets. If using these, you won't be able to form the dumplings into goldfish, but you can shape them like wontons. Make these for a cocktail party, and watch your guests devour them.

FILLING

8 ounces shrimp, shelled, deveined, and finely chopped
$^1\!/_2$ cup finely chopped canned bamboo shoots
2 tablespoons finely chopped green onion (white part only)
2 tablespoons minced fresh cilantro
2 tablespoons finely chopped pork fat (fatback)
$^1\!/_2$ teaspoon minced fresh ginger
2 teaspoons light soy sauce
1 teaspoon sugar
$^1\!/_8$ teaspoon salt
1 teaspoon Asian sesame oil
$^1\!/_4$ teaspoon ground white pepper
2 teaspoons tapioca starch (tapioca flour)
1 tablespoon Shaoxing wine or dry sherry

30 har gow wrappers (page 196) or square wonton wrappers
Red food coloring (optional)
Light soy sauce for dipping (optional)

- To make the filling: In a medium bowl, combine all the filling ingredients and stir to mix thoroughly. Cover and refrigerate for 2 hours.

- To form the dumplings: Place 1 tablespoon of the filling slightly off center on a har gow wrapper. Fold the edge closest to the filling up and over the filling. Fold each side over and pinch together in the center. Fold the opposite end into the filling. Pinch one end to form the goldfish's tail. Apply red food coloring with the tip of a wooden food pick to indicate eyes, if you like. Repeat to use the remaining filling and wrappers. Or, if using wonton wrappers, spoon 1 teaspoon filling in the center of a wrapper. Brush the top edge with a little water, fold the bottom half over, and press to seal the edges. Pull the bottom corners down and overlap them, then pinch them together. Repeat to use the remaining filling and wrappers. (If using wonton wrappers, the shrimp may be either steamed, as below, or deep-fried.)

- Soak both halves of a two-level bamboo steamer in water for about 10 minutes. Dry and lightly oil the inside bottom of each compartment. Pour hot water into a wok to come within 1 inch of the bottom of the steamer when it is set in the wok. Bring the water to a boil over high heat. Have additional hot water on hand for replenishing the wok if necessary. Arrange the goldfish in each steamer compartment, leaving ample space between the goldfish. Place the stacked compartments of the steamer over the boiling water, cover the top compartment, and steam for 15 minutes. Serve hot, directly from the steamer. (No dipping sauce is necessary, but if you like, use a light soy sauce.)

Har Gow Wrappers

MAKES ABOUT 30 WRAPPERS

The wheat starch and tapioca starch are available in Chinese markets.

1½ cups wheat starch (nonglutinous flour, or cheng fen)
2 tablespoons tapioca starch (tapioca flour)
1 cup boiling water
1 tablespoon lard

Sift the wheat starch and tapioca starch together into a bowl. Form a well in the center. Quickly pour in the boiling water while vigorously stirring the mixture until a ball forms. (This cooks the starches, resulting in a transparent wrapper.) Add the lard and stir it in, then transfer the dough to a lightly floured board and knead for a few minutes until soft and smooth.

Divide the ball in half. Using your hands, roll each piece of dough into a 1-inch-diameter cylinder. Cover with a damp towel and let rest for 15 minutes.

Cut each cylinder into ¾-inch pieces. Form each piece into a ball. Cover the balls with a damp towel. (You may let them rest for an hour or two if you don't have time to make the wrappers now.)

Oil each plate of a tortilla press, if you have one. Press 1 ball at a time (leaving the others covered) into a wafer about ⅛ inch thick and about 3¾ inches in diameter, oiling the press as necessary. Or, roll out each piece of dough on a floured board, using a rolling pin. Stack the wrappers as you roll them. Cover the wrappers with a damp towel if not using immediately. They should be used within a few hours of being made.

San Francisco Classics

Some of the classic San Francisco dishes from Gold Rush and Gay Nineties days have faded away. It's impossible to find boiled terrapin and Pudding à la Sultan on menus nowadays, and Chicken à la Raphael Weill hasn't been seen for some time. But others, like oyster loaf and Joe's Special, are still featured in some of the old-time places, and are sometimes revived by New California chefs who want to give a traditional dish a different spin. Rex sole and petrale sole, favorite San Francisco fish, are featured in restaurants like Sam's and the Tadich Grill, as they have been for years, and they occasionally appear in the kitchens of new young chefs as well.

Hangtown Fry, an oyster frittata born during the Gold Rush, is still on the menu at the Tadich Grill, San Francisco's oldest restaurant (page 44), and Green Goddess Salad is still found on the menu at the Garden Court in the Sheraton Palace Hotel, though in a lighter version. The Fly Trap Restaurant in SoMa specializes in Old San Francisco dishes such as Celery Victor and Chicken Jerusalem. Crab Louis may be a Pacific Northwest invention, but it's a San Francisco tradition on Fisherman's Wharf menus. Crab cocktails are sold on the street at the Wharf, and at the counter at Swan Oyster Depot. Cioppino, the San Francisco Italian fish stew made with Dungeness crab, is another Fisherman's Wharf staple, and it's also found on Rose Pistola's menu in season (see their recipe on page 74).

ADOS Y DEL PAIS
CHONTALEÑO DURO BLANDITO
QUESO FRESCO MONTERREY

3064

The Mission / Bernal Heights

O GRANDE

Alma

Charanga

Delfina

Foreign Cinema

The Liberty Cafe and Bakery

Limón

Luna Park

Slow Club

Ti Couz

Universal Cafe

THE MISSION DISTRICT, built around the old road running at an angle across the peninsula of San Francisco to Mission Dolores, basks in the sun most of the year and is filled with flashes of Latin culture and color. For many years a Latino

neighborhood, today the Mission is a mixture of people from Mexico, Central America, and South America; students, Gen-Xers, artists, and urban hipsters; and commuters to Silicon Valley, lured by the easy access to Highway 101. Now there are two Missions, the old Latino one, with its traces of former Irish and Italian populations, and the slowly gentrifying one, sprinkled with hip bars, cocktail lounges, and innovative restaurants. ⁓ THE MISSION BECAME A FAVORED MIDDLE-CLASS RESIDENTIAL AREA after the Great Quake. A few bars, a bakery, and a restaurant are all that remain of the Italian and Irish families who lived here then. When the Sunset and Richmond districts were built after World War I, many Mission residents moved there, and the neighborhood gradually became a haven for immigrants from Latin America, as well as artists, students, and others drawn by the low rents. During the late nineties, the eastern, industrial area of the Mission—known as the Trans-Mission—was clogged with construction zones and bristling with building cranes as Internet startups transformed the neighborhood. Now most of those startups have disappeared, but many of the city's most interesting restaurants, such as the Slow Club and Universal Cafe, remain. ⁓ THE HEART OF THE RESTAURANT SCENE IN THE NEW MISSION IS VALENCIA STREET. Along with other restaurants on parallel streets and side streets, it forms the city's most vibrant dining corridor. Once there was only Le Trou, a miniscule French bistro (which would eventually morph into several different eating places). Then, the eccentric Flying

Saucer landed over on Guerrero, and people began venturing out to the wilds of the Mission for the kind of inventive, constructed food that had formerly been available only in the city's most expensive downtown restaurants. Now the list is long and varied, from Delfina to Luna Park, including Nuevo Latino spots like Alma and Plátanos, and new restaurants pop up every year, adding to the mix of cuisines and cultures in the neighborhood. ⟶ IN MANY PLACES, the old and the new Mission are found side by side: the chic Foreign Cinema restaurant is right next to one of the huge abandoned Latino movie houses, and the Original McCarthy's Bar, once one of the few remaining Irish places, is now an outpost of Haight Street's Cha Cha Cha and serves their Caribbean and Latin-American cuisine around the original forty-five-foot-long wooden horseshoe bar. Groups of men still hang out night and day in front of corner liquor stores, while crowds of young urbanites fill trendy bars and lounges like Laszlo and Medjool. ⟶ THE OLD MISSION IS STILL HERE, of course: the huge new-and-used furniture stores, the taquerias, the Latino groceries, the clothing stores with frilly white confirmation dresses and elaborate *quinceañera* gowns, the many hole-in-the-wall Latino restaurants. Bins of mangos, papayas, and tomatillos line the fronts of local markets. There are bakeries where you can choose Mexican pastries from open racks with tongs, piling them on your metal tray. In the mornings, you can smell the churros deep-frying in the snack shops, and if you arrive at the right time, you can buy one warm and dusted with a snowfall of confectioners' sugar. At one of the last Italian outposts, Dianda's Italian American Pastry (2883 Mission), you can buy St. Honoré cake or one of their wonderful almond tortes with a thin layer of

OTHER NEIGHBORHOOD STARS

Andalú

Ankor Borei

Blue Plate

Cha Cha Cha

Firecracker

Geranium

La Taqueria

La Cumbre

Little Nepal

Pauline's Pizza

Pancho Villa

Plátanos

Tartine Bakery

Watercress

Walzwerk

Woodward's Garden

The Mission / Bernal Heights

201

raspberry jam on the bottom. At the Lucca Ravioli Company (1100 Valencia), fresh ravioli and pasta are made every day. (In the back of La Palma Mexicatessen (2884 Twenty-fourth Street), you can watch aproned women making tor-

tillas by hand from fresh masa (order handmade tortillas ahead for dinners or parties in either the regular or the cocktail size), or you can buy fresh masa and a tortilla press to make your own. The best burritos in town are sold at La Taqueria on the corner of Mission and Twenty-fifth Street (no rice, just beans and meat, plus any extras you want to add). PERCHED ABOVE THE MISSION IS BERNAL HEIGHTS, an urban hill town of twisting streets, quirky little workingman's houses, and a short main street (Cortland Avenue) of shops and cafes. Not too long ago, many of the streets in this area were unpaved, and some still are. Bernal Heights, too, is changing, as a new group of people come here to buy property. The city's first Nepalese restaurant is here, along with the Liberty Cafe, a quintessential neighborhood restaurant that draws devotees from all over the city for its classic American food, great desserts, and baked goods.

Asparagus and Cheese Flans
with Green Garlic–Chipotle Cream

SERVES 6 AS A FIRST COURSE

Johnny Alamilla's corner restaurant in the Mission is well named with the Spanish word for "soul," for his cuisine truly is soulful. The Nuevo Latino food served here includes stunningly fresh ceviche and such artful, savory dishes as these rich, silky flans to eat with a spoon or to spread on toast or crostini (and the margaritas and mojitos are special, too).

Alma
1101 Valencia Street
(at Twenty-second Street)

½ tablespoon canola oil
3 shallots, sliced
¼ teaspoon ground coriander
½ teaspoon cumin seeds, toasted and ground (see page 129)
1 tablespoon kosher salt
¼ teaspoon freshly ground pepper
2 cups heavy cream
1 bunch asparagus, trimmed, sliced, and blanched for 2 minutes
1 cup (4 ounces) shredded manchego cheese
5 large eggs
Green Garlic–Chipotle Cream (recipe follows)
Minced fresh chives for garnish
Toast triangles or crostini (page 279) for serving

Preheat the oven to 300°F. In a nonreactive saucepan, heat the canola oil over low heat and add the shallots, spices, salt, and pepper. Cook, stirring often, until the shallots are softened but not browned, about 5 minutes. Add the cream, bring to a simmer, and cook for 5 minutes. Add the asparagus and half of the cheese. Cook, stirring occasionally, until the cheese is melted, about 5 minutes. Remove from heat and transfer half of the mixture to a blender. Purée until smooth. Strain through a fine-meshed sieve. Repeat with the rest of the mixture. Taste and adjust the seasoning. Refrigerate until barely warm.

In a large bowl, whisk the eggs just until blended. Stir the asparagus mixture into the eggs. Stir in the remaining cheese. Let stand for 5 minutes. Spoon off any foam that has risen to the top.

Evenly divide the mixture among six 5-ounce flan molds or ramekins and set them in a baking pan. Add hot water to pan to come halfway up the sides of the molds or ramekins. Cover the pan with aluminum foil and carefully place in the oven on the center rack. Bake until a knife inserted in the center of a flan comes out clean, 45 minutes for flan molds, 1 hour for ramekins. Remove from the oven and pour some green garlic–chipotle cream over each warm flan. Sprinkle with the chives. Serve with toast or crostini.

Warm Green Garlic–Chipotle Cream

MAKES ABOUT $^3/_4$ CUP

$^1/_2$ tablespoon canola oil
2 large shallots, sliced
2 small stalks green garlic or green onions,
white and light green parts only, finely chopped
$^1/_2$ to 1 canned chipotle chili, sliced (depending on your heat tolerance)
$^1/_2$ teaspoon kosher salt
$^1/_2$ teaspoon piment d'Espelette (Basque chili powder),
or $^1/_4$ teaspoon sweet paprika and $^1/_4$ teaspoon cayenne pepper
$^1/_4$ teaspoon cumin seeds, toasted and ground (see page 129)
1 bay leaf
1 cup heavy cream
1 teaspoon fresh lemon juice

In a heavy, small saucepan, heat the oil over low heat and add the shallots, garlic or green onions, chipotle, salt, and piment d'Espelette or paprika/cayenne mixture. Cook for about 5 minutes, or until shallots are softened but not browned. Add the cumin, bay leaf, and cream. Slowly simmer to reduce volume by one half, about 10 minutes. Remove from heat and stir in the lemon juice. Taste and adjust the seasoning. Press through a fine-meshed sieve with the back of a large spoon. Set aside and keep warm, or reheat over low heat before serving.

Picadillo Cubano
with Black Beans

(Cuban-Style Ground Beef with Green Olives and Raisins)

SERVES 4 TO 6 AS A MAIN COURSE

Gabriela Salas, who cooked at Cha Cha Cha (page 252) for nine years, opened her own place on Mission Street in 1998 with Rita Abraldes. Salas is from Costa Rica, Abraldes is Cuban-American, and the cuisine at Charanga (named for a Cuban style of dance music) is pan-Latin. You'll find dishes from Spain, the Caribbean, and South America on the menu (don't be surprised to see some Asian touches as well), and the restaurant filled with happy diners who reflect the Mission's diversity. This recipe for a traditional Cuban dish is an adaptation of a recipe from Elena Abraldes (Rita's mom). Both the picadillo and the black beans use a sofrito, the aromatic mixture of vegetables and herbs that is the basis of so many Cuban dishes.

Charanga

2351 Mission Street (between Ninteenth and Twentieth Streets)

1¹/₂ pounds ground chuck

SOFRITO

2 tablespoons olive oil

1 onion, finely diced

1 bay leaf

¹/₂ red bell pepper, seeded, deribbed, and finely diced

¹/₂ green bell pepper, seeded, deribbed, and finely diced

1 tablespoon minced garlic

1 tablespoon ground cumin

1 tablespoon dried oregano leaves

Salt and freshly ground pepper to taste

¹/₄ cup sliced pimiento-stuffed manzanilla olives

¹/₄ cup raisins

¹/₄ cup dry white wine

³/₄ cup canned tomato sauce

Black Beans (recipe follows), rice (see note), and fried plantains for serving

- In a large, heavy sauté pan or Dutch oven over medium heat, brown the beef, breaking up large chunks with a spoon. Drain off the fat and transfer the beef to a bowl.

- To make the sofrito: In the same pan over medium-high heat, heat the olive oil and stir in the sofrito ingredients one at a time in the order listed. Cook, stirring frequently, until slightly thickened, about 10 minutes.

- Return the beef to the pan and stir in the olives, raisins, and white wine. Cook for 5 to 10 minutes to reduce the wine, then add the tomato sauce and stir the mixture well. Cover, reduce heat to a simmer, and cook until slightly thickened and well flavored, about 15 minutes. Taste and adjust the seasoning. Serve on warmed plates, with beans, rice, and fried plantains alongside.

Black Beans

SERVES 4 TO 6

2 cups (1 pound) dried black beans
1 bay leaf
8 cups water
2 to 3 tablespoons salt

SOFRITO

¹/₂ onion, chopped
¹/₂ green bell pepper, seeded, deribbed, and chopped
2 tablespoons chopped fresh flat-leaf parsley
2 tablespoons chopped fresh cilantro
1 teaspoon dried oregano leaves
2 teaspoons minced garlic
Olive oil for purée, if needed, plus 2 tablespoons
1 teaspoon cumin seeds
Salt and freshly ground pepper to taste

¹/₄ cup dry white wine
2 tablespoons olive oil
2 tablespoons distilled white vinegar

- Rinse and pick over the beans. In a large pot, combine the beans, bay leaf, and water. Bring to a boil, then reduce heat to low, stir in the salt, and cook, stirring frequently and adding more water as necessary, until tender, 1 to 1½ hours.

- While the beans are cooking, make the sofrito: In a blender or food processor, combine the onion, pepper, parsley, cilantro, oregano, and garlic. Blend to a smooth purée (add a little oil if necessary to purée). Set the purée aside.

- In a heavy, medium saucepan, heat the 2 tablespoons oil over medium heat and fry the cumin seeds until they are fragrant, sizzling, and beginning to brown. Add the purée and cook, uncovered, for 10 to 15 minutes. Set aside.

- Add the sofrito to the cooked beans, stirring well to blend the ingredients. Cook over low heat until the mixture is thickened and rich with the flavors of the sofrito, about 30 minutes. Add the wine, olive oil, and vinegar during the last 10 minutes of cooking. Taste and adjust the seasoning.

- Serve on warmed plates with the beans, rice, and plantains.

Note: To add color to steamed rice to serve 4 to 6 people, sauté ⅛ teaspoon achiote paste in a little oil and add the mixture to the liquid for steaming the rice.

Grilled Fresh Calamari
with Warm White Bean Salad

Delfina
3621 Eighteenth Street
(at Dolores)

Rarely has a small restaurant caused such excitement as when Delfina opened its doors in 1998. Soon, Anne and Craig Stoll's thirty-five-seat space expanded next door, adding thirty-five more tables. Named after a restaurant in Tuscany where Craig Stoll once cooked, Delfina serves up food that is rustic, simple, but perfectly executed, with every flavor standing out bright and clear, the hallmark of excellent food. This chef-owned enterprise, with its attention to detail and devotion to good cooking, is a prime example of one of the things San Francisco does best.

1 cup dried rice beans (tiny white beans) or navy beans
1/2 bunch sage
3 to 4 whole garlic cloves
Kosher salt to taste

PICADA
1 garlic clove
Kosher salt to taste
1 cup extra-virgin olive oil
1 bunch flat-leaf parsley, stemmed and minced

2 pounds calamari, cleaned but not skinned if possible
Olive oil for coating
Kosher salt and freshly ground pepper to taste
Leaves from 1 bunch frisée
1 bunch arugula, stemmed
6 tablespoons extra-virgin olive oil
1 1/2 tablespoons Champagne vinegar
Niçoise olives for garnish
Julienned zest of 1 lemon, blanched for 1 minute

- Rinse and pick over the beans. In a large pot, combine the beans, sage, and garlic. Add cold water to cover by about 4 inches and bring to a boil. Reduce heat to a very low simmer and cook, uncovered, for about 2 hours, or until the beans are completely tender. Season lightly with salt and set the beans aside in their broth.

- Soak six 9-inch-long wooden skewers in water for 30 minutes, then drain. Light a fire in a charcoal grill or preheat a broiler.

- Meanwhile, make the picada: In a mortar, combine the garlic and salt and pound to a paste with a pestle. Transfer to a stainless-steel bowl. Gradually whisk in the oil to make a smooth mixture. Stir in the parsley. Taste and adjust the seasoning.

- Thread 3 whole squid bodies on each skewer, piercing once through the bottom and once through the top of each body. Skewer the tentacles on the end. Coat with oil and season with salt and pepper. Grill 4 to 6 inches above hot coals or broil 2 inches from the heat source until the squid begins to firm up slightly and take on color on one side, about 3 minutes. Turn and cook on the other side for about 3 minutes.

- In a bowl, toss the greens with 2 tablespoons of the extra-virgin oil, the vinegar, and salt and pepper to taste. Transfer the beans with a little of their cooking liquid to a saucepan. Stir in the remaining 4 tablespoons extra-virgin olive oil and salt and pepper to taste. Heat over low heat until warmed through.

- To serve, arrange the greens in the center of each plate. Spoon the beans in a circle around them. Lay a skewer of calamari across the greens. Sprinkle with the olives, lemon zest, and picada. Serve at once.

Chocolate Pots de Crème

SERVES 6 AS A DESSERT

Foreign Cinema

*2534 Mission Street
(between Twenty-first and
Twenty-second Streets)*

The huge Latino movie houses on Mission Street are closed, but this splashy restaurant fills the gap by showing foreign films on a high wall of its patio. There are heat lamps to keep you warm, but if you're interested only in the Cal-Med food of Gayle Pirie and John Clark (formerly of the Zuni Cafe), you can dine in the vast warehouse space, which is brightened by an enormous fireplace. There's a bar at one end (and another, smaller one in the hall) and an open kitchen on the other. The noise and energy levels are high, and the food is alluringly good.

¹/₂ cup whole milk
³/₄ cup heavy cream
3 ounces bittersweet chocolate, chopped
3 large egg yolks
¹/₃ cup sugar
Sweetened whipped cream and chocolate shavings for garnish

- In a medium saucepan, combine the milk and cream. Cook over medium heat until bubbles form around the edges of the pan. Remove from heat, add the chocolate, and stir until melted. Set aside and let cool to room temperature.

- Preheat the oven to 325°F. In a medium bowl, whisk the egg yolks and sugar together just until blended. Do not let the mixture foam. Gradually stir the chocolate mixture into the egg yolk mixture, stirring constantly. Strain through a fine-meshed sieve into a bowl.

- Spoon off any foam that may have risen to the surface of the chocolate mixture. Pour it evenly into six 4-ounce pot de crème cups or ramekins. Again, spoon off any foam on top of the mixture.

- Set the cups or ramekins in a large baking dish or roasting pan and add hot water to the dish or pan to come halfway up the sides of the ramekins. Cover the pan loosely with aluminum foil to prevent a skin from forming on the creams. Place the pan in the center of the oven and bake until the creams are set at the edges, but still trembling in the center, about 25 minutes.

- Remove the pan from the oven and carefully remove the ramekins from the water. Let cool. Refrigerate for at least 2 hours or up to overnight. Serve with a dollop of whipped cream on top and a few chocolate shavings sprinkled over.

Chicken Potpies

SERVES 4 AS A MAIN COURSE

**The Liberty Cafe
and Bakery**
*410 Cortland Street
(between Bennington and Wool)*

Just when it seemed the Liberty couldn't get any better, they opened a combination bakery and wine bar in a little house in their backyard. Now you can come here for their wonderful baked goods during the day, and for a glass of wine at night. Both possibilities help ease the crush in the cafe, which takes no reservations and is always full of people who come to this neighborhood jewel for its New American food, like their famous banana cream pie and chicken potpies. The potpies are full of flavor because each ingredient in the filling is cooked separately, then combined. The gravy is made in the same pan used to brown the carrots and onions, and the crust is a simplified puff pastry known as "rough puff."

Note: If you want to save time when making these at home, use thawed frozen puff pastry. Although this recipe is painstaking, each of the three components—the crusts, filling, and gravy—can be made 1 day ahead and assembled just before baking.

PUFF PASTRY CRUSTS
3 cups unbleached all-purpose flour
1 teaspoon salt
1½ cups (3 sticks) cold unsalted butter
¾ cup cold water

FILLING
2 thyme sprigs
2 marjoram sprigs
One 2½-pound chicken
2 Yukon Gold potatoes, peeled and cut into ½-inch chunks (2 cups)
1 pound green peas, shelled (1 cup), or 1 cup frozen peas
4 tablespoons unsalted butter
2 carrots, peeled and cut into ½-inch chunks (2 cups)
1 garlic clove, minced
24 pearl onions

GRAVY

6 tablespoons unsalted butter
6 tablespoons all-purpose flour
4 cups chicken stock or canned low-salt chicken broth
Salt and freshly ground pepper to taste
1 egg yolk beaten with ½ cup heavy cream

- To make the crusts: In a medium bowl, stir the flour and salt together. Using a pastry cutter or 2 dinner knives, cut in the butter until the mixture resembles coarse cornmeal. Add the water a little at a time while stirring it into the mixture with a fork. On a lightly floured board, form the dough into a ball. It will be crumbly.

- On a lightly floured board, roll the dough out into a rectangle. It will be very crumbly still, but go ahead and fold the two sides into the center, then fold again as if you were closing a book. Turn the dough a half-turn and roll it out again into a larger rectangle, lightly dusting the dough with flour as needed to keep your rolling pin from sticking to the dough. Repeat the folding process. Keep rolling out and folding the dough until it is smooth, usually 3 or 4 times. Cover the dough tightly in plastic wrap and refrigerate for at least 2 hours or up to 24 hours.

- Have ready four 1½-cup ovenproof bowls. Place the dough on a floured board and roll it into a rectangle ⅛ inch thick. Place one of the bowls upside-down on the dough and cut around its perimeter using a knife or a pastry cutter. Place the round on a plate. Repeat to cut and stack 4 rounds in all, separating each with a piece of waxed paper or parchment paper. Cover with plastic wrap and refrigerate.

- To make the filling: Preheat the oven to 400°F. Insert the herb sprigs under the skin of the chicken. Place the chicken in a roasting pan and roast until the juices run clear when a thigh is pierced with a knife, about 45 minutes. Remove from the oven and let cool to the touch, then pull the meat from the carcass, reserving the skin and bones to make stock for another recipe. Cut the meat into bite-sized chunks. Set aside.

- Cook the potatoes in salted boiling water until just tender but not mushy, about 8 minutes. (They need to be firm enough to cook further in the oven.) Drain and set aside to cool.

- Blanch the fresh peas in boiling water for 3 to 5 minutes, or until cooked but still firm. If using frozen peas, no cooking is necessary.

- In a large skillet, melt 2 tablespoons of the butter over medium heat and sauté the carrots until tender, about 5 minutes. Add the garlic and cook until the carrots are slightly browned on the edges, about 5 minutes longer. Set aside.

- Blanch the onions in boiling water for 2 minutes; drain and let cool to the touch. Slip off the outer skin. Using the same pan, melt the remaining 2 tablespoons butter over medium heat and sauté the onions until lightly browned and tender, about 3 minutes. Set aside and let cool, reserving the pan.

- To make the gravy: In the pan used to sauté the vegetables, melt the butter over medium heat. Stir in the flour and cook, stirring constantly, until the mixture begins to brown lightly, about 4 minutes. Gradually stir in the stock or broth. Cook, stirring frequently until thickened, at least 15 minutes. Season with salt and pepper.

- To assemble: Preheat the oven to 375°F. Line up the 4 bowls on a counter. Divide the chicken among the bowls, putting both white and dark meat into each bowl. Do the same with each vegetable. Pour about 1 cup gravy into each bowl. Gently mix the ingredients in each bowl with a spoon. Top each bowl with a pastry round, pressing the edges against the rim of the bowl. Brush the top of each round with the egg mixture. Place the bowls on a baking sheet and bake until the crusts are thoroughly browned and puffed, 20 to 25 minutes.

Note: You can also make a single large potpie. Simply cut the pastry crust to fit the baking dish or pan you want to use. As the piece of puff pastry will be bigger, it may need to cook an additional 10 to 15 minutes. When the pastry is nicely browned, the filling will be heated through.

Lomo Saltado
(Sautéed Beef with Fried Potatoes)

Chef/owner Martin Castillo's Peruvian restaurant first opened in a minute space in the Mission, but it attracted so many people intrigued with his versions of a relatively unfamiliar cuisine that it was soon moved to larger quarters. Castillo, who formerly cooked at Jardinère, is now working on his own cookbook of Peruvian food, which shows traces of such cuisines as Chinese, Spanish, Japanese, and Italian. Lomo saltado, for example, is a traditional Peruvian dish that includes soy sauce, an ingredient originally brought to Peru by Chinese immigrants.

Limón
524 Valencia Street (between Sixteenth and Seventeenth Streets)

10 ounces top sirloin, thinly sliced
Pinch of salt
Pinch of freshly ground pepper
Pinch of ground cumin
¹/₂ tablespoon minced garlic
2 tablespoons corn oil or canola oil, plus 1 cup
¹/₂ cup thinly sliced red onion
³/₄ teaspoon white wine vinegar
2 tablespoons soy sauce
1 tomato, cut into ¹/₂-inch-thick slices, then into quarters
1 russet baking potato
Minced fresh flat-leaf parsley for garnish
Steamed basmati rice for serving

● Put the beef in a bowl and add the salt, pepper, cumin, and garlic. Toss to coat well. In a large, heavy sauté pan or skillet, heat the 2 table-spoons oil over medium heat until shimmering. Add the beef and sauté for about 45 seconds, stirring constantly. Add the onion, vinegar, and soy sauce and sauté for 30 seconds. Add tomato and sauté for about 20 seconds. Remove from heat and set aside.

- Peel and cut the potato into ½-inch-thick sticks, like French fries. Soak in water to cover for 10 minutes. Drain, rinse under cold running water, and pat dry with paper towels.

- In a heavy, 6-inch-diameter saucepan, heat the 1 cup oil to 365°F. Add the potato and cook until golden brown, 3 to 4 minutes. Using a wire skimmer, transfer to paper towels to drain. Mix the potatoes with the beef. Garnish with parsley and serve at once, with steamed rice.

Grilled Lamb Skewers
with Couscous "404" and Spicy Chickpea Stew

SERVES 4 AS A MAIN COURSE

Luna Park is a big, boisterous restaurant with big-flavored, crowd-pleasing food. Ever since it opened, it's been jammed with people who love the menu that ranges around the world, from Vietnamese Chicken Salad with Grapefruit and Candied Walnuts to Moroccan-influenced dishes like these grilled lamb skewers, served with chickpea stew and a couscous named for a Moroccan bistro in Paris (Le Bistro 404). Reasonable prices, large portions, and such audience-participation foods as their Make-Your-Own-S'Mores and Goat Cheese Fondue guarantee that the crowds will keep coming back.

Luna Park
694 Valencia Street
(at Eighteenth Street)

Notes: To simplify this recipe, make just the couscous or the stew to serve with the skewers. Pomi-brand chopped tomatoes are sold in cartons in specialty markets and some supermarkets.

SAFFRON SAUCE
2 tablespoons olive oil
1 cup diced onions
1 tablespoon minced garlic
1 teaspoon saffron threads
2 tablespoons dry white wine
³/₄ cup Pomi tomatoes
2 tablespoons tomato paste
1 tablespoon fennel seeds, toasted and ground (see page 129)
1 tablespoon coriander seeds, toasted and ground (see page 129)
2 tablespoons harissa
6 cups vegetable broth
Kosher salt to taste

CHICKPEA STEW

1 ½ tablespoons olive oil

½ cup finely diced onions

2 cups (1 pound) dried chickpeas,
picked over, rinsed, and soaked overnight in water to cover

2 tablespoons dry white wine

½ cup Pomi tomatoes

¾ teaspoon cayenne pepper

1 ½ teaspoons ground chile de árbol

Salt to taste

4 cups vegetable broth

1 carrot, peeled and cut into ½-inch dice

SEASONING MIX

¼ cup kosher salt

2 teaspoon ground fennel

2 teaspoons ground coriander

½ teaspoon ground cumin

1 tablespoon minced fresh rosemary

½ tablespoon ground chile de árbol

¼ teaspoon freshly ground black pepper

1 pound boneless lamb sirloin, cut into 1-inch cubes

2 bell peppers, seeded, deribbed, and cut into 1-inch squares

2 Japanese eggplants, cut into ½-inch-thick crosswise slices

2 lamb sausages, cut into 1-inch-thick crosswise slices

1 red onion, cut into 8 wedges

8 cremini mushrooms

Olive oil for coating

1 cup couscous

1 cup water

1 tablespoon salt

Pinch of saffron threads

Cilantro sprigs, mint sprigs, and lemon wedges for garnish

- To make the sauce: In a large, heavy saucepan, heat the olive oil over medium heat and sauté the onions and garlic until translucent, about 3 minutes. Add the saffron, stir for a minute, then add the wine and cook to reduce until almost dry. Stir in the tomatoes, tomato paste, fennel, coriander, and harissa. Add the vegetable broth and bring to a boil. Reduce heat to a simmer and cook for 20 minutes. Season with salt and set aside.

- To make the stew: In a soup pot, heat the olive oil over medium heat and sauté the onions until translucent, about 3 minutes. Drain the chickpeas and add to the pot. Cook, stirring, for 3 minutes to remove the excess water. Add the wine and cook to reduce until almost dry. Add the tomatoes, cayenne, chili powder, and salt. Stir well. Add the vegetable broth and cook, uncovered, until the beans are tender, about 2 hours, adding water if necessary. Add the carrot and simmer until tender, about 20 minutes; add water if necessary. The finished stew should be sticky and relatively dry.

- Soak 8 long wooden skewers in water for 30 minutes. Prepare a hot fire in a charcoal grill or preheat a gas grill to high. To make the seasoning mix: Combine all the ingredients in a medium bowl and stir until blended. In a large bowl, combine the lamb, vegetables, and oil and toss to coat. Sprinkle on the seasoning mix and toss again to coat evenly.

- Alternately thread the lamb on the skewers with the bell peppers, eggplants, sausages, onion, and mushrooms. Grill until browned on all sides, turning frequently, for about 5 minutes for medium-rare.

- Put the couscous in a bowl and stir in the boiling water. Cover and let stand for 15 minutes.

- Reheat the saffron sauce and add enough to the chickpea stew to make it moist. Serve in warmed earthenware Spanish casserole dishes, with a mound of couscous in the center, the stew poured around the couscous, and the skewers crisscrossed on top of the couscous. Garnish with the cilantro and mint and the lemon wedges.

Balsamic-Glazed Grilled Salmon

with Mashed Potatoes, Corn Salad, and Oregano Butter

SERVES 4 AS A MAIN COURSE

Slow Club
2501 Mariposa Street
(at Hampshire)

The first of the hip restaurants to open in this area between Potrero Hill and the Mission, sometimes known as the Trans-Mission, the Slow Club is still drawing crowds to its post-industrial setting. The kitchen is so small that if you come by in the afternoon for an espresso and the excellent assorted cookie plate, you'll find the kitchen staff prepping food at the tiny service counter and a few of the tables. But the cuisine that chef Sante Salvoni turns out in his minute kitchen is as sophisticated and imaginative as if it came from a state-of-the-art facility. The following dish is a Slow Club favorite.

CORN SALAD

3 cups fresh white corn kernels (about 6 ears)
2 ripe tomatoes, seeded and diced (see page 12)
1 small red onion, diced
¹/₂ cup coarsely chopped fresh basil
¹/₄ cup extra-virgin olive oil

OREGANO BUTTER

6 tablespoons unsalted butter at room temperature
4 tablespoons coarsely chopped fresh oregano
Grated zest of 2 lemons
¹/₂ teaspoon salt
¹/₄ teaspoon freshly ground pepper

MASHED POTATOES

4 russet (baking) potatoes, peeled, quartered, and
rinsed in several changes of cold water
1 tablespoon salt, plus more to taste if needed
1 cup heavy cream
6 tablespoons unsalted butter
2 tablespoons sour cream (optional)
$\frac{1}{2}$ teaspoon freshly ground pepper

Four 6- to 8-ounce salmon fillets, skin and pinbones removed
Olive oil for coating
Salt and freshly ground pepper to taste
4 handfuls arugula

To make the salad: In a bowl, combine all the ingredients and toss together. Cover and set aside.

To make the oregano butter: In the bowl of a heavy-duty mixer fitted with the paddle attachment, combine all the ingredients and mix thoroughly. Or, cream the ingredients together with a wooden spoon. Set aside at room temperature.

To make the mashed potatoes: In a large pot, combine the potatoes, 1 tablespoon salt, and cold water to cover. and add cold water to cover. Bring to a boil over high heat, immediately reduce heat to a simmer, and cook until the potatoes are tender when pierced with a knife, 20 to 25 minutes.

While the potatoes are cooking, combine the cream and butter in a small saucepan and melt the butter over very low heat. Remove from heat, cover, and keep warm until the potatoes are cooked. If using a charcoal grill for the salmon, prepare a hot fire now.

When the potatoes are done, remove them from heat and drain them in a large colander. Return the potatoes to the pot and stir over low heat for a few seconds to dry up excess moisture. Turn off heat and mash the potatoes with a potato masher. Take care that there are no lumps in the potatoes at this point, as it becomes more difficult to achieve a smooth texture once the liquid is added. Add the warm cream mixture to the potatoes and whip them briskly with a whisk. Whisk in the sour cream, if using. Stir in the pepper. Taste and adjust the seasoning. Cover and keep warm in a low oven until the salmon is cooked.

To grill the salmon: Preheat the broiler or heat a grill pan over high heat, if using. Coat each fillet well with oil, sprinkle with salt and pepper, and place on the grill 4 to 6 inches from the coals, in the grill pan, or 2 to 3 inches from the heat source under the broiler. Grill or broil the fillets for 3 to 4 minutes per side, or until browned on the outside and still slightly translucent in the center. Just before removing the salmon from the grill, broiler, or pan, add 1 tablespoon oregano butter to the top of each fillet to allow the butter to begin melting. Transfer the salmon to a warmed platter and set aside.

To assemble: Spread the corn salad in a thin layer in the center of 4 warmed plates. Spoon 1 cup mashed potatoes on top of the salad and top each portion with 1 handful of arugula. Place the salmon directly on top of the arugula and serve immediately.

Dessert Crêpes
with Caramelized Pears
and Crème Fraîche

MAKES ABOUT TWELVE 10-INCH CRÊPES; SERVES 6

It's an anomaly—an old-fashioned Breton crêpe house in the heart of the Mission—but it's long been a steady favorite of people who are in love with the savory buckwheat and sweet wheat-flour crêpes served here. Even though the restaurant (whose name means "the old house" in Breton) has expanded into the space next door, it's almost always crowded. A wide range of crêpe fillings are available, from mushrooms in cream sauce to Nutella, and you can custom order them as well. The prices are so low, you can eat crêpes to your heart's content, washing them down with fermented or unfermented cider. And because these dessert crêpes can be made with summer or winter pears, you can prepare them year-round for special dinners, or when you must have crêpes but just can't make it out to Sixteenth Street.

Ti Couz
3108 Sixteenth Street (between Guerrero and Valencia)

SWEET CRÊPE BATTER
$1\frac{1}{2}$ cups water

$4\frac{1}{2}$ cups milk

1 egg

$1\frac{1}{2}$ teaspoons vanilla extract

$2\frac{1}{2}$ cups unbleached white flour (organic if possible)

$\frac{1}{2}$ cup whole-wheat flour (organic if possible)

1 cup sugar

$1\frac{1}{2}$ teaspoons salt

2 tablespoons salted butter at room temperature, for cooking crêpes

CARAMELIZED-PEAR FILLING

³⁄₄ cup sugar
8 Anjou, Bosc, or Barlett pears, cored, peeled, and cut into ¹⁄₂-inch dice
1 vanilla bean, split lengthwise
¹⁄₂ cup (1 stick) salted butter, cut into small pieces

4 tablespoons salted butter at room temperature, for reheating and filling crêpes
Crème fraîche (recipe follows)

● To make the crêpe batter: In a large bowl, whisk the water, milk, egg, and vanilla together until blended. Gradually whisk the flour, then the sugar and salt, into the liquid mixture to make a smooth, thin batter. Cover and refrigerate for at least 1 hour or, preferably, overnight or up to 24 hours.

● Heat a nonstick 10-inch crêpe pan or skillet over medium-high heat. Add about ¹⁄₂ teaspoon butter to the pan and spread the melted butter over the bottom of the pan. Pour ¹⁄₃ cup batter into the pan and quickly tilt the pan to swirl the batter and evenly coat the bottom and a little of the sides. Cook until lightly browned on the bottom, about 1 minute, then turn the crêpe and cook it until lightly browned on the second side, about 30 seconds. Place the crêpe on a plate and repeat the process, stacking the crêpes as you go, until all the batter is used. If the first crêpe is too thick, whisk in 1 tablespoon of water at a time until the batter is the consistency of cream and is just thick enough to coat a wooden spoon.

● To make the filling: In a medium nonstick sauté pan or skillet, melt the sugar over medium heat and cook until it turns golden brown. Add the diced pears. Reduce heat to low. Scrape the seeds from the vanilla bean into the mixture and add the pod. Cook, stirring frequently, until the pears are tender and have cooked down almost to a compote, about 5 minutes. Gradually stir in the butter; remove the vanilla bean pod. Set the filling aside and keep warm.

To fill the crêpes: Heat the crêpe pan over medium-low heat, spread about ½ teaspoon of the butter over the surface, and reheat a crêpe for a few seconds on each side. Put the crêpe "face-side" down (the first side it was cooked on) on a work surface. Spread about ½ teaspoon more butter over the crêpe, then spread 1 heaping tablespoonful of the filling in the center. Fold the crêpe into a square over the filling. Place on a warmed plate and put in a low oven. Repeat the process to heat and fill the remaining crêpes. Remove the plates from the oven, garnish each crêpe with crème fraîche, and serve at once.

Crème Fraîche: In a bowl, combine 1 cup heavy cream and ⅓ cup buttermilk and stir to blend. Cover and let sit in a warm place (60° to 85°F) until thickened, about 12 hours. Refrigerate until thickened further, about 12 hours longer.

Farmers' Markets and CSA Farms

The Ferry Plaza Farmers' Market (page 85) is the superstar of farmers' markets in San Francisco, but it's not the only game in town. Home cooks (and professional chefs) have several others to choose from: the Alemany Farmers' Market on Saturdays at 100 Alemany Boulevard (the largest and oldest farmers' market in the city; this is where the produce market moved when the Embarcadero Center was built), the Heart of the City Market just off Market Street at Seventh Street on Wednesdays and Sundays (with a preponderance of Asian vegetables and herbs), and the Noe Valley market on Saturdays (3861 Twenty-fourth Street, Noe Valley Ministry parking lot). Other farmers' markets pop up from late spring to early fall (during the non-rainy season) at the Cannery (Fridays and Saturdays), Fillmore Street at O'Farrell (Saturdays), Kaiser SF at 2425 Geary Boulevard (Wednesdays), Bayview Hunters Point at Third and Galvez Streets (Saturdays), and the Marina on Chestnut between Fillmore and Bay in the Marina Middle School parking lot (Saturdays). You may have to ask whether the produce at some markets is organic, and it might not be.

Another way to buy fresh organic produce is from a Community Supported Agriculture farm, like Live Power Farm in Covelo and Eatwell Farm in Winter. Baskets of whatever is in season that week are delivered right to your door, or a group of people may divide a large shipment among themselves and take turns delivering it. You will find yourself eating your nine servings (or more) of fruits and vegetables every day, and they will all be organic and just picked from the plant or dug from the earth.

Brined Pork Chops
with Red Sauerkraut
and Juniper Butter

SERVES 6 AS MAIN COURSE

Leslie Carr-Avalos, a former line cook at Universal, and her husband, Armando, a former busboy there, bought the thriving cafe in 2003 with business partner Wendy St. John and have continued it on its course as an outstanding site for great food. The Universal has never faltered since it opened as one of the first industrial-chic restaurants in SoMa. Chef/owner Carr-Avalos changes the menu every week. Here is one of her dishes, from California by way of the former Istria, once part of northern Italy, along with her comments:

Universal Café
2814 Nineteenth Street
(between Bryant and Harrison)

"This is a simple but impressive preparation. The pork chops, juniper butter, and sauerkraut can all be prepared three days ahead. *Please* cook the pork chops medium-rare or medium; if guests are uncomfortable with the pinkness of the meat, explain to them that brined meats often take on a pink hue and that, especially if you offer organic meats, the best temperature to enjoy the full flavor of a beautiful brined pork chop is indeed medium-rare or medium! Potato purée and an arugula salad are a nice accompaniment to this dish."

Notes: You will need to start this dish one day before serving. Any leftover sauerkraut makes a great Reuben sandwich. If you prefer to use smaller chops, the brining time should be cut back. A 6-ounce pork chop, for example, will be brined in about 6 hours.

BRINE
1 gallon water
$^1/_2$ cup salt
$^1/_3$ cup sugar
2 bay leaves, preferably fresh, coarsely chopped

5 or 6 peppercorns
4 juniper berries
¹/₂ teaspoon red pepper flakes
3 garlic cloves
3 thyme sprigs

Six 10- to 12-ounce naturally raised pork chops with bone

RED SAUERKRAUT (BLAUKRAUT)

1 red onion, thinly sliced
2 pounds red cabbage, cored and thinly slice (about 6 cups)
3 fresh sage leaves
3 thyme sprigs
3 garlic cloves
2 cups red wine vinegar
2 tablespoons salt
2 tablespoons sugar

JUNIPER BUTTER

¹/₂ cup (1 stick) unsalted butter at room temperature
3 juniper berries, crushed in a mortar
1 teaspoon minced lemon zest
1 teaspoon minced shallot
Sea salt and freshly cracked pepper to taste

Sea salt and freshly cracked pepper to taste
Olive oil or peanut oil for cooking
Sage sprigs for garnish

- One to three days before serving, make the brine: Put the water in a stainless-steel stockpot and add all the remaining brine ingredients. Bring to a boil, then turn off heat and let cool completely. Add the pork chops, cover, and refrigerate for 24 hours.

- Remove the pork chops from the brine and pat dry with paper towels. Cover and refrigerate until needed.

- One to three days before serving, make the sauerkraut: In a large non-reactive saucepan, combine all the ingredients. Cover, bring to a boil, and reduce heat to a simmer. Cook for about 45 minutes, stirring frequently, until the cabbage is quite tender. Let cool, cover, and refrigerate overnight.

- One to three days before serving, make the juniper butter: In a small bowl, combine all the ingredients and mix well.

- On the day of serving, take the pork chops and juniper butter out of the refrigerator. Season the pork chops with salt and pepper. Let the chops and the butter stand at room temperature for at least 30 minutes.

- Heat a large grill pan over high heat for about 3 minutes. Coat the pan with oil, using paper towels. Brown the pork chops for about 5 minutes on each side for medium-rare or 8 minutes on each side for medium. Transfer the chops to a rack set on a platter. Place a dollop of juniper butter on each chop. Tent the chops loosely with aluminum foil and let them rest for about 5 minutes.

- Meanwhile, reheat the sauerkraut. Divide the sauerkraut among warmed plates. Top each mound of sauerkraut with a pork chop and spoon the juices from the platter around the plate. Add a little more juniper butter to the top of each pork chop, garnish with a sage sprig, and serve.

Upper Market / The Castro / Noe Valley

Chow

Firefly

Incanto

Ristorante Bacco

Tallula

2223 Market Street

THE WESTERN END OF MARKET STREET starts its slow rise toward Twin Peaks around Twelfth Street, the beginning of the Upper Market neighborhood, home to antiques stores and several sophisticated urban restaurants. On the expanse leading toward Castro Street (which can be reached by taking a vintage streetcar on the Market Street F-line), the broad thoroughfare is marked down its center with huge Canary palms, fitting symbols for a neighborhood of ornate Victorian houses. The shops and eating places along the

street, though, range from been-here-forever to retro, and from counterculture sixties-leftovers to the postmodern. Here you'll find a *real* diner (It's Tops), unchanged since the fifties, along with new diners in the Castro, styled to look old. Some of the best eating places on Upper Market have the open, sleek ambiance of New York restaurants (Zuni Cafe, Mecca), while others offer up comfort food in a homey atmosphere (Chow, Home). BRANCHING OFF MARKET STREET and leading up Liberty Hill, Castro Street is the central shopping throroughfare of the Castro district and the yellow brick road for generations of gay men all over the United States and the world. Tourists come from everywhere to visit this street of men in pairs and in groups. But the Castro is also a neighborhood of mixed gay and straight people and families, living in beautifully kept Victorians, shopping at Cliff's Hardware (one of the city's great stores), going to the gorgeously maintained Castro Theater with its live organ accompaniment, and dining in the small restaurants that sprinkle the area. ABOVE THE CASTRO REARS LIBERTY HILL, crisscrossed by winding streets and lined with more beautiful old homes. When you drive down the southern side of this ridge, you'll pass one of the city's two steepest streets (Twenty-second Street, between Church and Vicksburg) and descend into Noe Valley, a pleasant casual neighborhood that seems as if it's been airlifted out of Marin County, except that many more of the houses are Victorians, Queen Annes, Edwardians, and Craftsman cottages. The Valley's mainline is Twenty-fourth Street, which loses its Latin flavor on its journey out of the Mission to become the main street of this low-key, laid-back village. ONCE, BOTH THE CASTRO AND NOE VALLEY (as well as the Haight Street neighborhood) were part of a huge land grant belonging to José Noe, the last Mexican alcade, or mayor, of Yerba Buena (he is buried in the little cemetery at Mission Dolores). In 1887, the Castro (then known as Eureka Valley, after Eureka Street, at that time the main road to the Peninsula) was made accessible to development thanks to the new Market Street cable car system. Eventually, the cable cars crested the high ridge into Noe Valley, until then the site of dairies and truck farms. Today, it's a neighborhood of singles and young families, with a row of interesting shops and a full complement of small, homey restaurants, like Miss Millie's, Ristorante Bacco, and Firefly. THE EARLIEST RESIDENTS OF BOTH THE CASTRO AND NOE VALLEY WERE IRISH, German, and Scandinavian immigrants. Slowly, almost all traces of them disappeared; now, with the lamented departure of Speckmann's, only one German market remains in Noe Valley: Lehr's German Specialties at 1581 Church Street. It features all kinds of goods from Germany, including baking tools, and foods like Black Forest and Westphalian hams. This is the place to look for wooden cookie molds and Bundt pans for baking, as well as marzipan and other sweets from the Old Country. NOE VALLEY ALSO BOASTS ONE OF THE CITY'S BEST CHEESE STORES (the 24th Street Cheese Company, at 3893 Twenty-fourth Street), and one of its best

OTHER NEIGHBORHOOD STARS

Destino

Eric's

Chloe's

Home

Ma Tante Sumi

Mecca

Miss Millie's

Tita's

Zuni Cafe

bakeries, the Noe Valley Bakery (4073 Twenty-fourth Street). Since the bakery stopped selling their breads to other stores because they wanted to control the quality by making smaller batches, this is the only location other than the Ferry Plaza Farmers' Market where you can buy their outrageously fruit-laden fig bread, raisin bread, and—the most over-the-top—cherry-chocolate bread, studded with huge dark sweet cherries and big chunks of bittersweet chocolate. Sliced, toasted, and spread with crème fraîche or mascarpone, this loaf makes a sybaritic breakfast. Or, you could just go to Noe Valley for breakfast or brunch—this placid sunny neighborhood is the perfect destination for a lazy Sunday-morning meal, as well as an early weekend supper.

Coconut Cream Pie

SERVES 6 TO 8

This homey dessert is typical of the satisfying food at Chow, a casual, hugely popular restaurant on the edge of the Castro. As with any true neighborhood restaurant in San Francisco, you will find a diverse crowd of all ages, races, and sexual persuasions here, enjoying the large servings of robust pastas, good soups and salads, and classic American desserts at reasonable prices that have made this place such a hit.

Chow
*215 Church Street
(at Market)*

FILLING

³/₄ cup granulated sugar
¹/₃ cup cornstarch
3 cups milk
4 egg yolks, lightly beaten
1 tablespoon butter
2 teaspoons vanilla extract
Pinch of salt
One 9-inch pie crust (recipe follows)

TOPPING

1 cup shredded coconut
1 cup heavy cream
1 teaspoon vanilla extract
1 to 2 tablespoons sifted confectioners' sugar

To make the filling: In a heavy, medium saucepan, stir the sugar and cornstarch together, then gradually stir in the milk until smooth. Bring to a boil over medium heat, then cook, stirring, for 2 minutes. Stir a large spoonful of this mixture into the egg yolks, then return this mixture to the pan and cook over medium heat, stirring, until thickened, about 2 minutes. Stir in the butter, vanilla, and salt. Remove from heat. Let cool to room temperature. Pour the pudding into the pie shell and refrigerate for at least 1 hour but preferably not more than 2 or 3 hours (so the crust will not get soggy).

To make the topping: Preheat the oven to 350°F. Spread the coconut out in a rimmed baking sheet (jelly-roll pan). Toast, stirring frequently, until golden brown, 8 to 10 minutes.

In a deep bowl, combine the cream, vanilla, and confectioners' sugar. Beat with a whisk until stiff peaks form. Spread the whipped cream over the pie. Sprinkle the toasted coconut on top. Cut into wedges to serve.

Pie Crust

MAKES ONE 9-INCH CRUST

$1^{1}/_{2}$ cups unbleached all-purpose flour
1 tablespoon sugar
$^{1}/_{2}$ teaspoon salt
$^{1}/_{2}$ cup (1 stick) cold unsalted butter, cut into small pieces
4 tablespoons cold water

In a medium bowl, stir the flour, sugar, and salt together. Add the butter. Using a pastry cutter, 2 dinner knives, or your fingers, cut the butter into the flour mixture until it forms coarse crumbs. Using a fork, gradually stir in the water until all the crumbs are moistened. Gather the mixture into a ball. On a lightly floured board, form the dough into a disk. Place it in a self-sealing plastic bag and refrigerate for at least 30 minutes or up to 2 hours.

Preheat the oven to 400°F. Roll the dough out on the floured board to a round about ⅛ thick. Trim to an 11-inch round. Fit the round into a 9-inch pie pan. Fold the edges under and crimp to make a border. Prick the surface of the pastry all over with a fork. Line the pastry with a large square of aluminum foil and fill the foil with dried beans, rice, or pie weights.

Bake on the middle rack of the oven until set, about 10 minutes. Remove from the oven, remove the foil and its contents, and return the pastry to the oven to bake until golden brown, about 10 more minutes. Transfer to a wire rack and let cool completely.

Grilled Fuyu Persimmon and Red Oak Leaf Lettuce Salad
with Candied Pecans

SERVES 4 AS A FIRST COURSE

A giant firefly blinks and glows over the door in the relative darkness of this residential block, leading you to welcoming tables and eclectic dishes. The flavors are drawn from cuisines around the globe, but the overall effect is to make you feel at home in a venue dedicated to good food and comfortable dining. The menu changes with the season, and your choices can range from fried chicken with mashed potatoes, collard greens, and buttermilk biscuits to sesame-crusted tofu with sake-marinated Japanese eggplant. Here is a vivid salad from one of their fall menus.

Firefly
4288 Twenty-fourth Street
(between Diamond and Douglass)

WHITE BALSAMIC–HONEY VINAIGRETTE

¹/₂ teaspoon Dijon mustard
1 tablespoon honey
2 tablespoons white balsamic vinegar
Salt and freshly ground pepper to taste
6 tablespoons olive oil

2 firm, crisp Fuyu persimmons, cored
1 tablespoon olive oil
Salt and freshly ground pepper to taste
¹/₄ cup pecans
Canola oil for deep-frying
¹/₄ teaspoon cayenne pepper mixed with 1 tablespoon sifted confectioners' sugar
Leaves from 4 small heads red oak leaf lettuce
Pomegranate seeds for garnish

In a small bowl, whisk all the ingredients for the vinaigrette together until emulsified. Set aside.

Preheat a grill pan or large cast-iron skillet over medium-high heat. Cut the persimmons into ¼-inch-thick crosswise slices. Coat the slices with olive oil. Sprinkle with salt and pepper. Place on the grill pan or in the skillet and cook for about 1 minute on each side, or until lightly browned. Set aside.

Blanch the pecans in a saucepan of boiling water for 2 minutes. Drain well and dry on paper towels. In a medium, heavy skillet, heat 1 inch of the oil until the surface shimmers. Add the pecans and deep-fry for 1 minute. Using a wire-mesh skimmer, transfer the pecans to paper towels to drain. Toss in the cayenne mixture to coat.

Toss the lettuce leaves and persimmon slices in the vinaigrette. Divide among 4 salad plates and garnish with the pecans and pomegranate seeds.

Note: We have simplified Firefly's presentation of this dish.

Shaved Squash and Ricotta Bruschetta

SERVES 4 AS A FIRST COURSE

A large, slightly formal, ambitious restaurant in the tradition of the East Bay's Oliveto, Incanto serves authentic Italian dishes as well as Italian-influenced California cuisine. You may have to ask your server to explain some of the words on the menu here, as the kitchen loves to seek out unusual ingredients and preparations. They make their own cured Italian meats here, including lardo and prosciutto, and are dedicated to serving full-flavored food in an elegant setting.

Incanto
1550 Church Street
(at Duncan)

4 slices Italian bread
Extra-virgin olive oil for brushing, plus 4 tablespoons
2 unpeeled summer squash, such as yellow crookneck
Kosher or sea salt and coarsely ground pepper to taste
Juice of 2 lemons
Leaves from 4 basil sprigs
1 garlic clove, halved
1 cup whole-milk ricotta cheese, preferably Bellwether

- Heat a grill pan over high heat. Brush both sides of the bread slices with olive oil and grill until golden brown with darker grill marks, 1 to 2 minutes on each side. Remove from heat and set aside.

- With a mandoline or chef's knife, cut the squash into paper-thin slices lengthwise, horizontally, and diagonally to obtain different sizes and shapes. Place in a glass or ceramic bowl, season with salt and pepper, the lemon juice, and 2 tablespoons of the olive oil. Let stand for 5 minutes. Tear the basil leaves into pieces, add to the bowl, and toss.

- To serve: Rub the warm grilled bread with the cut side of the garlic clove, spread with a layer of ricotta, season with salt and pepper to taste, then dress the top with the squash slices. Cut the bread diagonally and serve drizzled with the remaining 2 tablespoons olive oil.

Pappardelle di Zafferano
con Salsa di Agnello
(Saffron Pappardelle with Lamb Sauce)

SERVES 6 AS A MAIN COURSE

Ristorante Bacco
737 Diamond Street
(between Elizabeth and
Twenty-fourth Streets

Step inside the velvet curtain and you're embraced by an Italian ambiance. This quiet restaurant with a restrained decor (even though it's named after Bacchus, the god of wine) has a charming Italian staff serving beautifully cooked food. The risotto is always excellent, as is this pasta of brilliant yellow wide noodles topped with a dark, deeply flavored lamb sauce. If you don't have time to make your own pasta, buy 1½ pounds of fresh pasta in sheets and cut your own pappardelle; most pasta shops carry saffron pasta.

LAMB SAUCE
½ cup olive oil
6 garlic cloves, minced
1 tablespoon minced fresh rosemary
1 pound lamb shoulder, cut into 1-inch cubes
Salt and freshly ground pepper to taste
1½ cups dry red wine
32 ounces canned diced Italian tomatoes
3 tablespoons tomato paste
2 cups chicken stock or canned low-salt chicken broth

SAFFRON PAPPARDELLE
1½ cups plus 2 tablespoons semolina flour
1½ cups unbleached all-purpose flour, plus more as needed
Pinch of salt
4 eggs
1 teaspoon saffron threads dissolved in 2 tablespoons water

Grated Parmesan cheese for serving

To make the sauce: In a large, heavy saucepan over medium heat, heat ¼ cup of the oil and sauté the garlic until golden. Stir in the rosemary; remove from heat and set aside.

Season the lamb with salt and pepper. In a large skillet, heat the remaining ¼ cup olive oil over high heat and sauté the lamb until browned on all sides, about 5 minutes. Add the red wine and cook, stirring to scrape up the browned bits from the bottom of the pan, for 3 or 4 minutes. Remove from heat and add the lamb and the pan liquid to the pan containing the rosemary and garlic. Stir in the tomatoes, tomato paste, and 1½ cups of the stock or broth. Bring to a simmer over low heat and cook, uncovered, stirring occasionally and adding the remaining ½ cup stock or broth as needed, until the lamb is very tender, about 2½ hours. Cover and set aside if using now, or let cool, then cover and refrigerate if making ahead.

Meanwhile, to make the pasta: In a bowl, stir the semolina flour, the 1½ cups all-purpose flour, and the salt together. Mound the flour mixture on a work surface. Form a well in the center of the mound. Break the eggs into the well. Add the saffron mixture to the well. Using a fork, beat the eggs until blended. Using your other hand, begin pushing some of the flour over into the eggs while mixing the flour into the eggs with the fork. Continue to do this until all but ½ cup or so of the flour has been added. Using your hands, work the mixture together to make a smooth dough, adding the reserved flour if the dough is too sticky. Wash and dry your hands, then stick your thumb into the center of the dough to see if it comes out clean. If not, dust the dough with a little more flour and work it into the dough.

Scrape the work surface clean of all flour and dough. Knead the dough, pressing it with the heel of your hand and turning it a half-turn each time, until the dough is silky smooth, about 8 minutes. Wrap the dough tightly in plastic wrap and let rest for 1 hour.

Set a pasta machine on its widest setting. Line a work surface with clean kitchen towels. Cut the dough into 12 pieces. Flatten one ball of dough and feed it through the machine. Fold each side of the dough over to make a piece one third as big and feed this piece through again. Repeat this process 2 or 3 times, then lay the rolled pasta out on a towel. Repeat to roll the remaining balls of dough.

Narrow the setting of the pasta machine by one notch and roll each pasta sheet through in turn. Continue to narrow the setting and roll the pasta sheets until the pasta is very thin. On a pastry board, roll a sheet of pasta into a cylinder and cut it into 1-inch-wide strips. Unroll the strips and spread them out on the towels. Repeat with the remaining pasta.

When ready to serve, reheat the sauce if necessary. Cook the pasta in a large pot of salted boiling water until al dente, about 2 minutes. Drain. Add to the sauce and toss to coat well. Divide among warmed individual pasta bowls and serve at once, with the Parmesan alongside for adding at the table.

Fennel-Crusted Golden Trout

SERVES 4 AS A FIRST COURSE, 2 AS A MAIN COURSE

The food at Tallula is as quirky and original as the rooms of the restaurant, which are small, stacked, and accessed by narrow, winding stairways. The cuisine combines a French sensibility with Indian spices and techniques, and the dishes are always both surprising and pleasing. Chef/owner Harveen Khera credits her sommelier, Duke Annibale, with helping her develop this dish of California golden trout stuffed with sprouted mung beans and flavored with raisins, ginger, and fennel. If serving it as a main course, accompany it with saffron rice and spinach.

Tallula
4280 Eighteenth Street (between Collingwood and Diamond)

$1/3$ cup green mung beans, or $1/4$ cup finely diced zucchini

VINAIGRETTE

$1/2$ fennel bulb, trimmed, cored, and finely diced
$1/2$ tablespoon minced shallot
$1/2$ teaspoon lemon zest
1 teaspoon minced fresh ginger
$1/2$ tablespoon fennel seeds, toasted (see page 129)
Salt to taste
1 tablespoon white wine vinegar
$1/4$ cup olive oil
$1/4$ cup golden raisins, soaked in water to cover for 30 minutes, then drained

1 whole golden or rainbow trout (12 to 16 ounces), boned
$1/4$ teaspoon grated fresh ginger
$1/2$ teaspoon grapeseed oil
Salt to taste
$1/4$ teaspoon fennel seeds
Splash of water

To sprout the mung beans, if using: Pick over and rinse the beans. Spread them in a small baking dish and add water to cover by ¼ inch. Place in an area with a temperature of at least 65°F. Let stand until they sprout, about 20 hours. Rinse the beans and blanch them in boiling water for 1 minute. Transfer to cold water, then drain and dry on paper towels. Set aside.

To make the vinaigrette: In a small bowl, combine all the ingredients except for the oil and raisins. Gradually whisk in the oil, then stir in the raisins. Taste and adjust the seasoning.

Preheat the oven to 350°F. Rinse the trout and clip off the fins. Rub the inside of the fish with the ginger and season with salt. Brush the outside of the fish with ¼ teaspoon of the oil and sprinkle with salt and fennel seeds. In a large ovenproof sauté pan or skillet, heat the remaining ¼ teaspoon oil over medium heat for 30 seconds. Gently take the fish, supporting the head and tail, and lay it in the pan. Cook for 1 minute. Give the pan a quick jiggle, and you will know it is time to flip when the fish moves freely. Confidently approach the fish from the back and, using a metal spatula (preferably a fish spatula), flip it over. Transfer the pan to the oven and cook for 5 minutes.

Meanwhile, put the sprouted mung beans or the zucchini in a small sauté pan or skillet and add the splash of water and a pinch of salt. Warm over medium heat for a minute; set aside.

Remove the pan from the oven and fill the fish with three fourths of the mung beans or zucchini. Return the fish to the oven and cook until opaque throughout, 5 to 6 minutes. Meanwhile, return the remaining mung beans or zucchini to medium heat and gently stir in ½ cup of the vinaigrette. Cook to heat through, about 2 minutes. Remove the fish from the oven and transfer to a warmed platter. Pour the vinaigrette around and over the fish. Serve at once.

Wine Suggestions: Sommelier Duke Annibale suggests a Sula Chenin Blanc 2003 from Nashik, India, or Thomas Fogarty Gewürztraminer 2002 from Monterey, California; on a warm day, serve with a rosé such as Les Devants de la Bonneliere 2002 from Touraine, France.

Spring Vegetable Potpies
with Parmesan Crust
and Creamy Herb Gravy

SERVES 6 AS A MAIN COURSE

The name of the restaurant is its street address on Market, where it combines people-watching and chef Melinda Randolph's "American bistro" cuisine, typified by these vegetarian potpies. Like the rest of the dishes on the menu, they're comforting and homey, but every component is made with care and great attention to achieving the best flavor.

2223 Market Street
2223 Market Street
(between Noe and Sanchez)

Note: You can save some time in making this dish by using canned vegetable broth, but remember this recipe for vegetable stock, as it is remarkably good.

HERBED VEGETABLE STOCK
2 tablespoons unsalted butter

2 tablespoons olive oil

6 large carrots, peeled and chopped (trimmings reserved)

1 bunch large leeks (white part only), sliced (trimmings reserved)

4 yellow onions, sliced (trimmings reserved)

$\frac{1}{2}$ cup dry white wine

3 bay leaves

$\frac{1}{2}$ bunch each thyme and parsley, chopped (stems included)

6 peppercorns

3 quarts water

CREAMY HERB GRAVY

¹/₂ cup (1 stick) unsalted butter
1 cup unbleached all-purpose flour
Herbed Vegetable Stock, above
1 cup heavy cream
1 teaspoon crumbled dried thyme
1 teaspoon crumbled dried parsley
Salt and freshly ground pepper to taste

SPRING VEGETABLES

1 large bunch asparagus, trimmed and diced
1 pound English peas, shelled (1 cup)
1 pound Blue Lake green beans, trimmed and diced
6 carrots, peeled and diced
1 pound cremini mushrooms, quartered (optional)
8 Yukon Gold potatoes, peeled and diced
2 bunches spring onions (white bulbs only), trimmed and quartered
3 tablespoons olive oil
1 teaspoon salt
1 teaspoon freshly ground pepper
Up to 2 cups other seasonal vegetables (¹/₂ cup each), such as shelled and peeled
fava beans, sliced baby zucchini, baby spinach leaves

PARMESAN CRUST

1 package frozen puff pastry, thawed
2 eggs, beaten with 1 tablespoon water
¹/₄ cup grated Parmesan cheese

To make the vegetable stock: In a medium, heavy stockpot, melt the butter with the olive oil over medium-high heat. Add the carrots, leeks, and onions and sauté until golden brown, 8 to 10 minutes. Add the white wine and stir to scrape up any browned bits from the bottom of the pan. Continue to cook, stirring, until the liquid is reduced by half. Add the bay leaf, thyme, parsley, peppercorns, and water and bring to a simmer. Reduce heat to low and continue to simmer for 1 hour, or until the stock has a good flavor.

- To make the gravy: In a medium, heavy sauté pan or skillet, melt the butter over medium-high heat without browning it. Stir in the flour. Cook, stirring constantly, to make a golden brown roux. Remove from heat and let cool.

- Strain the vegetable stock into a large, heavy saucepan. Stir in the cream, thyme, and parsley and bring to a low simmer. Whisk in small amounts of the roux, incorporating each addition fully before adding the next one, until the liquid thickens to the consistency of gravy. Simmer for 10 to 15 minutes. Strain through a fine-meshed sieve. Let cool. Taste and adjust the seasoning.

- To cook the vegetables: Preheat the oven to 400°F. Cook the asparagus, peas, and green beans separately in salted simmering water for 5 minutes. Drain and rinse with cold water until cool to the touch; set aside. Put the carrots, mushrooms (if using), potatoes, spring onions, and any other nongreen vegetables in a bowl and toss with the olive oil, salt, and pepper. Spread evenly on a baking sheet and roast in the oven for about 20 minutes, or until the vegetables are golden brown and tender. Remove from the oven and let cool. Combine all the vegetables and set aside.

- To make the crust: Choose six 2-cup ramekins. Cut the pastry into rounds with a diameter ½ inch greater than the diameter of the ramekins. Place the rounds on waxed paper or parchment paper and set aside.

- To assemble: Preheat the oven to 375°F. Divide the vegetable mixture among the ramekins. Cover the vegetables with just enough gravy so that you can still see them. Place a pastry round on top of each ramekin and crimp the pastry around the edges of the ramekin. Brush each pastry top with a small amount of the egg mixture. Sprinkle with grated Parmesan. Bake until golden brown, about 20 minutes. Serve at once.

The Haight / Cole Valley

Cha Cha Cha

Eos Restaurant and Wine Bar

Indian Oven

Rnm

Thep Phanom Thai Cuisine

Zazie

HAIGHT STREET RUNS IN A STRAIGHT SHOT from Market Street to Golden Gate Park; four blocks from the park it crosses Ashbury, the epicenter of the hippie movement in the late sixties. This neighborhood of large, beautiful Vic-

torian houses was originally a wealthy residential area. In 1928, a streetcar tunnel under Buena Vista Park helped to open up development in the Sunset District, and many families moved out of the Haight, leaving the big houses to be subdivided into apartments for an ethnic mixture of immigrants. In the late forties, students moved in to be near San Francisco State College; many of them stayed on after the school moved to its present location in 1952 (where it was eventually renamed San Francisco State University), because of the low rents. Soon came an influx of artists and writers, fleeing the rising rents of North Beach, which had become famous as the home of the Beats. Add drugs and an unpopular foreign war to the mixture, and all the elements were present for an explosion of revolution, self-expression, self-indulgence, and eventual self-destruction. ⸺ REMNANTS OF THE SIXTIES AND THE SUMMER OF LOVE ARE EVERYWHERE in the Haight, from head shops to tie-dyed T-shirts. Kids from all over are drawn to the neighborhood by the tattoo and piercing shops, the vintage-record stores, and the ghosts of Janis and Jerry. Many flock here to drop out of society, and the sidewalks are sometimes clogged with a profusion of street people, both young and old. At the same time, the Haight is a neighborhood of single people and young families who have refurbished the spacious old houses and are working to maintain Haight Street as a shopping area for both residents and tourists. The stores are an eclectic mix, from upscale bohemian to Gen-X grunge, and the food you can buy in the restaurants is equally diverse, ranging from hush puppies (Kate's Kitchen) to fried plantains (Cha Cha Cha) to Ethiopian flat bread (Axum Cafe). ⟶ ON COLE STREET, running perpendicular to Haight, is Cole Valley, one of San Francisco's most charming secret neighborhoods. This small area is right on the edge of the fog belt, so the air is sometimes clouded. The famed Tassajara Bakery, which had long lured customers here, closed a few years ago to the dismay of the neighborhood, but Pascal Rigo, of Bay Bread Boulangerie, extended his French empire to include this part of town, and the bakery shelves are once again filled with baguettes and fruit tarts and tempting cakes. Say Cheese, with a vast selection of cheeses and specialty foods, is here as well, as are several good, small restaurants and shops along Cole, surrounded by Victorian houses on streets with large trees and lots of flowers. Almost unknown to tourists, Cole Valley is a little oasis of quietude just off the sometimes-frantic Upper Haight. ⟶ THE LOWER

OTHER
NEIGHBORHOOD
STARS

Alamo Square

Axum Cafe

Kate's Kitchen

Memphis Minnie's

Rosamunde Sausage
  Grill

HAIGHT, which runs from Baker to Market, is a little rawer and lower in profile than the Upper Haight. Here, the tiny, funky shops are reminiscent of places in the East Village, while the Upper Haight is more like some parts of Greenwich Village. Most tourists and street youths focus on the Upper Haight, leaving the Lower to its residents and food-lovers attracted to such unassuming but excellent restaurants as Indian Oven and Thep Phanom.

Grilled Corn Salad

SERVES 4 TO 6 AS A FIRST COURSE

Cha Cha Cha

*1801 Haight Street
(at Shrader)*

Years ahead of the current Latin explosion, Cha Cha Cha opened on Upper Haight in 1985 and gradually evolved into a packed restaurant serving pan-Caribbean food, featuring elaborate Santería altars, and resounding to recorded Latin music. There are no reservations, the line is out the door, and chef Bill Higgins's Island soul food is as fun and colorful as the decor. This many-hued and lively flavored salad is one example; serve for a first course, or delete the lettuce leaves and serve as a side dish with grilled pork, ham, chicken, or turkey.

12 fresh ears yellow corn, ends cut off but husks left on
1 bunch cilantro, stemmed and chopped
2 red bell peppers, seeded, deribbed, and finely diced
2 poblano chilies, seeded, deribbed, and finely diced
3 red onions, finely diced
$^1/_2$ to 1 teaspoon cayenne pepper, depending on your tolerance for heat
A generous amount of freshly ground black pepper
Salt to taste
Juice of 4 lemons
$^1/_2$ cup rice vinegar
1 cup olive oil
Leaves from 1 head of red leaf lettuce

Prepare a medium-hot fire in a charcoal grill or preheat a gas grill to medium. Grill the corn, turning it occasionally, until the husks are charred black on all sides, 15 to 20 minutes. Transfer to a baking sheet and let cool to the touch.

Using a large knife, cut the kernels off the cobs; the corn should not be burned, but it should be tender and have some char marks. In a large bowl, combine the corn kernels and all the remaining ingredients except the lettuce leaves. Toss to blend. Serve on a bed of lettuce leaves.

Wok-Roasted Mussels
with Asian Aromatics

SERVES 4 AS A FIRST COURSE, 2 AS A MAIN COURSE

For ten years, chef/owner Arnold Eric Wong's chic corner restaurant has been luring people from the neighborhood and all over town to dine on his sophisticated Asian-fusion cuisine. One of the city's best and most consistently interesting eating places, Eos is always crowded and always worth a visit; the restaurant's next-door wine bar is a great amenity when waiting for your table. These wok-roasted mussels are a prime example of the food at Eos. At the restaurant, they are served as a first course, but at home you may want to serve them as a main course, along with steamed jasmine rice and a green vegetable.

Eos Restaurant and Wine Bar
901 Cole Street (at Carl)

6 tablespoons grapeseed or peanut oil

8 large garlic cloves, smashed

3 red Thai bird chilies, halved lengthwise,
or $\frac{1}{2}$ small red jalapeño chili, thinly sliced

One 2-inch piece fresh ginger, peeled and thinly sliced

1-inch piece fresh galangal, peeled and thinly sliced

1 lemongrass stalk (white part only),
peeled, crushed, and cut into four 2-inch sections

2 pounds Prince Edward Island black mussels, scrubbed and debearded

Leaves from 2 kaffir lime leaf sprigs

2 teaspoons sea salt

1 teaspoon coarsely cracked pepper

$\frac{1}{2}$ cup dry white wine

Slices of crusty bread, grilled or toasted

In a large wok, sauté pan, or cast-iron skillet, heat the oil over high heat until it just begins to smoke. Quickly add the garlic, chilies, ginger, galangal, and lemongrass to the pan and stir-fry until the garlic begins to turn golden, 1 to 2 minutes. Add the mussels. Toss or flip the mussels with a wok shovel or a large spoon, allowing them to reach the bottom of the pan and the garlic and chilies to come to the top.

Reduce the heat to medium and cook, uncovered, until the mussels just begin to open; watch carefully, as this can take as little as 2 minutes, though some mussels will take longer. Add the lime sprigs and season with salt and pepper. Stir in the white wine, scraping the bottom of the pan, and stir-fry for another minute or two, or until the wine has slightly reduced and the mussels have fully opened; they will have pulled away from the shell and will look plump and moist. Transfer the mussels and pan broth from the pan to large warmed bowls and serve with the grilled or toasted bread for dipping.

Saag Aloo

(Spinach and Potatoes with Onion, Ginger, and Garlic)

SERVES 4 AS A MAIN COURSE, 6 TO 8 AS A SIDE DISH

A bright, airy restaurant with uncluttered decor and an open kitchen, Indian Oven serves well-prepared, reasonably priced northern Indian food. Lovers of this fragrant, complex cuisine know to come here for the tandoori dishes and the samosas, as well as the vegetarian dishes that India excels in. This dish of spinach and potatoes, cooked with a mixture of aromatic spices, is one of them. Serve it as a main course for your vegetarian friends, or as a side dish with roasted or grilled meat, fish, or chicken.

Indian Oven
233 Fillmore Street
(between Haight and Waller)

3 boiling potatoes (about 3 inches in diameter),
peeled and cut into $^1/_2$-inch chunks
3 garlic cloves
Three 1-inch pieces fresh ginger, peeled
2 tablespoons canola oil
1 onion (about 3 inches in diameter), finely chopped
2 Roma (plum) tomatoes, finely chopped
$^1/_2$ teaspoon curry powder
$^1/_4$ teaspoon cayenne pepper
$^1/_4$ teaspoon ground coriander
$^1/_4$ teaspoon ground cumin
$^1/_2$ teaspoon salt
$^1/_2$ cup water, plus more as needed
2 pounds spinach, stemmed and finely chopped,
or two 10-ounce bags spinach leaves, finely chopped

● Cook the potatoes in medium saucepan of salted boiling water until almost tender when pierced with a knife, about 10 minutes. Drain and set aside.

On a cutting board, combine the garlic and ginger and mince them together using a chef's knife. In a large, heavy saucepan over medium heat, heat the oil and sauté the onion until translucent, about 3 minutes. Add the ginger mixture and sauté until fragrant, about 1 minute. Stir in the tomatoes, then stir in spices and salt and sauté until nicely fragrant, 1 or 2 minutes. Stir in the ½ cup water, the spinach, and potatoes. Cover and cook until the spinach is wilted and the potatoes are tender, about 5 minutes; check halfway through and add more water if needed. Serve at once, on warmed plates.

Porcini-Crusted Scallops
with Mushroom Ragout

SERVES 4 AS A FIRST COURSE, 2 AS A MAIN COURSE

Justine Miner, Rnm's young chef/owner, grew up in Pacific Heights, but opened her accomplished restaurant on the Lower Haight, where its sophisticated New York–style ambiance is a contrast to its funky surroundings. She named the place with her father's initials, and proceeded to use her culinary training to produce French-influenced food with personal and intriguing twists. These flavorful scallops, graced with white truffle oil, are typical of her cuisine. Miner serves them with a parsnip-potato purée and braised endives.

Rnm
598 Haight Street
(at Steiner)

Note: The recipe for mushroom stock makes more than you will need, but it's great to have on hand. To simplify the recipe, buy prepared mushroom stock.

2 tablespoons olive oil
8 ounces chanterelle mushrooms, torn into large pieces
1 teaspoon minced shallot
1 teaspoon minced fresh thyme
Salt and freshly ground pepper to taste
2 tablespoons dry white wine
1 teaspoon unsalted butter, plus 1 tablespoon
2 cups Mushroom Stock (recipe follows)
White truffle oil for drizzling
8 large day-boat scallops with the muscle removed
¼ cup porcini powder (see note) mixed with 2 tablespoons all-purpose flour

Place a large sauté pan or skillet over high heat for 1 to 2 minutes. Add 1 tablespoon of the olive oil and heat just until smoking. Add the mushrooms and sauté until browned, about 10 minutes. Add the shallot, thyme, salt, and pepper. Add the wine and cook until almost evaporated. Stir in the 1 teaspoon butter. Set aside and let cool.

Meanwhile, pour the mushroom stock into a saucepan and bring to a boil over high heat. Reduce heat to medium-high and cook until reduced by half. Add the mushroom mixture and the 1 tablespoon butter. Season with salt and pepper to taste. Cook until the butter melts and the sauce thickens. Reduce the heat and drizzle in a little truffle oil. Remove from heat and keep warm.

Heat a large sauté pan or skillet over high heat for 1 to 2 minutes. Season the scallops with salt and pepper to taste, then coat them in the porcini-flour mixture, shaking off the excess. Add the remaining 1 tablespoon olive oil to the skillet and let heat for a few seconds. Add the scallops, reduce heat to medium, and cook until golden brown, about 1 minute on each side. Divide the ragout among 4 warmed plates. Place 2 scallops on top of each serving of ragout and serve at once.

Mushroom Stock

MAKES 4 CUPS

¹/₂ tablespoon olive oil
¹/₃ cup mirepoix (finely chopped carrot, onion, celery, and leek)
1 garlic clove
1 pound button mushrooms, coarsely chopped
1 portobello mushroom, coarsely chopped
¹/₂ teaspoon crumbled dried porcini mushroom
¹/₂ cup dry white wine
¹/₄ cup port wine
Bouquet garni: 2 thyme sprigs, ¹/₂ bay leaf, and 5 peppercorns,
tied in a cheesecloth square

● In a soup pot, heat the olive oil over high heat until almost smoking. Add the mirepoix and garlic clove. Reduce heat to medium and cook, stirring frequently, for about 8 minutes, or until browned. Add the button mushrooms, portobello, and porcini. Cook, stirring, until the liquid from the mushrooms evaporates and they begin to brown. Add the white wine, port, and bouquet garni. Cook to reduce until the liquid is almost gone. Add enough water to cover the ingredients, then double that. Bring to a boil, reduce to a simmer, and cook for 45 minutes to 1 hour, skimming from time to time. Strain through a fine-meshed sieve. Set aside and let cool. Cover and refrigerate for up to 1 week, or freeze for up to 2 months.

Porcini Powder: You can purchase porcini powder, or make your own: Grind 2 ounces of dried porcini in a spice grinder or blender to make a fine powder.

Thaitanic Beef

SERVES 2 AS A MAIN COURSE

**Thep Phanom
Thai Cuisine**

400 Waller Street (at Fillmore)

In a city abundantly sprinkled with Thai restaurants, Thep Phanom consistently ranks at the top of the list. On a side street in the Lower Haight, its gracious service, pleasant setting, and excellent food mean that you'll almost always have to wait for a table. But the wait is worth it for such multiflavored dishes as this stir-fry of medium-rare steak and green pepper in a rich, savory-sweet sauce. Chef/owner Pathama Parikanont named this dish after the movie *Titanic* because of its huge flavor; the beef may be replaced with prawns, chicken, salmon, pork, or tofu, since, as Parikanont says, "It's the sauce that's Thaitanic!"

THAITANIC SAUCE

1 teaspoon Thai green curry paste
Pinch of ground turmeric
Pinch of ground white pepper
2 teaspoons Thai fish sauce
1 teaspoon oyster sauce
1 teaspoon sugar
3 fresh or thawed frozen kaffir lime leaves, finely sliced
1-inch piece lemongrass (white part only), peeled and thinly sliced
1/2-inch piece fresh ginger, peeled and thinly sliced

10 ounces rib-eye beefsteak
1 green bell pepper, seeded, deribbed, and cut into 1-inch-squares
2 tablespoons canola oil
2 garlic cloves, minced
2 tablespoons coconut milk
Steamed jasmine rice for serving

Shredded fresh Thai or sweet basil leaves
Julienned red bell pepper

- In a small bowl, combine all the sauce ingredients and stir to blend.

- Preheat the broiler. Place the steak on a broiler pan and broil about 4 inches from the heat source for 3 to 4 minutes on each side for medium-rare. Transfer the steak to a cutting board and cut into 1-by-$\frac{1}{4}$-inch slices.

- Broil the bell pepper squares, skin-side up, about 4 inches from the heat source for 4 to 5 minutes, or until softened.

- In a wok or skillet over medium heat, heat the oil and stir-fry the garlic just until golden. Remove the pan from heat. Using a slotted spoon, remove some of the garlic and reserve for garnish. Add the sauce to the pan and place the pan over medium-high heat. Add the beef and bell pepper squares and stir-fry for 2 to 3 minutes. Stir in the coconut milk until well blended.

- Serve at once over steamed rice, sprinkled with the reserved garlic and the basil and red bell pepper.

Lemon Ricotta Pancakes
with Lemon Curd and Raspberry Sauce

SERVES 4

This French cafe in the heart of Cole Valley defines the word *charming;* it has a small heated patio, an antique hutch, high ceilings, and French movie posters on the walls, a clue that the cafe's name comes from the film *Zazie dans le Métro.* Jennifer Piallat, the new owner, continues the Zazie tradition of lovely French lunches and dinners, and American-style breakfasts and brunches with a French twist, like these delicate pancakes.

Zazie
941 Cole Street (between Carl and Parnassus)

Note: The raspberry sauce below is an adaptation of Zazie's sauce.

4 eggs, separated
1 cup whole-milk ricotta cheese
5 tablespoons unsalted butter, melted
1/2 teaspoon vanilla extract
1/3 cup all-purpose flour
1/4 cup sugar
1/4 teaspoon salt
2 tablespoons grated lemon zest
Canola oil for cooking
Lemon Curd for serving (recipe follows)
Raspberry Sauce for serving (recipe follows)
Fresh berries and confectioners' sugar for garnish

In a large bowl, beat the egg whites until stiff, glossy peaks form. In a bowl, combine the ricotta, butter, egg yolks, and vanilla and stir until well blended. In another bowl, combine the flour, sugar, salt, and lemon zest; stir with a whisk to blend. Stir the dry ingredients into the ricotta mixture. Gently fold in the beaten whites just until blended.

Heat a griddle or a large sauté pan or skillet over medium heat and coat lightly with oil. Drop 1 cup batter on the pan and cook until golden brown, about 3 minutes per side. Transfer to a plate in a low oven.

Repeat to cook the remaining pancakes. Serve at once, accompanied with lemon curd and raspberry sauce, and garnished with berries and confectioners' sugar.

Lemon Curd

MAKES 1 CUP

Grated zest of 1 1/2 lemons
5 tablespoons fresh lemon juice
3/4 cup sugar
3 1/2 tablespoons unsalted butter
3 eggs

- In a double boiler over simmering water, combine the zest, juice, sugar, and butter. Stir occasionally until the butter melts and the sugar dissolves.

- In a medium bowl, whisk the eggs until blended. Whisk in a little of the lemon mixture to temper the eggs. Stir the eggs into the lemon mixture in the double boiler and cook, stirring constantly, until thickened to the consistency of mayonnaise, about 5 minutes. Remove from the heat and let cool.

Raspberry Sauce

MAKES 1 CUP

1/2 cup red currant jelly
1/4 cup raspberry jam
10 ounces thawed frozen raspberries
2 tablespoons sugar

- In a heavy, medium nonreactive saucepan, combine all the ingredients and simmer over low heat, stirring occasionally, until thickened, 10 to 15 minutes. Let cool.

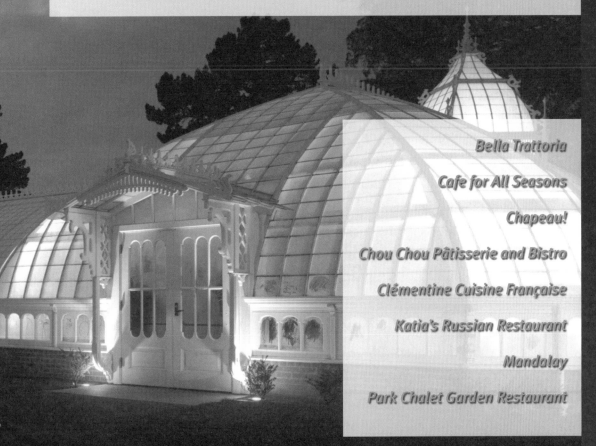

Presidio Heights / The Richmond /The Sunset / Forest Hills /West Portal

Bella Trattoria

Cafe for All Seasons

Chapeau!

Chou Chou Pâtisserie and Bistro

Clémentine Cuisine Française

Katia's Russian Restaurant

Mandalay

Park Chalet Garden Restaurant

THE WESTERN HALF OF SAN FRANCISCO begins at Van Ness below Pacific Heights and stretches away to where the wild, gray ocean crashes endlessly at Ocean Beach. Most of these flat reaches were once bare sand dunes, including the long rectangle of Golden Gate Park that divides the Sunset District, to the south, from the Richmond District, to the north. Tucked up on the

northern edge of the Richmond, on the southern flank of Pacific Heights, is Presidio Heights, clustered around Sacramento Street, a trove of elegant antiques stores, home-design stores, upscale clothing shops, and small restaurants. It's a quieter version of Union Street, far removed from the usual tourist paths. ⌐ FARTHER SOUTH, ON GEARY BOULEVARD, IS JAPANTOWN, a shopping center, theater, and hotel complex that contains several Japanese restaurants as well as a large Japanese bookstore and shops selling kimonos and other gift items. On the parallel streets are shops and stores where you can buy all the ingredients and utensils you will need to cook your own Japanese meal. Soko Hardware Company (1698 Post Street) sells beautiful cookware and serving pieces, and K. Uoki Sakai Company (1656 Post Street), a Japanese grocery store, has Asian vegetables, fresh fish, and almost any exotic Japanese ingredient you might need. Or, visit one of the sushi restaurants or noodle bars in the area and let a master chef do all the work. And if you've overindulged in sake and sushi, or anything else, the Kabuki Baths can help to restore you for another round of *futomaki*. ⌐ THE ARCHITECTURE OF MOST OF THE HOUSES in the Sunset and the Richmond is undistinguished, but these affordable homes were snapped up right after they were built in the decades following World War I. Although they are essentially suburbs that are geographically part of the city and tend to be more politically conservative than many other neighborhoods, in true San Francisco fashion these streets harbor a wide variety of ethnicities, from Russian to Korean, and Middle Eastern to Vietnamese. This is the fog belt, where the air is gray almost all summer, but where flashes of other cultures are visible almost everywhere you look. — CLEMENT STREET, the main shopping strip in the Richmond, is a newer, bigger, and wider Chinatown, but mixed in among the Chinese markets are Thai, Vietnamese, Russian, Italian, French, Korean, American, and Mexican restaurants, along with coffeehouses, antiques shops, clothing stores, and bookstores. (If you're shopping for exotic ingredients, be sure to check out Haig's Delicacies at 642 Clement, rich with Middle Eastern, Indian, and Southeast Asian spices and condiments.) — ACROSS THE PARK, the equivalent Sunset thoroughfare is Irving, an equally diverse street of shops and homes. Ninth Avenue, which bisects Irving right across from the Japanese Tea Garden and the new deYoung Art Museum, is a pleasant little restaurant row. On the other side of Nineteenth Avenue, in just a few blocks you'll find three huge Asian supermarkets (one of them next to Tel Aviv Kosher Meats, with a deli selling piroshki) and a medium-sized one; the Van Phat Herb and Ginseng Company; a pizza place, a pho restaurant, an Irish pub, two sushi restaurants, two health food stores, a Chinese sausage company and a Chinese bakery, Marnee Thai restaurant—and a Taco Bell, a Kentucky Fried Chicken, and a Starbucks. — BETWEEN THE SUNSET AND WEST PORTAL is Forest Hills, a manicured residential area with trees, lawns, and many Tudor-style homes. West Portal, farther south, is a place many residents depart from

OTHER NEIGHBORHOOD STARS

Bistro Clement

Brother's Korean Restaurant

Casa Aguila

Ebisu

Ella's

The House

Kabuto Sushi A & S

Khan Toke Thai House

Korea House

Marnee Thai

Mayflower

Mescolanza

Narai

Old Krakow

Pacific Cafe

Park Chow

Pizzetta 211

Royal Thai

Straits Cafe

Ton Kiang

and arrive at each day through the Muni Metro tunnel, and it has the aura of belonging in another place and time. Most tourists never venture here, but it's another San Francisco village, this one reminiscent of a small Midwestern town. Fittingly enough, the draw for food-lovers is Cafe for All Seasons, an all-American neighborhood restaurant.

Portobellos Balsamico

SERVES 4 AS AN APPETIZER

Bella Trattoria, in a narrow corner location in the Avenues, really is *bella*: warm and cozy, with bright exterior and interior walls, and gratifying, authentic Italian food. In the best small-restaurant tradition, the former sous-chef, Antonio Mastroianni, is now the head chef, and his brother, Davide Mastroianni, the former sommelier, is now the owner. Everything is made in-house here, including the bread and pasta. These intensely flavorful portobello mushrooms in a balsamic vinegar reduction are one of their most popular starters.

Bella Trattoria
3854 Geary Boulevard
(at Third Avenue)

2 tablespoons olive oil
2 teaspoons minced garlic
$^{1}/_{2}$ cup dry white wine
Pinch of salt
Pinch of freshly ground white pepper
4 portobello mushrooms, stemmed
About 1 cup chicken stock or canned low-salt chicken broth
$^{1}/_{3}$ to $^{1}/_{2}$ cup balsamic vinegar
2 tablespoons unsalted butter
$^{1}/_{4}$ teaspoon flour
1 teaspoon minced fresh flat-leaf parsley
Grilled Bruschetta with Gorgonzola (recipe follows)

- In a nonreactive skillet just large enough to hold the mushrooms, heat the oil over medium heat. Add the garlic and sauté until golden, about 2 minutes. Add the wine and cook to reduce slightly, about 2 minutes. Add the salt and pepper.

- Add the portobellos, then pour enough broth or stock over the mushrooms to cover them. Cover and cook the mushrooms until tender but not mushy, about 10 minutes on each side. Transfer the mushrooms, stem-side down, to warm plates, reserving the pan juices.

● Add the balsamic vinegar to the pan juices and cook over medium heat until slightly reduced, about 2 minutes. Whisk in the butter until melted, then whisk in the flour and cook for about 2 minutes, whisking frequently, just until slightly thickened (don't cook it too long, or the sauce will separate). Spoon the sauce over the mushrooms and sprinkle with the parsley. Serve at once, garnished with the bruschetta.

Grilled Bruschetta with Gorgonzola: Cut four ½-inch-thick slices from a large loaf of Italian bread. Broil under a preheated broiler until golden brown on each side, about 2 minutes. Remove from the broiler, leaving it on, and rub one side of each toast with a garlic clove, then drizzle with olive oil. Top each toast with about 2 tablespoons crumbled Gorgonzola. Place under the broiler for 1 to 2 minutes, or just until the cheese is barely melted. Cut each bruschetta in half on a diagonal and serve at once.

Mexican Chicken Salad

SERVES 4 AS A FIRST COURSE, 2 AS A MAIN COURSE

The locals love this cafe, and even those who don't live nearby will travel to the old-fashioned neighborhood of West Portal to dine here. (Note: Plan a meal for before or after a movie at the nearby theater.) Good-sized portions of American favorites, like this chicken salad, are the draw, and brunch is also highly popular. This is home cooking, just like Mom's, if Mom happens to be a really good cook.

Cafe for All Seasons
150 West Portal Avenue (between Fourteenth Avenue and Vicente)

SPICY SOUR CREAM SAUCE

1 cup sour cream
1 tablespoon minced seeded jalapeño chili
2 tablespoons chopped fresh cilantro
³/₄ teaspoon salt

SALAD

2 heads romaine (outer leaves removed), thinly sliced
8 ounces seasoned cooked chicken breast, thinly sliced
¹/₂ cup cooked black beans
¹/₂ cup blanched fresh or thawed frozen corn kernels
¹/₂ cup chopped firm, ripe tomato
¹/₄ cup chopped red onion
1 small avocado, peeled, pitted, and chopped
²/₃ cup shredded mild Cheddar cheese
1 cup Cumin Dressing (recipe follows)

TOPPINGS

Deep-fried tortilla strips (see note)
¹/₃ cup finely chopped green onions, including green parts

To make the sauce: In a blender or food processor, combine all the ingredients and process until well blended, 1 to 2 minutes. Cover and refrigerate for at least 1 hour to develop the flavors.

To make the salad: Toss all the ingredients together in a large bowl. Divide among individual plates, stacking the salad like a mountain. Spoon the sauce over the salads. Sprinkle the toppings evenly over the salads and serve.

Cumin Dressing

MAKES 2½ CUPS

3 tablespoons water

3 tablespoons apple cider vinegar

2 teaspoons salt

1 teaspoon ground pepper

1½ teaspoons Worcestershire sauce

½ teaspoon dry mustard

1 tablespoon sugar

1 tablespoon fresh lemon juice

1 teaspoon chopped garlic

3 tablespoons ketchup

¼ teaspoon red pepper flakes

3 tablespoons olive oil

⅓ cup salad oil

1 tablespoon ground cumin

In a medium bowl, whisk all the ingredients together until blended. To store, cover and refrigerate for up to 10 days.

Deep-Fried Tortilla Strips: Cut 4 corn tortillas into 1½-by-¼-inch strips. In a large skillet, heat 1 inch of peanut oil or canola oil over medium-high heat until the surface shimmers. Add the strips and cook until golden brown, 2 to 4 minutes. Using a wire-mesh skimmer, transfer the strips to paper towels to drain.

Far Breton with Dried Plums

SERVES 6 AS A DESSERT

This glowing, intimate restaurant is a civilized outpost of French cuisine on upper Clement Street. Owners Philippe and Ellen Gardelle make everyone feel welcome here, even though these days Philippe spends much of his time in the kitchen, preparing classic dishes like this warming, easy-to-make clafoutis-like Breton dessert, studded with rum-soaked prunes.

Chapeau!

1408 Clement Street
(at Fifteenth Avenue)

2 cups pitted prunes
2 tablespoons rum
2 tablespoons water
1²/₃ cups sifted confectioners' sugar
2 cups unbleached all-purpose flour
Pinch of ground cinnamon
Pinch of salt
4 cups milk
1 vanilla bean, split lengthwise
6 eggs
6 tablespoons unsalted butter, melted

- In a medium bowl, combine the prunes, rum, and water. Let sit for 1 hour.

- Preheat the oven to 300°F. Butter a shallow 10-cup baking dish.

- In a medium bowl, stir the sugar, flour, cinnamon, and salt together. Pour the milk into a medium saucepan and add the vanilla bean. Heat over medium-low heat until bubbles form around the edges of the pan. Strain through a fine-meshed sieve.

- In a large bowl, whisk the eggs until just blended. Whisk in the dry mixture in 4 batches alternately with the milk to make a smooth batter. Stir in the butter until blended.

- Pour the batter into the prepared dish. Distribute the prunes evenly over the top of the batter; they will sink in. Bake until browned and set, about 50 minutes. Serve warm.

Pork Tenderloin
with Mustard Sauce, Sage, Onion Confit, and Grapes

SERVES 4 AS A MAIN COURSE

*Chou Chou Pâtisserie
and French Bistro*

*400 Dewey Boulevard
(at Woodside Avenue)*

Named for a French term of endearment (*chou chou* means "cutie pie"), this Gallic spot *is* endearing in its devotion to French pastries and comfort food like *cassolettes*: French country stews served in clay pots with pastry shell "lids." The sweet pastries couldn't be more authentic: Samy Dida, the owner and pastry chef, also owns a traditional pastry shop in Paris. This company dish from chef Eduardo Guti is a seductive combination of spicy, herbal, and sweet; serve it to your own dear ones.

One 1 ½-pound pork tenderloin, cut into ½-inch-thick slices
Olive oil for coating, plus 1 tablespoon
Salt, freshly ground pepper, and paprika to taste
1 onion, cut into ½-inch-thick slices
1 tablespoon canola oil
1 cup dry white wine
2 cups chicken broth
4 tablespoons unsalted butter
4 teaspoons whole-grain mustard
4 fresh sage leaves, minced
16 seedless red grapes, halved
Mashed Yukon Gold potatoes for serving
1 green onion, including green parts, finely chopped, for garnish

- Coat the pork with olive oil and season with salt, pepper, and paprika. Set aside.

- In a medium saucepan, heat the 1 tablespoon olive oil over medium heat and sauté the onion until translucent, about 5 minutes. Set aside.

- In a large sauté pan or skillet, heat the oil over high heat until smoking. Add the pork and sauté for about 45 seconds on each side for medium-rare. Transfer the pork to a plate and pour off the oil.

- Add the white wine to the pan and stir over medium heat to scrape up the browned bits from the bottom of the pan. Add the chicken broth, butter, mustard, sage, and cooked onions and cook to reduce to 1½ cups. Add the pork and grapes to the sauce and heat for 1 minute. Spoon the mashed potatoes onto warmed plates, place slices of pork on top, and spoon some of the pan sauce over. Garnish with the green onion and serve at once.

Veal Filet
with Blue Cheese–Potato Gratin and Red Wine Sauce

SERVES 4 AS A MAIN COURSE

Clémentine

126 Clement Street (between Second and Third Avenues)

The name of the restaurant cleverly combines the French word for a kind of tangerine with an allusion to its location on Clement, where the food is sumptuous and gratifying in the French style. The setting is intimate and the staff is unfailingly friendly. Come early for the reasonable prix fixe dinner. This is the place to come for a celebration or when you just want to be especially nice to yourself. A more casual offshoot, Bistro Clement, recently opened across the street.

BLUE CHEESE–POTATO GRATIN

4 russet potatoes, peeled and thinly sliced ($^1/_8$ inch)

$1^1/_2$ cups whole milk

$1^1/_2$ cups heavy cream

$^1/_4$ cup minced garlic

1 tablespoon minced shallot

Salt and freshly ground pepper to taste

$^3/_4$ cup (4 ounces) crumbled blue cheese

$^1/_2$ cup (2 ounces) shredded Gruyère cheese

1 tablespoon butter, cut into small pieces

RED WINE SAUCE

$^1/_2$ teaspoon canola oil

$^1/_2$ shallot, minced

$1^1/_2$ cups dry red wine

2 cups unsalted veal stock, or

half unsalted chicken stock and half unsalted beef stock

Salt and freshly ground pepper to taste

1 tablespoon canola oil
Four 6-ounce veal loin filets
Chervil sprigs for garnish

○ To make the gratin: Preheat the oven to 350°F. In a saucepan, combine the potatoes, milk, cream, garlic, and shallot. Bring to a low simmer over medium heat and cook for 10 minutes. Butter a 6-cup gratin dish. Add half of the potato mixture and sprinkle with salt and pepper. Sprinkle evenly with the blue cheese. Cover with the remaining potatoes, sprinkle again with salt and pepper, and sprinkle evenly with the Gruyère. Dot the cheese with the butter. Bake in the oven for 45 minutes, or until the top is golden brown and the potatoes are tender when tested with a knife. Remove from the oven, set aside, and keep warm.

○ To make the sauce: In a large saucepan, heat the oil over medium heat and sauté the shallot until translucent, about 3 minutes. Add the red wine and cook to reduce by half. Add the stock or broth and cook to reduce a glaze. Season with salt and pepper and strain through a fine-meshed sieve. Set aside and keep warm.

○ In a large sauté pan or skillet, heat the oil over high heat and sauté the veal for 4 to 5 minutes on each side for medium-rare. Transfer the meat to a platter, tent loosely with foil, and let rest for 5 minutes. Transfer the meat to a cutting board and cut into thin slices. Using a large serving spoon, spoon one fourth of the gratin onto each of 4 warmed plates and arrange the sliced veal on top. Pour the sauce over the veal, garnish with the chervil, and serve.

Eggplant Caviar

MAKES ABOUT 2 CUPS

Katia's Russian Restaurant

600 Fifth Avenue (at Balboa)

The Russian presence in the Richmond goes back to 1917, when thousands of White Russians emigrated here after the Revolution. Katia Troosh's restaurant is a pleasing taste of that culture, with a menu that serves classic Russian dishes like beef Stroganoff. The restaurant's own blend of tea is served in a *podstakannik* (a glass in a silver holder), and group teas, featuring samovar service, savories (such as blini and tea-sized piroshki), tea sandwiches, and sweets, are available by reservation. Come here on a foggy night for a warming meal and live guitar and accordion music. Or, make this roasted-eggplant spread at home to serve as an appetizer with bread, crackers, or crostini.

1 large globe eggplant
1 teaspoon corn or olive oil
1 large onion, finely chopped
1 carrot, peeled and grated
1/2 to 1 cup tomato sauce or crushed fresh tomatoes
1 teaspoon sugar
1/2 teaspoon salt
1/4 teaspoon freshly ground pepper
3 garlic cloves, minced
1 teaspoon chopped fresh dill
Freshly sliced bread, crackers, or crostini (recipe follows)

Preheat the oven to 350°F. Pierce the eggplant on all sides with a fork, place it on a baking sheet lined with parchment paper, and bake for about 45 minutes, or until tender when pierced with a knife. Let cool to the touch, then peel off the skin. Chop the eggplant flesh into very small dice.

- In a large skillet over medium heat, heat the oil and sauté the onion until translucent, about 3 minutes. Add the grated carrot and cook for a minute or two. Stir in the eggplant, tomato sauce or tomatoes, sugar, salt, and pepper, and simmer for about 5 minutes. Add the garlic and simmer for a few more minutes to blend the flavors. Taste and adjust the seasoning. Stir in the dill.

- Let cool slightly or completely. Serve on freshly sliced bread, crackers, or crostini.

Crostini: Preheat the oven to 350°F. Cut a baguette into crosswise slices ¼ inch thick; for larger crostini, cut on a sharp diagonal. Spread the slices on a baking sheet and bake until just golden, 10 to 15 minutes. Remove from the oven and let cool. Store in an airtight container for up to 1 day.

Mango Chicken

SERVES 4 AS A MAIN COURSE

Mandalay
4348 California
(at Sixth Avenue)

The first Burmese restaurant in town, the recently remodeled Mandalay is still cooking the aromatic dishes of this cuisine in its outpost on California Street. The mango chicken, one of their signature dishes, is typical of Burmese cooking, which combines Chinese, Thai, and Indian flavors and techniques. This dish is simple, quick, and colorful, especially when served over saffron rice (with golden raisins and green peas); serve it over coconut rice for a different exotic flavor. Although Mandalay doesn't use cilantro sprigs on this dish, you could add them for a colorful garnish.

SPICE PASTE

¹/₂ teaspoon Madras curry powder
¹/₂ teaspoon chili powder
¹/₂ teaspoon ground ginger
¹/₂ teaspoon garam masala
¹/₂ teaspoon fish sauce
8 ounces boneless, skinless chicken breast, cut into 1-inch cubes
1 teaspoon canola oil
1 tablespoon finely chopped
1 mango, peeled, cut from the pit, and cut into 1-inch cubes
Saffron rice or coconut rice for serving

In a medium bowl, combine all the ingredients for the spice paste. Add the chicken cubes and toss to coat evenly. Let sit at room temperature for 20 minutes.

In a large skillet over medum-high heat, heat the oil and sauté the chicken until lightly golden on the outside and cooked through, 3 to 5 minutes. Add the onion and sauté for 2 to 3 minutes. Add the mango and toss just to heat through. Serve at once, over rice.

Shepherd's Pie

SERVES 5 AS A MAIN COURSE

Park Chalet is a separate restaurant and brewpub accessed through the Beach Chalet and opening out onto Golden Gate Park. It's the best of two worlds: a casual spot between the park and the ocean, where you can sit outside on a sunny day (or inside, by the floor-to-ceiling windows and the huge stone fireplace, on a cool day) and enjoy their own freshly brewed porters, ales, and beers along with such comforting pub fare as pizza, hamburgers, and shepherd's pie.

Park Chalet Garden Restaurant
1000 Great Highway (between Fulton Street and Lincoln Way)

Note: The lamb shanks can be cooked one day ahead and refrigerated in their pan juices. Remove and discard the fat on top before heating the shanks and liquid to room temperature over low heat. The garlic can be roasted in the oven along with the lamb shanks.

3 lamb shanks
All-purpose flour for dredging, plus 6 tablespoons flour for roux
2 tablespoons canola oil
2 large carrots, peeled and finely diced
2 celery stalks, finely diced
1 onion, cut into 1/2-inch dice
1 turnip, peeled and finely diced
1 bay leaf
1 tablespoon minced fresh rosemary
1 teaspoon minced fresh thyme
2 tablespoons minced fresh flat-leaf parsley
2 cups low-salt beef broth, plus more as needed
1/2 cup (1 stick) unsalted butter
2 cups (16 ounces) Beach Chalet Golden Gate Park Porter or other dark beer
2 teaspoons kosher salt
2 teaspoons freshly ground pepper
Garlic Mashed Potatoes (recipe follows)

Preheat the oven to 350°F. Dredge the shanks in flour to coat evenly. In a large Dutch oven or flameproof casserole, heat the oil and sear the shanks on all sides until browned, about 3 minutes. Turn off heat. Add the carrots, celery, onion, turnip, rosemary, thyme, and 1 tablespoon of the parsley. Add the 2 cups beef stock or broth and bake for 3½ hours, or until very tender. Remove from the oven. Using a wire skimmer, transfer the meat to a platter to cool to the touch.

Strain the pan juices through a medium-meshed sieve, pushing on the solids with the back of a large spoon to force them through the sieve. Reserve the liquid and discard the leftover solids. Let the liquid stand and pour off the fat that rises to the top. Pull the meat of the lamb shanks from the bones.

In a large, heavy saucepan, melt the butter over medium heat and stir in the 6 tablespoons flour. Cook, stirring, for about 3 minutes; do not let the flour color. Gradually whisk in the porter and pan juices and cook, stirring frequently, until thickened, about 10 minutes. Add more beef broth as needed to make a gravylike sauce. Add the meat to the sauce and season with the salt and pepper. Stir until blended. Taste and adjust the seasoning.

Preheat the oven to 350°F. Transfer the meat and sauce to an 8-cup casserole dish. Top with the warm mashed potatoes and spread them evenly. Bake in the oven until golden brown, about 30 minutes. Sprinkle the remaining minced parsley over the potatoes and serve at once.

Garlic Mashed Potatoes

2 pounds russet potatoes, peeled and chopped into 1-inch chunks
1/2 teaspoon kosher salt, plus 2 teaspoons
1 cup heavy cream
2 tablespoons unsalted butter
2 tablespoons roasted garlic (see note)
1 teaspoon freshly ground pepper

- Put the potatoes in a saucepan and add cold water to cover and the 1/2 teaspoon salt. Bring to a boil, reduce heat to a rapid simmer, and cook until potatoes are tender, 10 to 15 minutes. Meanwhile, combine the cream, butter, and garlic in a small saucepan and cook over low heat until the butter melts. Set aside and keep warm.

- Drain and return potatoes to the pan; set over low heat and shake pan for 30 seconds or so to dry excess liquid. Push the potatoes through a ricer into a bowl and return to the pan, or mash them in the pan with a potato masher. Gradually stir in the warm cream mixture, the 2 teaspoons salt, and the pepper until smooth. Keep warm in a low oven or over hot water for up to 30 minutes.

Roasted Garlic: Preheat the oven to 350°F. Cut off the top of a garlic bulb by about 1/2 inch to expose the flesh of all the cloves. Brush the bulb with olive oil and sprinkle with salt and pepper. Line a small baking dish with aluminum foil, add the garlic, and bake for about 30 minutes, or until the garlic skin is dark brown. Let cool to room temperature. Separate the cloves and squeeze out the pulp.

List of Contributors

ABSINTHE
398 Hayes Street
San Francisco, CA 94102
415/551-1590

ALBONA RISTORANTE
ISTRIANO
545 Francisco Street
San Francisco, CA 94133
415/441-1040

ALMA
1101 Valencia Street
San Francisco, CA 94110
415/401-8959

ANTICA TRATTORIA
2400 Polk Street
San Francisco, CA 94109
415/928-5797

APERTO
1434 Eighteenth Street
San Francisco, CA 94107
415/252-1625

AQUA
252 California Street
San Francisco, CA 94111
415/956-9662

A 16 RESTAURANT
AND WINE BAR
2355 Chestnut Street
San Francisco, CA 94123
415/771-2216

BACAR RESTAURANT
AND WINE SALON
448 Brannan Street
San Francisco, CA 94107
415/904-4100

BARAKA
288 Connecticut Street
San Francisco, CA 94107
415/255-0370

BELLA TRATTORIA
3854 Geary Boulevard
San Francisco, CA 94118
415/221-0305

BETELNUT PEJU WU
2030 Union Street
San Francisco, CA 94123
415/929-8855

BISTRO CLOVIS
1596 Market Street
San Francisco, CA 94102
415/864-0231

BIX RESTAURANT
56 Gold Street
San Francisco, CA 94133
415/433-6300

BOCADILLOS
710 Montgomery Street
San Francisco, CA 94111
415/982-2622

CAFE FOR ALL SEASONS
150 West Portal Avenue
San Francisco, CA 94127
415/665-0900

CAFÉ JACQUELINE
1454 Grant Avenue
San Francisco, CA 94133
415/981-5565

CAFE KATI
1963 Sutter Street
San Francisco, CA 94115
415/775-7313

CHA CHA CHA
1801 Haight Street
San Francisco, CA 94117
415/386-5758

CHAPEAU!
1408 Clement Street
San Francisco, CA 94118
415/750-9787

CHARANGA
2351 Mission Street
San Francisco, CA 94110
415/282-1813

CHEZ NOUS
1911 Fillmore Street
San Francisco, CA 94115
415/441-8044

CHEZ PAPA BISTROT
1401 Eighteenth Street
San Francisco, CA 94107
415/824-8210

CHOU CHOU PÂTISSERIE
AND BISTRO
400 Dewey Boulevard
San Francisco, CA 94116
415/242-0960

CHOW
215 Church Street
San Francisco, CA 94114
415/552-2469

CITIZEN CAKE
399 Grove Street
San Francisco, CA 94102
415/861-2228

CLÉMENTINE CUISINE
FRANÇAISE
126 Clement Street
San Francisco, CA 94118
415/387-0408

COLIBRÍ
438 Geary Street
San Francisco, CA 94102
415/440-2737

DA FLORA
701 Columbus Avenue
San Francisco, CA 94133
415/981-4664

DELFINA
3621 Eighteenth Street
San Francisco, CA 94110
415/552-4055

ENRICO'S SIDEWALK CAFE
504 Broadway
San Francisco, CA 94133
415/982-6223

EOS RESTAURANT
AND WINE BAR
901 Cole Street
San Francisco, CA 94117
415/566-3063

FARALLON
450 Post Street
San Francisco, CA 94102
415/956-6969

1550 HYDE CAFÉ
AND WINE BAR
1550 Hyde Street
San Francisco, CA 94109
415/775-1550

FIREFLY
4288 Twenty-fourth Street
San Francisco, CA 94114
415/821-7652

FOREIGN CINEMA
2534 Mission Street
San Francisco, CA 94110
415/648-7600

FRINGALE
570 Fourth Street
San Francisco, CA 94107
415/543-0573

GLOBE
290 Pacific Avenue
San Francisco, CA 94111
415/391-4132

GRAND CAFE
501 Geary Street
San Francisco, CA 94102
415/292-0101

GREAT EASTERN
649 Jackson Street
San Francisco, CA 94133
415/986-2500

GREENS RESTAURANT
Fort Mason, Bldg. A
San Francisco, CA 94123
415/771-6222

HELMAND
430 Broadway
San Francisco, CA 94133
415/362-0641

HOG ISLAND OYSTER
COMPANY
One Ferry Building 11A
San Francisco, CA 94111
415/391-7117

INCANTO
1550 Church Street
San Francisco, CA 94131
415/641-4500

INDIAN OVEN
233 Fillmore Street
San Francisco, CA 94134
415/626-1628

ISA
3324 Steiner Street
San Francisco, CA 94123
415/567-9588

JACK FALSTAFF
300 Brannan Street
San Francisco, CA 94107
415/836-9239

KATIA'S RUSSIAN
RESTAURANT
600 Fifth Avenue
San Francisco, CA 94118
415/668-9292

KOH SAMUI
AND THE MONKEY
415 Brannan Street
San Francisco, CA 94107
415/369-0007

KOKKARI ESTIATORIO
200 Jackson Street
San Francisco, CA 94111
415/981-0983

KULETO'S ITALIAN
RESTAURANT
221 Powell Street
San Francisco, CA 94102
415/397-7720

LA FOLIE
2316 Polk Street
San Francisco, CA 94109
415/776-5577

LA SUITE
100 Brannan Street
San Francisco, CA 94107
415/593-5900

LE CHARM FRENCH BISTRO
315 Fifth Street
San Francisco, CA 94107
415/546-6128

LE COLONIAL
20 Cosmos Place
San Francisco, CA 94109
415/931-3600

LE PETIT ROBERT
2300 Polk Street
San Francisco, CA 94109
415/922-8100

THE LIBERTY CAFE AND
BAKERY
410 Cortland Avenue
San Francisco, CA 94110
415/695-1223

LIMÓN
524 Valencia Street
San Francisco, CA 94110
415/252-0918

L'OSTERIA DEL FORNO
519 Columbus Avenue
San Francisco, CA 94133
415/982-1124

LUNA PARK
694 Valencia Street
San Francisco, CA 94110
415/553-8584

MANDALAY
4348 California Street
San Francisco, CA 94118
415/386-3895

MAYA
303 Second Street
San Francisco, CA 94107
415/543-2928

MOOSE'S
1652 Stockton Street
San Francisco, CA 94133
415/989-7800

OOLA RESTAURANT
AND BAR
860 Folsom Street
San Francisco, CA 94107
415/995-2061

PALIO D'ASTI
640 Sacramento Street
San Francisco, CA 94111
415/395-9800

PARK CHALET
GARDEN RESTAURANT
1000 Great Highway
San Francisco, CA 94121
415/386-4125

PAZZIA CAFFÈ PIZZERIA
ROSTICCERIA
337 Third Street
San Francisco, CA 94107
415/512-1693

PESCE SEAFOOD BAR
2227 Polk Street
San Francisco, CA 94109
415/928-8025

PIPÉRADE
1015 Battery Street
San Francisco, CA 94111
415/391-2555

PLOUF
40 Belden Street
San Francisco, CA 94104
415/986-6491

PLUMPJACK CAFE
3127 Fillmore Street
San Francisco, CA 94123
415/563-4755

POSTRIO
545 Post Street
San Francisco, CA 94102
415/776-7825

QUINCE
1701 Octavia Street
San Francisco, CA 94109
415/775-8500

RESTAURANT LULU
816 Folsom Street
San Francisco, CA 94107
415/495-5775

RISTORANTE BACCO
737 Diamond Street
San Francisco, CA 94114
415/282-4969

RISTORANTE MILANO
1448 Pacific Avenue
San Francisco, CA 94109
415/673-2961

RNM
598 Haight Street
San Francisco, CA 94117
415/551-7900

ROSE PISTOLA
532 Columbus Avenue
San Francisco, CA 94133
415/399-0499

ROSE'S CAFE
2298 Union Street
San Francisco, CA 94123
415/775-2200

RUBICON
558 Sacramento Street
San Francisco, CA 94111
415/434-4100

SCALA'S BISTRO
432 Powell Street
San Francisco, CA 94102
415/395-8555

SHANGHAI 1930
133 Steuart Street
San Francisco, CA 94105
415/896-5600

SLANTED DOOR
Ferry Building
One Ferry Plaza
San Francisco, CA 94111
415/861-8032

SLOW CLUB
2501 Mariposa Street
San Francisco, CA 94103
415/241-9390

SOCIALE CAFFÈ
AND WINE BAR
3665 Sacramento Street
San Francisco, CA 94118
415/921-3200

SOUTH PARK CAFÉ
108 South Park Avenue
San Francisco, CA 94107
415/495-7275

SUPPENKÜCHE
601 Hayes Street
San Francisco, CA 94102
415/252-9289

TABLESPOON
2209 Polk Street
San Francisco, CA 94109
415/268-0140

TADICH GRILL
240 California Street
San Francisco, CA 94111
415/391-1849

TALLULA
4280 Eighteenth Street
San Francisco, CA 94114
415/437-6722

TAYLOR'S AUTOMATIC
REFRESHER
One Ferry Building
San Francisco, CA 94111
866/328-3663

THEP PHANOM
THAI CUISINE
400 Waller Street
San Francisco, CA 94117
415/431-2526

TI COUZ
3108 Sixteenth Street
San Francisco, CA 94103
415/252-7373

TOWN HALL
342 Howard Street
San Francisco, CA 94105
415/908-3900

TOWN'S END RESTAURANT
AND BAKERY
2 Townsend Street
San Francisco, CA 94107
415/512-0749

2223 MARKET STREET
2223 Market Street
San Francisco, CA 94114
415/431-0692

UNIVERSAL CAFE
2814 Nineteenth Street
San Francisco, CA 94110
415/821-4608

VIVANDE PORTA VIA
2125 Fillmore Street
San Francisco, CA 94115
415/346-4430

YANK SING
Rincon Center
101 Spear Street
San Francisco, CA 94107
415/957-9300
    and
49 Stevenson Street
San Francisco, CA 94107
415/541-4949

ZARZUELA
2000 Hyde Street
San Francisco, CA 94109
415/346-0800

ZAZIE
921 Cole Street
San Francisco, CA 94117
415/564-5332

Ethnic Index

AFGHAN
Helmand

AMERICAN
Cafe for All Seasons
Hog Island Oyster Company
(seafood)
The Liberty Cafe and Bakery
2223 Market Street

AMERICAN/
OLD SAN FRANCISCO
Tadich Grill (seafood)

BAKERY/CAFE
Citizen Cake
Chou Chou Pâtisserie Artisanale
and French Bistro
The Liberty Cafe and Bakery
Town's End Restaurant and
Bakery

BASQUE
Bocadillos
Pipérade

BREWPUB
Park Chalet Garden Restaurant

BURMESE
Mandalay

CALIFORNIA
Citizen Cake
Firefly
Jack Falstaff

CALIFORNIA/ASIAN
Eos

CALIFORNIA/FRENCH
Aqua (seafood)
Bix
Farallon (seafood)
Grand Cafe
Luna Park
Restaurant LuLu
Rubicon

CALIFORNIA/ITALIAN
Incanto
Pesce Seafood Bar

CALIFORNIA/
MEDITERRANEAN
bacar restaurant and wine salon
Enrico's Sidewalk Cafe
1550 Hyde Cafe and Wine Bar
Moose's
Plumpjack Cafe
Slow Club

CARIBBEAN/
LATIN AMERICAN
Cha Cha Cha

CHINESE
Great Eastern (seafood)
Shanghai 1930
Yank Sing (dim sum)

ECLECTIC
Chow

FRENCH
Absinthe
Bistro Clovis
Café Jacqueline (soufflés)
Chapeau!
Chez Papa Bistrot
Chou Chou Pâtisserie and Bistro
Clémentine Cuisine Française
Isa
La Folie
La Suite
Le Charm
Le Petit Robert
Plouf (seafood)
South Park Café
Ti Couz (crêpes)
Zazie

FRENCH/BASQUE
Fringale

GERMAN
Suppenküche

GREEK
Kokkari Estiatorio

INDIAN
Indian Oven

INDIAN/FRENCH
Tallula

ITALIAN
Albona Ristorante Istriano
(Istrian)
Antica Trattoria (northern
Italian)
Aperto
A 16 Restaurant and Wine Bar
(Campanian)
Bella Trattoria
Da Flora (Venetian)
Delfina
Kuleto's Italian Restaurant
L'Osteria del Forno
Palio D'Asti
Pazzia Caffè Pizzeria Rosticceria
(Tuscan)
Pesce Seafood Bar
Ristorante Bacco (northern
Italian)
Ristorante Milano (northern
Italian)
Rose Pistola (Ligurian)
Rose's Cafe (Ligurian)
Sociale Caffè and Wine Bar
Vivande Porta Via

ITALIAN/FRENCH
Quince
Scala's Bistro

MEDITERRANEAN
Chez Nous
Delfina
Enrico's
Foreign Cinema
Plumpjack Cafe

MEDITERRANEAN/
MOROCCAN
Baraka

MEXICAN
Colibrí
Maya

NEW AMERICAN
Cafe Kati
Globe
The Liberty Cafe and Bakery
Oola Restaurant and Bar
Postrio
RNM
Tablespoon
Taylor's Automatic Refresher
    (diner)
Town's End Bakery and
    Restaurant
Town Hall
Universal Cafe

NUEVO LATINO
Alma

PAN-ASIAN
Betelnut PejuWu

PAN-LATIN
Charanga

PERUVIAN
Limón

RUSSIAN
Katia's Russian Restaurant

SEAFOOD
Aqua (California / French)
Farallon (California / French)
Great Eastern (Chinese)
Hog Island Oyster Company
    (American)
Pesce Seafood Bar (Italian)
Plouf (French)
Tadich Grill (Old San Francisco)

SPANISH
Zarzuela

THAI
Koh Samui and the Monkey
Thep Phanom

VEGETARIAN
Greens Restaurant

VIETNAMESE
Le Colonial
Slanted Door

General Index

Names of contributing restaurants are in **boldface**.

A

A 16 Restaurant and Wine Bar, 124
Abraldes, Elena, 205
Absinthe, 152
Ahi Burgers, 94–95
Aioli, 142
Alamilla, Johnny, 203
Albona Ristorante Istriano, 52
Alma, 203
Almonds
    Asian Pear Ajo Blanco, 117
    Red Bell Pepper, Almond, and Garlic Sauce,
      83–84
    Swedish Oatmeal Pancakes with Pears and,
      96–97
Anchovy Vinaigrette, 106–7
Annibale, Duke, 243, 244
Antica Trattoria, 104
Aperto, 167
Appetizers, see also First courses
    Eggplant Caviar, 278–79
    Grilled Fresh Calamari, 208–9
    Minced Duck in Lettuce Petals, 90–91
    Pissaladière, 152–54
    Portobellos Balsamico, 269–70
    Shrimp Goldfish, 194–96
Apricot-Cherry Crisp, 132–33
Aqua, 25
Artichokes
    about, 176
    Ahi Tuna au Poivre, 174–76
    hearts, preparing, 175
Artisan breads, 98–99
Artisan cheeses, 191
Asian Pear Ajo Blanco, 117
Asparagus
    Asparagus and Cheese Flans, 203–4
    Spring Asparagus Soup, 136–37

B

bacar restaurant and wine salon, 169
Bakeries
    artisan breads sold in, 98–99
    Noe Valley Bakery, 234
    The Liberty Cafe and Bakery, 212
    Town's End Restaurant and Bakery, 96
Balsamic-Glazed Grilled Salmon, 220–22
Banducci, Eurico, 59
Baraka, 171
Barbary Coast Trail, 23
Basil oil, 8
Basil Syrup, 109, 110
Bazirgan, David, 171
Beans
    Crab in Black Bean Sauce, 63–64
    Fava Bean Tartines, 111–12
    Grilled Fresh Calamari with Bean Salad,
      208–9
    Picadillo Cubano with Black Beans, 205–7
Béchamel Sauce, 68–70
Beef
    Braised Short Ribs, 171–73
    Lomo Saltado, 215–16
    Picadillo Cubano with Black Beans, 205–7
    Thaitanic, 260–61
Bella Trattoria, 269
Betelnut Pejui Wu, 126
Beurre Blanc, 27
Bistro Clovis, 155
Bix Restaurant, 28
Blasi, Aldo, 115
Blood Orange-Glazed Fresh Sardines, 6–7
Blue Cheese-Potato Gratin, 276, 277
Bocadillos, 31
Borgatti, Susanna, 68
Braised Oxtails with Garlic and Feta, 35–36
Braised Short Ribs, 171–73
Brine, 59–60, 227–28
Brined Pork Chops, 227–29
Brioza, Stuart, 42
Bronzini à la Provençale, 8–9
Broth (Shellfish), 25
Brownies, 158–59
Brown, John Henry, xii
Bulow, Jocelyn, 87, 174
Butter
    clarified, 170
    Juniper, 228
    Oregano, 220, 221

C

Cabbage
  Soy-Braised, 128–29
  Warm Cabbage Salad, 181–83
Cacciucco, 16–17
Cafe for All Seasons, 271
Café Jacqueline, 55
Cafe Kati, 128
Calamari, Grilled Fresh, 208–9
California cuisine, xv
Cal-Med cuisine, xv
Candied Pecans, 93, 237, 238
Capers
  Melanzane al Forno, 146–47
  Olive-Caper Sauce, 113–14
Caramelized Garlic Soup, 42–43
Caramelized-Pear Filling, 224–25
Carr-Avalos, Armando and Leslie, 227
Castillo, Martin, 215
The Castro, see Upper Market/The Castro/Noe
  Valley
Celery and Herb Salad, 172–73
Cha Cha Cha, 252
Chapeau!, 273
Charanga, 205
Cheeses, see also Ricotta cheese
  artisan, 191
  Asparagus and Cheese Flans, 203–4
  Blue Cheese-Potato Gratin, 276, 277
  Braised Oxtails with Garlic and Feta, 35–36
  Fava Bean Tartines, 111–12
  garnish of feta, 35
  Grilled Bruschetta with Gorgonzola, 270
  Macaroni Gratin, 190
  Warm Piquillo Peppers with Goat, 31–32
Chemel, Bruno, 87
Chez Nous, 130
Chez Papa Bistrot, 174
Chicken
  Chicken Fricassee, 155–56
  Chicken Hash à la Bix, 28–30
  Chicken Potpies, 212–14
  Herb-Marinated Brick, 10–11
  Lemongrass-Marinated, 14–15
  Mango Chicken, 280
  Mexican Chicken Salad, 271–72

  Pollo alla Marsala con Spinaci Siciliani,
    37–38
Chicken stock, 156
Chickpea Stew, 218, 219
Chili-Spice Paste, 181–83
Chinatown, see North Beach/Chinatown
Chipotle Rouille, 183
Chocolate
  Chocolate Pots de Crème, 210–11
  S'More Brownies, 158–59
Chou Chou Pâtisserie and French Bistro,
  274
Chow, 235
Chowpan, 65–67
Cioppino, 74–75
Citizen Cake, 158
Civic Center/Hayes Valley
  about, 150–51
  contributing restaurants of, 149
  natural foods stores of, 157
  other neighborhood restaurants of, 151
  Pissaladière, 152–54
Clams (fish stew), 115–16
Clarified Butter, 170
Clark, John, 210
Clémentine, 276
Clement, Thierry, 177
Coconut Cream Pie, 235–36
Coconut Tapioca, 108–10
Coconut Tuiles, 109–10
Coffeehouses, 62
Cole Valley, see The Haight/Cole Valley
Colibrí Mexican Bistro, 4
Coniglio in Agrodolce (Braised Rabbit), 52–54
Corn Salad, 220
Cosselman, Erik, 35
Couscous, 8, 9
Cow Hollow, see Marina/Cow Hollow/Pacific Heights
Crab Cakes, see also Dungeness Crab, 39–40
Cranberry Bean and Dandelion Soup, 124–25
Creamy Herb Gravy, 246
Crème Fraîche, 225
Crêpes, see also Pancakes
  Crespelle alla Boscaiola, 68–70
  Dessert Crêpes with Caramelized Pears and
    Crème Fraîche, 223–25

Crespelle alla Boscaiola, 68–70
Crostini, 279
CSA (Community Supported Agriculture) farms, 226
Cumin Dressing, 272

D

Da Flora, 57
Delfina, 208
Desserts
    Apricot-Cherry Crisp, 132–33
    Chocolate Pots de Crème, 210–11
    Coconut Cream Pie, 235–36
    Coconut Tapioca, 108–10
    Coconut Tuiles, 109–10
    Dessert Crêpes with Caramelized Pears and Crème Fraîche, 223–25
    Far Breton with Dried Plums, 273
    Huckleberry Soufflés, 138–39
    Lemon Ricotta Pancakes, 262–63
    Lemon Soufflé, 55–56
    Orange Crème Brûlée, 180
    Passion Fruit Sorbet, 108, 109
    Pear Tarte Tatin, 177–78
    S'More Brownies, 158–59
Dida, Samy, 274
Doob, Jared A., 188
Dough
    Parmesan Crust, 246, 247
    Pie Crust, 236
    Pizza, 141–42
    Puff Pastry Crusts, 212–13, 214
    Saffron Pappardelle, 240–42
Downtown, see Union Square/Downtown
Dressings, see also Vinaigrettes
    Cumin, 272
    for Grapefruit Salad with Jicama, 92–93
Duck
    Duck à l'Orange Provençale, 87–88
    Duck in Pipian Sauce, 4–5
    Minced Duck in Lettuce Petals, 90–91
Dungeness Crab, see also Crab Cakes; Seafood
    about, 41
    Caramelized Garlic Soup with, 42–43
    Cioppino, 74–75
    Crab in Black Bean Sauce, 63–64
    King Salmon with fondue of, 25–27

E

Eggplant
    Eggplant Caviar, 278–79
    Melanzane al Forno, 146–47
    sautéed, 66–67
The Embarcadero, see Fisherman's Wharf/The Embarcadero/South Beach
Emerald Fire Noodles, 126–27
Emporio Rulli, 2
Enrico's Sidewalk Cafe, 59
Eos Restaurant and Wine Bar, 253
Evangelista, Rose ("Pistola"), 74

F

Falkner, Elizabeth, 158
Falstaff, Jack, 83
Farallon, 6
Far Breton with Dried Plums, 273
Farmers' markets
    CSA (Community Supported Agriculture) farms and, 226
    Ferry Plaza Farmer's Market, 79–80, 85–86, 226
Fava Bean Tartines, 111–12
Fendert, Ola, 184
Fennel-Crusted Golden Trout, 243–44
Fennel-Rucola Salad, 106–7
Ferry Plaza Farmer's Market, 79–80, 85–86, 226
Field of Greens (Somerville), 132
1550 Hyde Cafe and Wine Bar, 106
Financial District, see Jackson Square/Financial District
Firefly, 237
First courses, see also Appetizers
    Asian Pear Ajo Blanco, 117
    Asparagus and Cheese Flans, 203–4
    Blood Orange-Glazed Fresh Sardines, 6–7
    Caramelized Garlic Soup, 42–43
    Crab in Black Bean Sauce, 63–64
    Cranberry Bean and Dandelion Soup, 124–25
    Fava Bean Tartines, 111–12
    Fennel-Crusted Golden Trout, 243–44
    Gazpacho Andaluz, 118–19
    Gnudi, 18–19
    Grapefruit Salad with Jicama, 92–93
    Grilled Corn Salad, 252

Grilled Fuyu Persimmon and Red Oak Leaf
  Lettuce Salad, 237–38
Hog Island Oysters Rockefeller, 81–82
Italian Fish Soup, 16–17
Marinated Shrimp with Peach and Cucumber
  Salad, 71–72
Melanzane al Forno, 146–47
Mexican Chicken Salad, 271–72
Oven-Dried-Tomato Tarts, 184–85
Pipérade, 89
Porcini-Crusted Scallops, 257–59
Seafood Risotto, 186–87
Seared Day-Boat Scallops, 169–70
Shaved Squash and Ricotta Bruschetta, 239
Sicilian Swordfish Rolls, 113–14
Tuna Confit, 106–7
Warm Piquillo Peppers, 31–32
Wok-Roasted Mussels, 253–54
Fish, see also Salmon; Seafood; Tuna
  Blood Orange-Glazed Fresh Sardines, 6–7
  Bronzini à la Provençale, 8–9
  Cioppino, 74–75
  Fennel-Crusted Golden Trout, 243–44
  Huachinango a la Talla (red snapper), 181
  Italian Fish Soup, 16–17
  Polenta alla Coda di Rospo (monkfish, clams,
    mussels), 115–16
  Potato-Wrapped Bluenose Sea Bass, 134–35
  Sicilian Swordfish Rolls, 113–14
  Whole Fish with Tomato and Fennel Ragout,
    188–89
Fisherman's Wharf / The Embarcadero / South
  Beach
  about, 78–80
  artisan breads sold in, 98–99
  contributing restaurants of, 77–99
  Ferry Plaza Farmers' Market, 79–80, 85–86
  other neighborhood restaurants of, 79
Fish stew, 115–16
Fish stock, 17
Foley, Aom and Chris, 179
Foreign Cinema, 210
Forest Hills, see Presidio Heights / The Sunset /
  The Richmond / Forest Hills / West Portal
Franz, Mark, 6
Fried green tomatoes, 192–93

Fringale, 177
Fruits, see also Pears
  Grapefruit Salad with Jicama, 92–93
  heirloom, 13
  Meyer lemons, 56
  Passion Fruit Sorbet, 108, 109
  peeling and segmenting citrus, 7

G
Gadaldi, Ruggero, 113
Gardelle, Philippe and Ellen, 273
Garlic
  Braised Oxtails with Garlic and Feta, 35–36
  Caramelized Garlic Soup, 42–43
  Mashed Potatoes with, 10, 12, 283
  Red Bell Pepper, Almond, and Garlic Sauce,
    83–84
  Roasted, 283
  Warm Green Garlic-Chipotle Cream, 204
Garnish
  feta cheese, 35
  Thaitanic Beef, 260–261
Gaspar, Flora, 57
Gazpacho Andaluz, see also Soups, 118–19
Ginger-Wasabi Mayo, 95
Glazed Shallots, Garlic, and Sherry Vinegar Sauce,
  155–56
Globe, 33
Gnocchi
  Gnocchi al Tartufo, 104–5
  spinach-ricotta, 18–19
Gnudi, 18–19
Grand Cafe, 8
Grapefruit Salad with Jicama, 92–93
Gravy
  Chicken Potpies, 212–214
  Creamy Herb, 246
Great Eastern, 63
Greens Restaurant, 132
Grilled Bruschetta with Gorgonzola, 270
Grilled Corn Salad, 252
Grilled Fuyu Persimmon and Red Oak Leaf Lettuce
  Salad, 237–38
Grilled Herbes de Provence Lamb Chops, 130–31
Grilled Lamb Skewers, 217–19
Grits, 28–30
Guérard, Michel, 138

H

The Haight / Cole Valley
  about, 250–51
  contributing restaurants of, 249, 252–63
  other neighborhood restaurants of, 251
Ham, see also Pork
  Crespelle alla Boscaiola, 68–70
  Fava Bean Tartines with prosciutto, 111–12
Hangtown Fry, 44–45
Har Gow Wrappers, 196
Hayes Valley, see Civic Center / Hayes Valley
Heirloom Tomato Jam, 10–11
Heirloom vegetables and fruits, 13
Helmand, 65
Herbed Vegetable Stock, 245
Herbes de Provence, 130
Herb-Marinated Brick Chicken, 10–11
Herb Paste, 130
Higgins, Bill, 252
Hille, Christopher, 124
Hirigoyen, Gerald, 89
Hog Island Oyster Company, 81
Hog Island Oysters Rockefeller, 81–82
Huachinango a la Talla, 181
Huckleberry Soufflés, 138–39

I

Incanto, 239
Indian Oven, 255
"The Inside Scoop" (SF Chronicle), xiii
Isa, 134
Italian Fish Soup, 16–17

J

Jack Falstaff, 83–84
Jackson Square / Financial District
  about, 22–24
  contributing restaurants of, 21, 25–45
  other neighborhood restaurants in, 23
Jacobson, Morgen, 71
Jicama, Grapefruit Salad with, 92–93
Juniper Butter, 228

K

Kale-Wrapped Wild Salmon, 83–84
Karzai, Jamilla, 65
Katia's Russian Restaurant, 278

Khera, Harveen, 243
King Salmon with Dungeness Crab Fondue,
  25–27
Kitchen God shrine, 50
Koh Samui and the Monkey, 179
Kokkari Estiatorio, 35
Kuleto, Pat, 6, 16
Kuleto's Italian Restaurant, 10

L

La Folie, 108
Lamb
  Chowpan, 65–67
  Grilled Herbes de Provence Lamb Chops,
    130–31
  Grilled Lamb Skewers, 217–19
  Pappardelle di Zafferano con Salsa di Agnello,
    240–42
  Shepherd's Pie, 281–82
Lamb Sauce, 240
La Suite, 87
Lavender Salt, 130–31
Le Charm French Bistro, 180
Le Colonial, 14
Lee, Shek Wo, 63
Lemon Curd, 263
Lemon Ricotta Pancakes, 262–63
Lemon Soufflé, 55–56
Lemon Vinaigrette, 111–12
Le Petit Robert, 111
The Liberty Cafe and Bakery, 212
Limón, 215
Little Saigon, 3
Lobster Stock, 17
Local Favorites, 73
Lomo Saltado, 215–16
L'Osteria del Forno, 68
Luchetti, Emily, 6
Luna Park, 217

M

McMahon, Jen, 57
Main courses
  Ahi Burgers, 94–95
  Balsamic-Glazed Grilled Salmon, 220–22
  Braised Oxtails with Garlic and Feta, 35–36
  Braised Short Ribs, 171–73

Brined Pork Chops, 227–29
Bronzini à la Provençale, 8–9
Chicken Fricassee, 155–56
Chicken Hash à la Bix, 28–30
Cioppino, 74–75
Coniglio in Agrodolce (Braised Rabbit), 52–54
Crespelle alla Boscaiola, 68–70
Duck à l'Orange Provençale, 87–88
Duck in Pipian Sauce, 4–5
Emerald Fire Noodles, 126–27
Fava Bean Tartines, 111–12
Fennel-Crusted Golden Trout, 243–44
Gnudi, 18–19
Grilled Fresh Calamari, 208–9
Grilled Herbes de Provence Lamb Chops,
    130–31
Grilled Lamb Skewers, 217–19
Grilled Salmon Paillards, 33–34
Hangtown Fry, 44–45
Herb-Marinated Brick Chicken, 10–11
Huachinango a la Talla, 181
Italian Fish Soup, 16–17
Kale-Wrapped Wild Salmon, 83–84
King Salmon with Dungeness Crab Fondue,
    25–27
Lemongrass-Marinated Chicken, 14–15
Lomo Saltado, 215–16
Mango Chicken, 280
Mexican Chicken Salad, 271–72
Pappardelle di Zafferano con Salsa di Agnello,
    240–42
Picadillo Cubano with Black Beans, 205–7
Pipérade, 89
Polenta alla Coda di Rospo, 115–16
Pollo alla Marsala con Spinaci Siciliani,
    37–38
Porcini-Crusted Scallops, 257–59
Pork Tenderloin, 274–75
Portobello Mushroom Pasta, 57–58
Pumpkin Curry Tofu, 179
Roasted Pork Loin, 59–61
Saag Aloo, 255–56
Salmon Salad Cozies, 140–42
Sausage Ravioli, 144–45
Seafood Risotto, 186–87
Sicilian Swordfish Rolls, 113–14

Spring Vegetable Potpies, 245–47
Tagliolini Pepati, 167–68
Thaitanic Beef, 260–61
Veal Filet, 276–77
Warm Piquillo Peppers, 31–32
Whole Fish with Tomato and Fennel Ragout,
    188–89
Wok-Roasted Mussels, 253–54
Mandalay, 280
Mango Chicken, 280
Manrique, Laurent, 25
Manzare, Joseph, 33
Margulis, Jacqueline, 55
Marina / Cow Hollow / Pacific Heights
    about, 122–23
    contributing restaurants of, 121, 124–47
    other neighborhood restaurants of, 123
Marindas
    Lemongrass-Marinated Chicken, 14–15
    Three-Mustard-Crusted Pork Tenderloin, 128
Marks, Mary Beth, 57
Mashed Potatoes, 221
Mashed Potatoes with Garlic, 10, 12, 283
Mastroianni, Antonio and Davide, 269
Maya, 181
Melanzane al Forno, 146–47
Mexican Chicken Salad, 271–72
Meyer lemons, 56
Middione, Carlo, 146
Minced Duck in Lettuce Petals, 90–91
Miner, Justine, 257
The Mission / Bernal Heights
    about, 200–202
    contributing restaurants of, 199, 203–29
    other neighborhood restaurants of, 201
Monkfish, 115–16
Moose, Ed, 71
Moose's, 71
Moscatel Vinaigrettes, 31–32
Moose, Mary Etta, 71
Mushroom Sauce, 57–58
Mushroom Stock, 258–59
Mussels
    fish stew, 115–16
    Seafood Risotto, 186–87
    Wok-Roasted, 253–54

N

Natural foods stores, 157
Newsom, Gavin, 136
Nob Hill, see Russian Hill/Nob Hill/Polk Street
Noe Valley, see Upper Market/The Castro/Noe
    Valley
North Beach/Chinatown
    about, 48–51
    coffeehouses of, 62
    contributing restaurants in, 47, 48–75
    other neighborhood restaurants in, 49

O

Old San Francisco restaurants, 45
Olive-Caper Sauce, 113–14
Olvera, Luis, 59
Onion Jam, 184–85
Oola Restaurant and Bar, 184
Orange Crème Brûlée, 180
Oregano Butter, 220, 221
Ormsby, James, 83, 136
"Other Neighborhood Stars"
    Civic Center/Hayes Valley, 151
    described, xvi
    Fisherman's Wharf/The Embarcadero/South
        Beach, 79
    The Haight/Cole Valley, 251
    Jackson Square/Financial District, 23
    Marina/Cow Hollow/Pacific Heights, 123
    The Mission/Bernal Heights, 201
    North Beach/Chinatown, 49
    Presidio Heights/The Richmond/The Sunset/
        Forest Hills/West Portal, 267
    Russian Hill/Nob Hill/Polk Street, 103
    South of Market/Potrero Hill, 165
    Union Square/Downtown, 3
    Upper Market/The Castro/Noe Valley, 233
Oven-Dried Tomatoes, 184–85
Oven-Dried-Tomato Tarts, 184–85
Oxtails, 35–36
Oysters
    Hangtown Fry, 44–45
    Hog Island Oysters Rockefeller, 81–82

P

Pacific Heights, see Marina/Cow Hollow/Pacific
    Heights

Padilla, Alex, 4
Palio D'Asti, 37
Pallow, 65
Pancakes, see also Crêpes
    Lemon Ricotta, 262–63
    Swedish Oatmeal Pancakes with Pears and
        Almonds, 96–97
Paniagua, Armando, 74
Pappardelle di Zafferano con Salsa di Agnello,
    240–42
Parikanont, Pathama, 260
Park Chalet Garden Restaurant, 281
Parmesan Crust, 246, 247
Passion Fruit Sorbet, 108, 109
Passot, Roland, 108
Pasta
    Macaroni Gratin, 190
    Portobello Mushroom, 57–58
    Saffron Pappardelle, 240–42
Pazzia Caffè Pizzeria Rosticceria,
    186–87
Pears, see also Fruits
    Asian Pear Ajo Blanco, 117
    Dessert Crêpes with Crème Fraîche and
        Caramelized, 223–25
    Pear Tarte Tatin, 177–78
Pepper confit, 8
Peppers, see also Vegetables
    Gazpacho Andaluz, 118–19
    Pipérade, 89
    Red Bell Pepper, Almond, and Garlic Sauce,
        83–84
    Red Bell Pepper Sauce, 144–45
    Red Pepper Alioli, 192, 193
    roasting and peeling bell, 40
    Warm Piquillo, 31–32
Perfect Puree Website, 108
Pesce Seafood Bar, 113
Phan, Charles, 92
Piallat, Jennifer, 262
Picada, 208, 209
Picadillo Cubano with Black Beans, 205–7
Pie Crust, 236
Pine nuts, toasting, 32
Pipérade, 89
Pipérade, 89

Pirie, Gayle, 210
Pissaladière, 152–54
Pistola, Rose, 140
Pizza Dough, 141–42, 152
Pizzas
- *Asparagus and Cheese Flans, 203–4*
- *Oven-Dried-Tomato Tarts, 184–85*
- *Pissaladière, 152–54*
- *Salmon Salad Cozies, 140–41*

Placencia, Alex, 4
***Plouf,** 39*
***Plumpjack Café,** 136*
Poached chicken, 28–30
Polenta, 54
Polenta alla Coda di Rospo, 115–16
Polk Street, see Russian Hill / Nob Hill / Polk Street
Pollo alla Marsala con Spinaci Siciliani, 37–38
Porcini-Crusted Scallops, 257–59
Porcini Powder, 259
Pork, see also Ham
- *Brined Pork Chops, 227–29*
- *Pork Tenderloin, 274–75*
- *Roasted Pork Loin, 59–61*
- *Three-Mustard-Crusted Pork Tenderloin, 128–29*

Portobello Mushroom Pasta, 57–58
Portobellos Balsamico, 269–70
***Postrio,** 16*
Potatoes, see also Vegetables
- *Blue Cheese-Potato Gratin, 276, 277*
- *Chicken Potpies, 212–14*
- *dumplings with truffle sauce, 104–5*
- *Garlic Mashed, 10, 12, 283*
- *Lomo Saltado, 215–16*
- *Mashed, 221*
- *Potato-Wrapped Bluenose Sea Bass, 134–35*
- *Saag Aloo, 255–56*

Potpies
- *Chicken, 212–14*
- *Spring Vegetable, 245–47*

Potrero Hill, see South of Market / Potrero Hill
Presidio Heights / The Richmond / The Sunset / Forest Hills / West Portal
- *about, 266–68*
- *contributing restaurants of, 265, 269–83*
- *other neighborhood restaurants of, 267*

Puff Pastry Crusts, 212–13, 214
Pumpkin Curry Tofu, 179

Q

***Quince,** 138*

R

Rabbit (Coniglio in Agrodolce), 52–54
Radish and Mint Salad, 136–37
Randolph, Melinda, 245
Raspberry Sauce, 263
Rau ram, 92
Ravioli, Sausage, 144–45
Red Bell Pepper Sauce, 144–45
Red Pepper Alioli, 192, 193
Red Sauerkraut (Blaukraut), 228–29
Red snapper (Huachinango a la Talla), 181
Red Wine Reduction, 174–75
Red Wine Sauce, 276–77
***Restaurant LuLu,** 188*
Rice, Pallow, 65
The Richmond, see Presidio Heights / The Richmond / The Sunset / Forest Hills / West Portal
Ricotta cheese, see also Cheeses
- *Gnudi, 18–19*
- *Lemon Ricotta Pancakes, 262–63*
- *Shaved Squash and Ricotta Bruschetta, 239*

Rigo, Pascal, 111
***Ristorante Bacco,** 240*
***Ristorante Milano,** 115*
***RNM,** 257*
Roasted Garlic, 283
Roasted Pork Loin Pork, 59–61
Rosenthal, Mitchell and Stephen, 16, 192
***Rose Pistola,** 74*
***Rose's Café,** 140*
Russian Hill / Nob Hill / Polk Street
- *about, 102–3*
- *contributing restaurants of, 101, 104–19*
- *other neighborhood restaurants of, 103*

S

Saag Aloo, 255–56
Saffron Pappardelle, 240–42
Saffron Sauce, 217, 219
St. John, Wendy, 227

Salads, see also Vegetables
   Celery and Herb, 172–73
   Corn, 220
   Fennel-Rucola, 106–7
   Grapefruit Salad with Jicama, 92–93
   Grilled Corn, 252
   Grilled Fuyu Persimmon and Red Oak Leaf
     Lettuce, 237–38
   Mexican Chicken, 271–72
   Peach and Cucumber, 71–72
   Radish and Mint, 136–37
   Salmon Salad Cozies, 140–42
   Spicy Watercress and Orange, 6–7
   Warm Cabbage, 181–83
   Warm White Bean, 208–9
Salas, Gabriela, 205
Salmon, see also Fish
   about, 143
   Balsamic-Glazed Grilled, 220–22
   Grilled Salmon Paillards, 33–34
   Kale-Wrapped Wild, 83–84
   King Salmon with Dungeness Crab Fondue,
     25–27
   Salmon Salad Cozies, 140–42
   Seafood Risotto, 186–87
Salmon Salad Cozies, 140–42
Salsa Verde, 33–34
Salvoni, Sante, 220
Sandoval, Richard, 181
San Francisco
   artisan breads of, 98–99
   artisan cheeses of, 191
   coffeehouses, 62
   CSA (Community Supported Agriculture)
     farms of, 226
   early days of, xii-xiii
   Ferry Plaza Farmer's Market, 79–80, 85–86,
     226
   Local Favorites, 73
   natural foods stores of, 157
San Francisco Chronicle, xiii, xvi
San Francisco restaurants., see also specific
   neighborhoods
   classic dishes of, 197
   contributors among, xvi
   diversity reflected in, xiv-xv

   early days of, xii-xiii
   Old San Francisco, 45
Sauces
   Béchamel, 68–70
   for Crab Cakes, 39
   Fig Sauce with Mint and Marsala, 60
   Ginger-Wasabi Mayo, 95
   Glazed Shallots, Garlic, and Sherry Vinegar,
     155–56
   Lamb, 240
   for Minced Duck in Lettuce Petals, 90–91
   Mushroom, 57–58
   Olive-Caper, 113–14
   Pipian, 4–5
   Raspberry, 263
   Red Bell Pepper, 144–45
   Red Bell Pepper, Almond, and Garlic, 83–84
   Red Wine, 276–77
   Saffron, 217, 219
   served with Emerald Fire Noodles, 126–27
   Spicy Sour Cream, 271
   Thaitanic, 260
   Tomato, 168
   Truffle, 104
Sausage Ravioli, 144–45
Scala's Bistro, 18–19
Scallops, see Seafood
Scherotter, Daniel, 37
Sea bass
   Bronzini à la Provençale, 8–9
   Potato-Wrapped Bluenose, 134–35
Seafood, see also Dungeness Crab; Fish; Shrimp
   Grilled Fresh Calamari, 208–9
   Hangtown Fry, 44–45
   Hog Island Oysters Rockefeller, 81–82
   Lobster (fish or shrimp) Stock, 17
   Porcini-Crusted Scallops, 257–59
   Seafood Risotto, 186–87
   Seared Day-Boat Scallops, 169–70
   Wok-Roasted Mussels, 253–54
Seared Day-Boat Scallops, 169–70
Seasoning Mix, 218
Shanghai 1930, 90
Shaved Squash and Ricotta Bruschetta, 239
Shellfish Broth, 25
Shepherd's Pie, 281–82

Sherry Vinaigrette, 25–26
Shrimp
    Cioppino, 74–75
    Marinated Shrimp with Peach and Cucumber
        Salad, 71–72
    Seafood Risotto, 186–87
    Shrimp Goldfish, 194–96
Shrimp stock, 17
Side dishes
    Macaroni Gratin, 190
    Mashed Potatoes with Garlic, 10, 12
    Melanzane al Forno, 146–47
    Pipérade, 89
    Polenta, 54
    Saag Aloo, 255–56
    Spätzle, 160–61
    Wok-Tossed Asian Vegetables, 14–15
Slanted Door, 92
Slow Club, 220
S'More Brownies, 158–59
Sociale, 144
Sofrito, 205–7
Somerville, Annie, 132
Soufflés
    Huckleberry, 138–39
    Lemon, 55–56
Soups, see also Gazpacho Andaluz
    Asian Pear Ajo Blanco, 117
    Caramelized Garlic, 42–43
    Cranberry Bean and Dandelion, 124–25
    Italian Fish, 16–17
    Spring Asparagus, 136–37
South Beach, see Fisherman's Wharf / The
    Embarcadero / South Beach
South of Market / Potrero Hill
    about, 164–66
    contributing restaurants of, 163, 167–97
    other neighborhood restaurants of, 165
South Park Café, 190
Soy-Braised Cabbage, 128–29
Spätzle, 160–61
Spice Paste, 280
Spicy Sour Cream Sauce, 271
Spicy Watercress and Orange Salad, 6–7
Spinach, see also Vegetables
    Hog Island Oysters Rockefeller, 81–82

Pollo alla Marsala con Spinaci Siciliani,
    37–38
Saag Aloo, 255–56
spinach-ricotta gnocchi, 18–19
Spring Asparagus Soup, 136–37
Spring Vegetable Potpies, 245–47
Squash
    Pumpkin Curry Tofu, 179
    Shaved Squash and Ricotta Bruschetta, 239
Stocks
    fish or shrimp, 17
    Herbed Vegetable, 245
    Lobster, 17
    Mushroom, 258–59
    rich chicken, 156
Stoll, Anne and Craig, 208
Suleiman, Hanna, 51
Sunchick Purée, 169–70
Sung, Luke, 134
The Sunset, see Presidio Heights / The Sunset /
    The Richmond / Forest Hills / West Portal
Suppenküche, 160
Swedish Oatmeal Pancakes with Pears and
    Almonds, 96–97
Sweet Crêpe Batter, 223, 224
Swordfish (Sicilian Swordfish Rolls), 113–14

T
Tabasco Vinaigrette, 192–93
Tablespoon, 117
Tadich Grill, 44
Tagliolini Pepati, 167–68
Tallula, 243
Tattamanti, Wally, 68
Taylor's Automatic Refresher, 94
Terje, Staffan, 18
Thaitanic Beef, 260–61
Thep Phanom Thai Cuisine, 260
Three-Mustard-Crusted Pork Tenderloin, 128–29
Ti Couz, 223
Tomatoes, see also Vegetables
    Gazpacho Andaluz, 118–19
    Heirloom Tomato Jam, 10–11
    Lamb Sauce, 240
    Oven-Dried-Tomato Tarts, 184–85
    peeling and seeding, 12
    Pipérade, 89

Seafood Risotto, 186–87
Tuna Tartare and Fried Green, 192–93
Whole Fish with Tomato and Fennel Ragout, 188–89
Tomato Sauce, 168
Tortilla Strips (deep-fried), 272
Town Hall, 192
Town's End Restaurant and Bakery, 96
Troosh, Katia, 278
Trout, Fennel-Crusted Golden, 243–44
Truffle Sauce, 104
Tuna
    Ahi Burgers, 94–95
    Ahi Tuna au Poivre, 174–76
    Tuna Confit, 106–7
    Tuna Tartare with Fried Green Tomatoes, 192–93
Tusk, Lindsay and Michael, 138
2223 Market Street, 245

U

Union Square / Downtown
    about, 2–3
    contributing restaurants of, 1, 4–19
    other neighborhood restaurants in, 3
Universal Café, 227
Upper Market / The Castro / Noe Valley
    about, 232–35
    contributing restaurants of, 231, 235–47
    other neighborhood restaurants of, 233

V

Veal Filet, 276–77
Vegetables, see also Peppers; Potatoes; Salads;
  Spinach; Tomatoes
    Chicken Potpies, 212–14
    Grilled Lamb Skewers with, 217–19
    heirloom, 13
    Pumpkin Curry Tofu, 179
    Red Sauerkraut (Blaukraut), 228–29
    Sautéed Eggplant, 66–67
    Shaved Squash and Ricotta Bruschetta, 239
    Soy-Braised Cabbage, 128–29
    Spring Asparagus Soup, 136–37
    Spring Vegetable Potpies, 245–47
    Warm Piquillo Peppers, 31–32
    Wok-Tossed Asian, 14–15

Vinaigrettes, see also Dressings
    Anchovy, 106–7
    Lemon, 111–12
    Moscatel, 31–32
    served with Crab Cakes and greens, 40
    served with Fennel-Crusted Golden Trout, 243
    Sherry, 25–26
    Tabasco, 192–93
    White Balsamic-Honey, 237
Viti, Nicola, 115
Vivande Porta Via, 146

W

Walden, GraceAnn, xiii
Warm Green Garlic-Chipotle Cream, 204
Warm Piquillo Peppers, 31–32
Watercress
    Grilled Salmon Paillards on Bucatini with, 33–34
    Spicy Watercress and Orange Salad, 6–7
Webber, Kirk, 128
West Portal, see Presidio Heights / The Richmond /
    The Sunset / Forest Hills / West Portal
White Balsamic-Honey Vinaigrette, 237
Whole Fish with Tomato and Fennel Ragout, 188–89
Wine pairings, 27, 38, 244
Wok-Roasted Mussels, 253–54
Wok-Tossed Asian Vegetables, 14–15
Wong, Arnold Eric, 169, 253

X

Xu, Jason, 90

Y

Yakura, Mike, 14
Yank Sing, 194
Yerba Buena, xii

Z

ZAGAT Survey, xvi
Zarzuela, 118
Zazie, 262

Acknowledgments

We would like to thank the chefs, sous-chefs, owners, partners, general managers, and front-of-the-house people who sent us recipes from their restaurants, then patiently answered our queries on ingredients and techniques. In the high-stakes, consuming profession of running a restaurant in San Francisco, they were generous with their time. We found that it's really true that many chefs don't write recipes down, that they don't always use measuring cups, that they work ridiculously long hours, and that they love the demanding art of making great food available to those who live in and visit San Francisco.

We would also like to thank the staff at Silverback Books; our undaunted star tester, Theresa Burton, and gracious testers Greg and Libby Smith, Bruce Binn, Peter Melendy, and Andrew Baker; friends and supporters Joan Cogen, Mike Chaplin, and Randy Dunagan, for their insight and levity; Kate Basart, for our artful design; Joan Olson, for production and page layouts; David Wakely, our ace photographer, who brought the neighborhood images to this book; and last, but hardly least, the city of San Francisco, which has nourished us, body and soul, for so many years.